Cross Border Terrorism
Road Block to Piece Initiatives

CROSS BORDER TERRORISM

Road Block to Piece initiatives

Brig. (Retd.) S. P. Lohia

Gaurav Book Centre Pvt Ltd

Delhi

Publisher
GAURAV BOOK CENTRE PVT LTD
4832/24,Prahlad Lane,S-207 Ansari
Road, Daryaganj, Delhi-110002
Ph.: 43570976, 23278261
Email: gauravbookcentre@gmail.com

Edition: 2016

ISBN: 978-93-83316-46-5

Laser Typesetting
JEE-VEE Graphics, Delhi

Price: 1150/-

Printed
Vikas Computers, Delhi

Preface

India has been battling with the surge in terrorism driven by religious extremism for many years. Now, the Central Asian Republics (CARs) have also began to feel the impact of an overflow of terrorism linked activities into their countries. Militant groups in these republics have been influenced by the religious extremism spreading outward from this region. The growing threat of violence has led the CARs not only to cooperate among thenselves1 but also to seek the help of like-minded countries so as to evolve a framework of cooperation to contain the movement of terrorists as well as arms.

In this regard convergence between India and the CARs could be arrived at on the issue of terrorism led by religious fundamentalists, which is best exemplified by the Afghanistan-Pakistan complex, exporting men and material not only to India but also to Central Asian Republics. Thus, nations have to look beyond their boundaries with a common vision to stem the growth of this phenomenon. In this book, the problem of cross-border terrorism in India and the CARs has been examined and focus made on how India in association with the CARs can work together to meet the challenge of terrorism.

Terrorism has become the most powerful hazard to international security, and terrorism driven by religious extremism, is even doubly so. India and Central Asia share this common threat just by virtue of sharing their borders with Pakistan and Afghanistan. Having a common threat can also be a positive thing because cooperation by like-minded nations can help in combating the common adversary and strengthening future ties. This book deals with the areas of commonality between India and Central Asia, the problems they face when it comes to cross-border terrorism and how these problems can be resolved through cooperation.

This book is a modest attempt to discuss all these issues.

—Editor

Contents

1

Introduction

India has a unique history and singular geographical location, and because of this its internal peace and security is especially vulnerable to subversive forces.

The country is a cultural mosaic, with a multiplicity of racial, religious, ethnic and linguistic groups. Nearly all of these groupings clamour for the special attention of the Central government and seek special social and legal privileges to protect their identities. In this way these groups often behave as competing groups, and therefore the relationship between groups can be very fragile.

Even if different groups bond together in one cohesive whole the fault-lines remain. A clever manipulation of deep-seated prejudices and suspicions through the use of controversial symbols and motivated acts of offence has often led to outbreak of terrible violence.

This is specially true of India because of its colonial experience and the British legacy of playing one group against another in a system of distribution of political and economic rewards. It has entrenched groups against one another and also put up the group against the state itself.

Moreover, a residual loyalty to a region, a religious community, an ethnic background, etc., are still strong enough to challenge the ideals and assumptions which form the base on which the edifice of modern nationhood rests. The problem is compounded when external forces get involved with the internal tensions. They manipulate the sentiments and fears of groups and posit before them the inevitability and necessity of armed rebellion against the state.

All the armed insurgent outfits that are active in different parts of the country have the tenacity to raise arms against the state, wreak havoc on security forces and civilians alike and sustain their movement for decades primarily because of external support. The aim of these external forces is to destabilise India or at the least keep it engaged in worrying about the suppurating wounds.

The demographic and geographical reality is such that affinities cut across societies and political boundaries. Many ethnic groups, especially in the areas bordering the international boundary, have as much in common with the population living across the boundary as with their own nationals.

These social continuities across territorial frontiers have given rise to demands for redrawing national and international boundaries. However, due to the involvement of external forces, the scope for the resolution of conflicts at internal level is greatly reduced.

Countries surrounding India have been actively exploiting the volatile situation in the northeast and Jammu and Kashmir, as well as the disturbed law and order situation in various other parts of the country. Through political backing, economic assistance, military training and arms supplies, these countries have contributed varying to destabilise the internal security situation in India.

The Chinese support to the insurgents came in the early 1960s and continued through the 1970s. Both Issac Swu and Muivah Thangkhul, leaders of the NSCN, received guerrilla training in the Yunan province of China in 1967. It was because of the Chinese support that the Naga outfit became one of the best organised insurgent outfits.

Taking the cue from the Nagas, other insurgent groups also sought and got moral and material support from China. The Mizo and Meitei insurgents were also trained in guerrilla warfare and subversion tactics in Yunan and Lhasa. However, in their endeavour to normalise relations with India support to the insurgents in the northeast has been practically stopped by China since the 1980s. Dr. Rajpal Budania (in his book, India's Security Dilemma) points out that sponsored-terrorism is abetted from outside a country with a view to weakening or destroying the political cohesion of the targeted country. Pakistan has indulged in such an exercise targeting India with definite strategic and political motives for destabilising or breaking up India. Pakistan has been instrumental in spreading terrorism and secessionism not only in Jammu and Kashmir but also in Punjab, and North-eastern states.

Its security and military establishments have attempted to establish operational links with drug syndicates and fundamentalist groups in India, Pakistan and Afghanistan. Pakistan's assistance to militants in Kashmir goes much beyond, what Pakistan acknowledges, moral, political and diplomatic support. Pakistan, has been providing the militants with weapons and training. Pattern of Pakistani involvement in terrorist activities in Kashmir has involved: training of Kashmiri militants; induction of Pakistani nationals and other alien mercenaries into the valley, mainly Afghans, Libyans, Sudanese and Iranians; providing safe sanctuaries to leaders of militant groups kept in Pakistan to manipulate, control and guide the terrorists; supply and continued induction of weapons and communication equipment; providing funds; subversive propaganda through electronic and print media; and attempts at garnering international support by raising the issue of human rights violation in Jammu and Kashmir. Interrogation of the captured militants indicates that militancy is being orchestrated by the Inter-Services Intelligence (ISI) in Pakistan. Attempts have been made to establish close coordination between the militants in Kashmir and Punjab.

Pakistan's encouragement to terrorism in J&K did not remain unnoticed by other important countries of the world which have been sympathetic towards Pakistan. In January 1993, the Clinton Administration in the US placed Pakistan on a "Watch List" of nations suspected of giving support to international terrorism. However, in July, the US decided to remove Pakistan from the list of suspected terrorist state. Yet America has never categorically denied that Pakistan is not involved in giving material support to militants in Kashmir. India has accused Pakistan of its involvement in terrorist activities also in other parts of the country such as blasts in Bombay stock exchange in March 1993, airdropping of arms in Purulia district in West Bengal in December 1995, bomb blasts in Delhi and Red Fort firing in December 2000, the attack on Parliament in 2002 and elsewhere with the motives of destabilising the Indian polity and economy. ISI is active in north-eastern India and it is reported to be operating from Nepal, Bangladesh and even Bhutan.

India faces yet another threat in the form of narco-terrorism from Pakistan. The narco-link between the drug smugglers from Pakistan and ' the Punjab terrorists is known to exist. Reports show the narco-link playing a role in the north-east.

In a plural and developing society like India differences between the political units of the state as well as between various sections of society are bound to come up. Pakistan has taken advantage of these vulnerabilities and encouraged separatist tendencies in India.

When the Naga National Council was established in 1956, Pakistan (East) was the first to give the outfit moral and material training. The Naga leadership shares a very close relationship with the Pakistani government.

Till the time of the independence of Bangladesh, all major north-eastern insurgent outfits including MNF and NSCN were trained by Pakistan in what is now Bangladesh. Even after the break-up of Pakistan, the relationship with the insurgent groups continued.

Pakistani efforts at provoking the people of Jammu and Kashmir failed to fructify for a long time. But it took advantages of internal disturbances in the late 1980s and managed to incite a full-fledged armed insurgency.

Its experience in exploiting the tension in Punjab proved useful. The raising of the Taliban and providing it with the material and logistical support gave the necessary morale boost to the Pakistani agencies vis-a-vis their activities against India. Till 1971, Bangladesh (then East Pakistan) was the base of most insurgent groups. The situation changed after the liberation of Bangladesh but only until Mujibur Rehman was in power. After the assassination of Mujibur Rehman, subsequent governments in Bangladesh have allowed ISI activities directed against India to flourish.

The extremely porous Indo-Bangladesh border is prone to illegal immigration and has often been used by the ISI to push in its agents. Similarly, due to the open borders between India and Nepal the latter country serves as the easiest entry route. The hijacking of Indian Airlines aircraft IC814 from Kathmandu shows that the network is widespread.

Why India is vulnerable India is a large democratic state marked by diversity of ethnic/religious groups. Disaffection can easily be fanned into eruptions against other communities and state symbols.

Much the largest state in a neighbourhood of less successful or smaller states (excepting China), which are for most of the time ruled by dictators or military, India becomes a target for cross-border terror groups.

India's borders are not 'secure' in the sense they are vast and difficult at any one time to watch over, given the terrain in the north and northwest as well as in the northeast. The borders are porous, and easy to infiltrate. Illegal immigration is a major problem in the east.

Economic deprivation and low development levels among many regions occupied by some communities have been grounds for disturbances.

The states of Assam and Nagaland have over the years received a large influx of immigrants. Shifting demographics in an area already prone to tribal friction have helped touch off a number of religious and cultural conflicts.

Poverty is endemic in the region, and many groups are demanding independence, citing neglect and discrimination on the part of the Indian government as grounds for separation. Militant groups like the United Liberation Front of Assam have targeted politicians and infrastructure in an attempt to force out government influence.

INDIA RAKES UP ISSUE OF CROSS BORDER TERROR, 26/11 WITH PAKISTAN

India raised a number of issues with Pakistan on Tuesday, including cross-border terrorism, 2008 Mumbai terror attacks, and the ongoing ceasefire violations across the Line of Control (LoC), during the visit of Foreign Secretary S Jaishankar to Islamabad. The foreign secretary, who was in Pakistan as part of Prime Minister Narendra Modi's 'SAARC Yatra' initiative, also met Pakistan Prime Minister Nawaz Sharif; Sartaj Aziz, Sharif's advisor on foreign affairs and national security; and Tariq Fatemi, special assistant to Sharif. Jaishankar met Sharif later in the day and handed over a letter written by Prime Minister Narendra Modi to him.

The talks were held in a "constructive and positive atmosphere" and both neighbours were able to reach a "common ground and narrow the differences." "My visit provided an opportunity to discuss our bilateral relations. I reiterated our known concerns on cross-border terrorism, including on the Mumbai case. We agreed that ensuring peace and tranquillity on the border was vital," Jaishankar said after an hour-long meeting with his Pakistani counterpart Aizaz Ahmad Chaudhry in Islamabad.

According to a senior official in the ministry of external affairs, India has made it clear to Pakistan that talks will not continue unless the guns fall silent on the border. It has also suggested a strategy in terms of regular contact between both the director generals of military operations (DGMOs) and border security forces. The DGMOs had last met on December 2013 after incidents involving a dozen of soldiers along the LoC came to light. It was then decided the DGMOs of both countries would have regular discussion over a hotline every week. However, it has become irregular and incidents of ceasefire violation have continued unabated.

"Since diplomats cannot resolve tensions taking place on the border, it will be best to engage people who are on the ground. So we have proposed to Pakistan that let the DGMOs and BSF rangers work out the daily issues. We will start with that. If that works out, then we will look at other CBMs (confidence building measures). We are not very ambitious, but at least it will set in process engagement and normalcy on the border," the official added. Pakistan on its part took up the issue of 2007 Samjhauta Express bombings and the ongoing disputes concerning Kashmir, Sir Creek and Siachen. It also urged India to not to encourage hostile propaganda against each other and adherence to the 2003 LoC cease-fire agreement.

"We have discussed all issues with India. There was a common resolve to work towards all bilateral issues. On the LoC, we expressed our concerns and agreed to utilise the existing channels that can maintain the cease-fire. Both sides agreed to stay engaged and then move on the next steps," Chaudhry told reporters there. Jaishankar and Chaudhry also had another hour-long discussion over luncheon where both were learnt to have discussed matters related to South Asian Association for Regional Cooperation (SAARC) and what Modi envisioned during the last SAARC Summit held in Kathmandu.

On SAARC, India has asked Pakistan to cooperate and take appropriated steps. The foreign secretary is believed to have told Pakistan that if it does not cooperate in making SAARC a successful entity, India will move ahead with a new initiative — BBIN (Bhutan, Bangladesh, Indian and Nepal). This is the same message the foreign secretary is expected to impart to Afghanistan, which he would visit on March 4. In Kabul, Jaishankar will meet key officials from the new administration led by President Ashraf Ghani.

Jaishankar is expected to visit Sri Lanka on March 6-7 during the second phase of the 'SAARC Yatra'. He will be accompanying external affairs minister Sushma Swaraj.

CROSS BORDER TERROR IS A BIGGER THREAT THAN ISIS

The hold acquired by ISIS in the Iraq-Syria region in recent months has produced media despatches claiming that the terrorist group was now rapidly spreading towards South Asia. What is ironic, however, is that many strategic analysts are being quick to suggest that the prime threat that India now faces was coming from the ISIS, rather than from ISI-sponsored cross border terrorism for which as is well known, India-specific outfits like LeT and HuM were used all along by Pakistan.

ISIS, no doubt, has the potential to grow into a global threat to all non-Muslims, since its basic ideology and thrust is to reestablish the Caliphate for the entire Umma by going back to the days of the four Rashidun Khalifas. The Caliphate put an obligation on all Muslims to make the supreme sacrifice to destroy the enemies of Islam and other infidels. Islamic radicals see nothing wrong in "beheading" the enemy. They look at the position of women as something determined by the religious injunction, "Men are in charge of women."

Indian strategic analysts, studying the ISIS phenomenon, must note that in the "war on terror", the two targets of the US-led offensive, Iraq and Afghanistan, became the focal points of radical consolidation — through ISIS in Iraq and Syria and the Al Qaeda-Taliban combine in the Pak-Afghan belt. In a superficial reading of the developments, many media "specialists" started writing of the mutually destructive rivalry between ISIS and Al Qaeda, until reports came in of a growing convergence between them.

For Islamic radicals, the US-led West and their allies are the prime enemies; this is something rooted in their historical memory of the Crusades as well as the Wahhabi revolt of the Indian subcontinent. For historical, ideological and political reasons, radical Islam — given to extremism — goes also after the Shias, apart from keeping its wrath alive for other deviants including the idol-worshipping kafirs. The question is: How far will the voices from within the Muslim world go to resist the rise of extremism in the name of religion?

It should be mentioned that a set of geopolitical and socioeconomic factors have enabled the Islamic radicals to gather strength on the ground and spread to places like Somalia, Algeria and Yemen in a decisive way. The tentativeness of military response from the West led to the ISIS consolidating its hold on the oil wealth of Iraq. In both the Syria-Iraq and Pak-Afghan theatres, there are enough supporters and admirers of the ISIS, Al Qaeda and Taliban to facilitate the advance of the radicals. And now the removal of Al Baghdadi, Osama bin Laden and Mullah Omar from the scene is having the effect of operationally bringing the two radical groupings closer to each other.

ISIS has the potential to grow into a global threat to all non-Muslims, since its basic ideology and thrust is to reestablish the Caliphate for the entire Umma by going back to the days of the four Rashidun Khalifas. The Caliphate put an obligation on all Muslims to make the supreme sacrifice to destroy the enemies of Islam and other infidels.

A firm indicator of this convergence comes from the contents of a recruitment document that the American Media Institute claims to have found in the Pakhtoon frontier of Pakistan. It seeks to unite factions of Taliban in Pakistan and Afghanistan into a single army and expects the latter — together with Al Qaeda — to rally behind the Islamic State for establishing the Caliphate for all of the one billion Muslims. The document in Urdu (not Arabic) talks of an attack "in India" (not on India) to provoke an apocalyptic confrontation with America. The security set up of India would do well to research the origin of this document.

From India's perspective, the threat of terrorism has revolved round the covert offensive that the Pak ISI had planned against India years ago, by infiltrating the Mujahideen into the Kashmir valley to replicate the Afghan jihad there and using the porous borders of India with Nepal and Bangladesh to send in trained elements to carry out acts of terrorism in other parts of India as well. Even after India came on board with the US-led world coalition against the new global terror perpetrated by Islamic radicals, the Pak-sponsored cross border terrorism went on unabated.

India's naive step at Havana of bracketing itself with Pakistan as being at the receiving end of terrorism gave our adversary a plea of deniability that it used even for 26/11. This stand, disregarding, for whatever reason, our assessment of the Pak sponsored proxy war, served the purpose of getting India in line with what was clearly the American stand on Pakistan. It is not surprising that the US policymakers now want India to go along with the US-Pak approach on Afghanistan's future. The desire of the US to somehow have an India-Pak dialogue resumed, reflects this approach. This is happening at a time when the Pak army has sensed an increased dependence of the US on it for protecting American assets in Afghanistan. Interestingly, those behind the ISIS document mentioned above, highlight an alleged plan of this outfit to attack US army personnel moving out of Afghanistan and the American diplomats staying on in that country.

India's intelligence agencies are aware that Pakistan's plea that "we are also a victim of terrorism" has been used by the Pak ISI as a ploy to palm off its own operations against India to the "radicals", as was seen in the attacks sometime back made on our missions in Afghanistan. The Pakistani army has the potential of striking an equation with Taliban in a post-American Afghanistan. The strategy of countering the influence of Islamic radicals on India's Muslim youth should take into account the distinct possibility of Pakistani agencies being able to use both India-specific groups like LeT and the outfits of the radical umbrella in the "proxy war" against this country.

ISLAMIST MILITANCY IN KASHMIR: THE CASE OF THE LASHKAR-I TAYYEBA

The emergence of radical Islamist groups in Kashmir over the last decade has added a new dimension to the ongoing conflict in the region. It has led to a rapid transformation in the terms of discourse in which the conflict is represented, by India, Pakistan and by many Kashmiris themselves. The current stage in the Kashmir conflict can be dated to 1989, when the Jammu and Kashmir Liberation Front (JKLF) inaugurated an armed uprising against Indian rule. By the mid-1990s, however, the JKLF had been increasingly taken over by Pakistan-based Islamist groups. The wiping out of many of its cadres in confrontation with the Indian armed forces, the withdrawal of Pakistani support and the growing realisation of the need for peaceful, as opposed to military, means for the eventual resolution of the Kashmir dispute, seem to be among the major reasons for the gradual decline of the JKLF as a military force in Kashmir, despite the fact that its goal of an independent Kashmir still commands the support of many Kashmiri Muslims. On the other hand, military and other forms of support from the Pakistani establishment, from private *jihad*ist groups in Pakistan and elsewhere, in addition to a passionate zeal for what is seen as a 'holy' cause, account, in large measure, for the gradual take-over of the armed struggle in Kashmir by militant Islamist groups, mainly based in Pakistan and led, for the most part, by Pakistani nationals.

Despite the active involvement of Islamist groups in the on-going struggle in Kashmir, little written has been written about them from a scholarly and detached point of view. This chapter seeks to provide an account of the ideology, organization and development of one of the leading Islamist groups active in Kashmir today, the Lashkar-i Tayyeba. Of the several Pakistan-based Islamist groups active in Kashmir today, the Lashkar is, by far, the most well-organised, well-trained and heavily armed. From the mid-1990s, this once little known group has emerged today as the most serious challenge to the Indian armed forces, being responsible for several attacks in Kashmir, killing a large number of Indian soldiers as well as civilians, both Hindu as well as Muslim. This chapter looks at the emergence of the Lashkar as a key player in the present stage of the Kashmiri struggle. Owing to the relative paucity of published material, the chapter relies heavily on the official Internet web site of the Markaz Da'wat wa'l Irshad ('Centre for Invitation and Instruction'), of which the Lashkar is the armed wing.

The Lashkar: Early Origins

The Lashkar is the military wing of the Markaz Da'wat wa'l Irshad, with its headquarters at the town of Muridke in the Gujranwala district in Pakistani Punjab. The Markaz was established in 1986 by two Pakistani university professors, Hafiz Muhammad Sa'eed and Zafar Iqbal. They were assisted by the late 'Abdullah Azam' a close aide of Osama bin Laden, who was then associated with the International Islamic University, Islamabad. Funds for setting up the organization are said to have come from Pakistan's dreaded secret services agency, the Inter Services Intelligence (ISI).

The Markaz is affiliated to the Ahl-i Hadith school of thought, a reformist Islamic movement, which had its origins in early nineteenth century north India. The founders of the Ahl-i Hadith, men such as Maulana Nazir Husain (1805-1902), Nawab Siddiq Hasan Khan Bhopali (d1832-90) and Maulana Sanaullah Amritsari (1870-1943), believed that they were charged with the divine responsibility of purging popular Muslim practice of what they saw as 'un-Islamic' accretions and borrowings from their Hindu neighbours, regarding these as 'unlawful innovations' (*bida'at*), and as akin to *shirk*, the sin of associating anything with God. They insisted that Muslims must go back to the original sources of their faith, the Qur'an and the Hadith, the Traditions of the Prophet, and abandon all beliefs and practices not sanctioned therein.

They called for Muslims to abide strictly by the Islamic law (*shari'ah*) and to abandon 'imitation' (*taqlid*) of the traditional schools of Islamic jurisprudence (*mazhab*. pl. *mazahib*), attempting to refashion the worldwide Muslim community in the mould of the Companions of the Prophet. The '*ulama*of the Hanafi *mazhab*, representing the vast majority of the Muslims of South Asia, entered into bitter conflict with the Ahl-i Hadith on the matter of *taqlid*. The latter defended their opposition to *taqlid* on the grounds that the schools of jurisprudence had developed more than two hundred years after the death of the Prophet, and that, therefore, the Companions of the Prophet did not follow *taqlid*. Since, they argued, Muslims should follow the model of the Companions, there was no need for them to 'blindly follow' the schools of jurisprudence, for this would be tantamount to 'personality worship' of the founders of the *mazahib*, a heinous sin. Further, they claimed, the Hanafis had fabricated numerous *hadith* to prove the claims of their *mazhab*, and quoted a *hadith* to the effect that 'he who fabricates *hadith* shall be thrown into hell-fire'.

Besides attacking the Hanafi '*ulama*, the Ahl-i Hadith directed their attention to bitterly critiquing Sufism, which they saw as a 'wrongful innovation', for, they argued, it had no sanction in the practice of the Prophet and his Companions. Every 'wrongful innovation', they insisted, was a heinous sin, the punishment for which was damnation in hell. They stiffly opposed the adoration of the Prophet as a superhuman being as well as the devotion to the saints and the cults centred on their shrines that are an integral part of popular Sufi tradition in South Asia, seeing this as a deviation from the practice of the Prophet and the early Muslims. Faith in the powers of Sufi preceptors and the widespread belief in the Sufi saints as intermediaries with God were condemned as akin to polytheism. So, too, was the belief in the supernatural powers of the Prophet and of his being ever-present and all-seeing.

Given the immense popularity of the Sufi traditions and the influence of the Hanafi 8*ulama* among the Muslims of South Asia, it was hardly surprising that the Ahl-i Hadith faced stiffed opposition, being banned from worship at mosques and condemned as apostates and enemies of Islam. For their part, the Ahl-i Hadith appeared to have revelled in controversy, not losing any opportunity of attacking their Muslim opponents for what they branded as their 'un-Islamic' ways. Engaged in constant conflict with other Muslims, drawing clear lines of division between themselves as the only truly Muslim group and the rest, seems to have played a crucial role in the development of a separate Ahl-i Hadith identity.

Confrontation with other Muslim groups created an atmosphere conducive to militancy, and the Ahl-i Hadith saw themselves as carrying on in the long tradition of *jihad*, which they accused other Muslims as having abandoned. The founders of the Ahl-i Hadith claimed the legacy of the early nineteenth century jihad movement led by Sayyed Ahmad Barelvi and Isma'il Shahid against the Sikhs in the Punjab. In the failed revolt of 1857 against the British, several Muslim *ulama* associated with Ahl-i Hadith-style activism played a role in leading uprisings at some places. After 1857, while some Ahl-i Hadith leaders accommodated themselves to British rule and devoted themselves to peaceful preaching, others continued to carry on violent struggles against the British in the North-West Frontier Province, till they were finally crushed by the end of the nineteenth century. Although from the early twentieth century onwards the Ahl-i Hadith, as a whole, gave up the path of violence in the face of British arms, an Ahl-i Hadith scholar writes that they 'refused to accept the supremacy of the British and the Hindus', and vowed to carry on the struggle through other means to 'convert India into an abode of Islam (*dar-ul islam*) through *jihad'*. While they desisted from entering into violent confrontation with the British, their opposition to Sufism and to the Hanafis brought them into conflict with many traditional Muslims, which sometimes took violent forms. However, they were doomed to a marginal existence owing to their vehement opposition to popular Muslim practice, and hence were not able to emerge as a mass movement. Rather, they remained an elitist group, characterised, as Barbara Metcalf writes, by a sense of 'moral superiority' and 'self-righteousness', tinged with 'a certain harshness', and with a small following among urban Muslims, particularly in north India.

THE AHL-I-HADITH IN PAKISTAN AND THE RISE OF THE LASHKAR

Since the Lashkar has its headquarters in Pakistan and most of its fighters in Kashmir are Pakistani nationals, the role of the Lashkar in Kashmir must be seen in the context of the growing salience within Pakistan itself of the Ahl-i Hadith, to which it owes allegiance. Following the creation of Pakistan in 1947, the Ahl-i Hadith began making gradual progress in the country, establishing mosques and *madrasas* of its own. It had to face with stiff resistance from traditional Sufis, for its opposition to Sufism and *taqlid*. It tended to have a more visible presence in urban areas, its strict scripturalist literalism appealing to groups such as urban traders who were not tied down to local Sufi shrines.

Although the Ahl-i Hadith still has a limited following in Pakistan, from the 1980s onwards it was able to make considerable inroads in Pakistani society. A number of factors have combined to make for this. Firstly, the growing appeal of scripturalist Islam as a result of the rapid expansion in the number of *madrasa*s or Islamic seminaries in the country in recent decades, many of which are sponsored by the Saudis and preach a conservative yet militant form of Islam that has a close resemblance with that of the Ahl-i Hadith. Secondly, the active sponsorship and patronising of such *madrasa*s by the Pakistani state, under and after General Zia-ul Haq (d. 1988). Thirdly, the Afghan *jihad* against the Soviets, which saw a great expansion of resources for groups such as the Ahl-i Hadith, with massive amounts of aid, in the form of money and arms, pouring in from Saudi Arabia and other Arab countries. Many Ahl-i Hadith and other Sunni *madrasas* emerged at this time as training grounds for militants active in the Afghan *jihad*. After expelling the Soviets from Kabul, these *mujahids* turned their attention to fresh pastures, Kashmir being one of them. Thus, from being a relatively minor group in Pakistan's Islamic landscape, the Ahl-i Hadith grew, by the end of the 1980s, into a major force, with scores of *madrasas* all over the country, particularly in the Punjab and the North-West Frontier Province, and several newspapers and journals articulating its vision of an Islamic revolution.

Along with other Islamist groups, the Ahl-i Hadith immersed itself in the *jihad* in Afghanistan. In 1986 it set up the Markaz Da'wat wa'l Irshad, based in a sprawling 160-acre campus at Muridke, a town some 30 kilometres from Lahore, to train *mujahidin* to fight the Soviets. Thus, in 1993, the Markaz established its separate '*jihadic* and warfare' wing, the Lashkar. The Lashkar later set up four training centres in Pakistan and Afghanistan, where, 'thousands of *mujahidin* from all over the world are being trained'. Markaz authorities claim that the militants produced at these centres have played a leading role in armed struggles, first in Afghanistan, and then in countries as far afield as Bosnia, Chechenya, Kosovo, the southern Philippines, Kashmir and 'in other areas where Muslims are fighting for freedom'. All Muslims, it believes, are members of one global community. Oppression of Muslims anywhere makes it incumbent on Muslims everywhere to assist them, if necessarily through active engagement in violent conflict with their non-Muslim opponents. As the Lashkar case so strikingly illustrates, one of the characteristic features of some contemporary Islamist movements is precisely this global agenda, a marked contrast with the local or national scope and ambitions of Islamist movements in the past.

According to one report, in recent years the spread of the Markaz/Lashkar in Pakistan has been 'phenomenal', and today it has some five hundred offices all over the country, most of them in Punjab, which operate as recruitment centres for would-be *mujahidin*. At its Muridke headquarters, the Markaz runs an Islamic school and university, most of whose students are local Pakistanis, with some from both Pakistan-administered Kashmir and Kashmiris from the Indian-ruled part of the state, and several Afghans and Arabs. Established in 1994, several hundred students have already graduated from the school.

Scores of smaller schools run on the same lines have been set up in various other parts of Pakistan, and, by mid-2001, their number was said to be almost 130, with some 15,000 students and 800 teachers on their rolls. Young boys of the age of eight are taken in and are given a 12-year training, which includes the standard Islamic disciples, taught from an Ahl-i Hadith perspective, English, Arabic, and Science, as well as the handling of weapons and techniques of armed combat. A strict military atmosphere is enforced. Students must wear military uniforms, abide by military discipline and 'properly assimilate the commandments of their theologians and military instructors that their future profession-as *mujahidin*-will be in great demand in the Muslim world on the threshold of the new millennium'. Students from different countries and ethnic groups live together, and every effort is made to discourage ethnic differences. They must wear the same clothes, speak the same language (Urdu, Arabic). Names that might suggest local, clan, tribal or caste origins must be effaced. The only identity that should matter to them is of being Muslim, ethnic differences being seen as working to divide and weaken the worldwide Muslim *ummah*.

At its four training centres, would-be *mujahidin* are given rigorous military training. This is of two kinds. Firstly, a short twenty-one day course, the *daura-i 'ama* ('general course'). Secondly, a three-month intensive course, the *daura-i khasa* ('special course'), geared to guerrilla warfare, in which trainees learn how to handle small arms as well as survival and ambush techniques. These courses, it is claimed, 'change the course of life' of the trainees completely', and a sign of this is said to be that they 'no longer shave' and 'wear their *shalwars*(baggy trousers) above their ankles, as enjoined by the Prophet Muhammad (peace be upon him)'. They are fired with a passionate zeal in what is said to be a 'holy' cause, willing to sacrifice their lives and attain 'martyrdom' for it. Families whose sons die in battles with the Indian forces are said to celebrate and rejoice their deaths, rather than mourn, for they are confident of their securing a place for themselves in heaven. This has particularly crucial implications for how Kashmiri Lashkar activists see themselves. If, traditionally, Kashmiri Muslims were depicted as 'cowards', 'passive' or 'mild', and lax as far as religious observances were concerned, at least compared to their Pathan and Punjabi Muslim neighbours, they are now sought to be made 'true', 'brave' and 'fearless' Muslims, fired by the zeal of would-be 'martyrs' for the faith.

THE IDEOLOGY OF THE LASHKAR

Like other Islamist groups, the Markaz/Lashkar sees Islam as a perfect, all-embracing system (*nizam*). Islam is said to govern all aspects of personal as well as collective life, in the form of the *shari'ah*. For the establishing of an Islamic system, an Islamic state is necessary, which will impose the *shar'iah* as the law of the land. This is seen as 'the solution to all our problems'. If such a state were to be set up and all Muslims were to live strictly according to 'the laws that Allah has laid down', then, it is believed, 'they would be able to control the whole world and exercise their supremacy'. Since the laws have already been laid down by God, there is no room for human beings to exercise their judgement in creating fresh legislation. Hence, democracy, in the sense of a system where people make their own laws, is condemned as completely un-Islamic. Since Islam is seen as the very antithesis of nationalism, it demands the establishment of one universal Islamic state, ruled by a single *khalifah*. Thus, the present division of the Muslims into many nation-states must be overcome. Since 'the *ummah* is one', it follows from this that 'the system of *khilafah* does not recognise the physical borders or the independence of one Muslim country from another'. Hence, 'the state is one, the army is one, the flag is one, the budget is one, etc.'.

The struggle for the establishment of the Islamic state can take various forms, peaceful as well as violent. Islam, the Lashkar admits, is 'a religion of peace and harmony', and seeks to 'eliminate mischief and disorder, and to provide peace, not only to Muslims but also to the entire humanity'. However, Muslims are commanded to take to armed struggle, or *jihad*, to defend their co-religionists suffering from the oppression of others. Such a situation is said to prevail over much of the world today. While *jihad* in defence of Islam and of Muslims labouring under oppression is presented as a liberation struggle, it is also seen as a means for Islam to 'prevail on this earth', for Islam is seen as the only true religion. Armed *jihad* must continue 'until Islam, as a way of life, dominates the whole world and until Allah's law is enforced everywhere in the world'. Since Islam is meant for all peoples, the Islamic State must spearhead a movement to spread the Islamic 'ideology' all over the world. In the course of this struggle, it is 'expected' that it will encounter 'conflict' with other states and their ideologies. The conflict can be resolved through peaceful diplomacy, but, if that fails, then the only course left open for the Muslims is armed*jihad*. In this sense, the Markaz/Lashkar believes, *jihad* is 'the foreign policy' of the Islamic State. This does not, however, mean that force can be used to coerce others into accepting Islam. Rather, *jihad* is seen as providing them with the 'security that comes from the application of Islam', while leaving them free to follow their own religion or to become Muslims.

The subject of armed *jihad* runs right through the writings and pronouncements of the Markaz/Lashkar and is, in fact, the most prominent theme in its discourse. Indeed, its understanding of Islam maybe seen as determined almost wholly by this preoccupation, so much so that its reading of Islam seems to be a product of its own political project. Being born as a result of a war (in Afghanistan), fighting for a holy cause has become the very raison d'être of the Lashkar, and its subsequent development has been almost entirely determined by this concern. The contours of its ideological framework are constructed in such a way that the theme of armed *jihad* appears as the central element of its project. In the writings and speeches of Markaz spokesmen *jihad* appears as violent conflict (*qittal*) waged against 'unbelievers' who are said to be responsible for the oppression of the Muslims. Indeed, it is projected as the one of the most central tenets of Islam, although it has traditionally not been included as one of the 'five pillars' of the faith. Thus, it is claimed that 'There is so much emphasis on this subject that some commentators and scholars of the Qur'an have remarked that the topic of the Qur'an is *jihad'*. Further, a Markaz statement declares, 'There is consensus of opinion among researchers of the Qur'an that no other action has been explained in such great detail as *jihad'*.

The global *jihadist* programme of the Markaz presents itself as a 'liberationist' project, basing itself on widespread feelings of discontent and suffering of sections of Muslims who see themselves as being persecuted by Western-oriented elites in their own countries, as well as by the 'West' more generally. The greatest problem of the Muslims, says Hafiz Muhammad Sa8eed, head of the Markaz, is their 'subjugation to the West'. Thus, the Markaz is reported to have gone so far as to call for a *jihad* against the USA. 'All Muslims', the Markaz believes, are oppressed today, by such 'enemies' as the Hindus, the Jews or Christians. 'Wherever you look, you will find that non-believers are everywhere trying to enslave Muslims and destroy them', it argues. Hence, Muslims must form a 'solid bloc' to defend themselves from these 'enemies', and if all peaceful means fail they must resort to armed *jihad* for their liberation. This Muslim bloc must be led by both Pakistan and Saudi Arabia, and have its headquarters at Mecca. It must aim at forming a pan-Islamic union based on strong trade, education and defence links, including a joint military command. *Mujahidin* from various Muslim countries would be trained to undertake *jihad* against unbelievers if peaceful means to put an end to oppression of Muslims fail. However, the Markaz insists, *jihad* is to be directed only at military and not civilian targets. It is contrasted with other forms of war that are pursued for purely worldly concerns, and is described as 'the act of supreme sacrifice to preserve human rights bestowed by Allah'. *Jihad* is thus a means for challenging 'oppression' and of establishing the rule of Islam.

Jihad is seen as the secret of Muslim power in the past when much of the known world was under Muslim rule, and it is argued that when Muslims 'abandoned *jihad* and other injunctions they began to degenerate'. In Markaz/Lashkar discourse, *jihad* is projected as a religious duty binding on *all* Muslims today. Thus, it is claimed that the prevailing global situation warrants *all* Muslims to be involved in some way or the other in *jihad* against non-Muslim 'oppressors'. In this grand enterprise there are different roles for different people to play. Those who are ordered by the *khalifah* to fight must do so, while others may be required to assist the *mujahidin* by supplying them food, arms and other supplies, providing medical assistance, looking after their families in their absence or even simply by exhorting others to participate in the war. Thus, *every* Muslim, man or woman, must be mobilised to assist in the struggle in some form or the other, and if any Muslim has 'never intended to fight against the disbelievers', his or her faith 'is not without traces of hypocrisy'. Those believers who have the capacity to participate or assist in the *jihad* but do not do so are said to 'be living a sinful life'. On the other hand, Muslims are promised that they would receive great rewards, both in this world and in the Hereafter, if they were to actively struggle in the path of *jihad*. Not only would they be guaranteed a place in Heaven, but they would also 'be honoured in this world', for *jihad* is also 'the way that solves financial and political problems'.

THE JIHAD IN KASHMIR AND INDIA

The Markaz sees its active involvement in the armed struggle in Kashmir as only one stage of a wider, indeed global, *jihad* against the forces of disbelief, stopping at nothing short of aiming at the conquest of the entire world. As Qari 'Abdul Wahid, former *amir* of the Lashkar in Indian-administered Kashmir, puts it, 'We will uphold the flag of freedom and Islam through *jihad* not only in Kashmir but in *the whole world*'. Likewise, Nazir Ahmed, in-charge of the public relations department of the Markaz, declares that through the *jihad* that the *mujahidin* have launched, 'Islam will be dominant all over the world, *Inshallah* (God willing)'. This war is seen as a solution to all the ills and oppression afflicting all Muslims, and it is claimed that 'if we want to live with honour and dignity, then we have to return back to *jihad'*. Through *jihad*, it is believed, 'Islam will be supreme throughout the world'. The *mujahidin* are promised that with the launching of the global *jihad* against all the 'unbelieving oppressors' of the world, 'The day is just round the corner when Islam will prevail in this earth, *Insha Allah'*.

In Markaz/Lashkar discourse, the conflict in Kashmir is seen not as a territorial dispute between India and Pakistan, but as nothing less than a war between two different and mutually opposed ideologies: Islam, on the one hand, and disbelief [*kufr*], on the other. This is portrayed as only one chapter in a long a struggle between the two that is said to have characterised the history of Hindu-Muslim relations for the last 1400 years ever since the advent of the Prophet Muhammad. The Prophet is claimed on the basis of a *hadith* to have singled out India as a special target for *jihad*. 'Whosoever will take part in *jihad* against India', Markaz leader Muhammad Ibrahim Salaf claims that the Prophet had declared, 'Allah will set him free from the pyre of hell'.

The Markaz/Lashkar sees the roots of the Kashmir problem as lying in its Muslim rulers having been replaced, first by the Sikhs and then by the Hindu Dogras through British assistance. With India (the 'Hindus') having taken over Kashmir in 1947, a long and protracted reign of bloody terror is said to have been unleashed on the Kashmiri Muslims. This is seen as a direct and logical consequence of the teachings of Hinduism itself, because, it is alleged, 'the Hindus have no compassion in their religion'. Hence, it is the duty of Muslims to wage *jihad* against the 'Hindu oppressors', for 'it is the Hindu who is a terrorist'. All Hindus are tarred with the same brush, described in such essentialist terms as 'terrorists', 'traitors', 'cowards', 'enemies', etc., these powerfully echoing widely shared sentiments among Pathan and Punjabi Muslims of Hindus being 'weak' and 'slavish', having been subjected to 'Muslim' rule for centuries, and of being 'crafty' and 'cunning', probably owing to Hindu near-monopoly of trade and commerce in India. This also builds on Pathan sentiments of 'manly honour', 'chivalry' and 'bravery', which Hindus are supposed to lack, being allegedly 'effeminate' and 'cruel'. Thus, Hafiz Muhammad Saeed declares: 'In fact, the Hindu is a mean enemy and the proper way to deal with him is the one adopted by our forefathers who crushed them by force. We need to do the same'. India is a special target for the Markaz's *mujahidin*. According to the *amir* of the Markaz, Hafiz Muhammad Sa'eed, 'The *jihad* is not about Kashmir only. It encompasses all of India'. Thus, the Markaz sees the *jihad* as going far beyond the borders of Kashmir and spreading through all of India. The final goal is to extend Muslim control over what is seen as having once been Muslim land, and, hence, to be brought back under Muslim domination, creating 'the Greater Pakistan by dint of *jihad*'. Thus, at a mammoth congregation of Markaz supporters in November 1999, Hafiz Muhammad Sa'eed declared, 'Today I announce the break-up of India, *Inshallah*. We will not rest until the whole of India is dissolved into Pakistan'. On the same occasion, Amir Hamza, senior Markaz official and editor of its Urdu organ, *ad-Da'wa*, thundered: 'We ought to disintegrate India and even wipe India out'. Those who take part in this anti-Indian *jihad* are promised that 'Allah will save [them] from the pyre of hell', and 'huge palaces in paradise' await those who are killed in fighting the 'disbelieving enemies'.

This project for the disintegration of India, followed by its take-over by Pakistan and the establishing an Islamic state in the entire sub-continent, is sought to be justified by an elaborate set of arguments that use the rhetoric of liberation. Thus, instances of human-sacrifice, untouchability, infanticide, the oppression of the 'low' castes by the Brahmins and the suppression of women in Hinduism are described in great detail, and on this basis it is sought to be shown that such a religion as Hinduism should not 'be allowed to flourish'. In Markaz literature, the mass slaughter of Muslims by Hindu chauvinist groups, often in league with the Indian state and its agencies, and the growing wave of attacks on other marginalised groups in India such as the 'low' caste Dalits, Shudras and Christians, are presented in stark colours, and the point forcefully made that such a country 'where non-Hindus are not allowed to exist' should break-up. The Markaz/Lashkar poses as a 'champion' of not just the oppressed Muslims of Kashmir or India but even of the 'low' caste Shudras and Dalits. It sees itself as having a divinely appointed mission of saving the Shudras from Brahminical tyranny. Thus, it says, 'It is incumbent upon us to save the Shudras of India from the clutches of Brahmins', and insists that 'the Brahmin Authority' must be 'ransack'. Although it claims that its *jihad* is aimed only against 'the tyrannical government and the army' and that 'nowhere do the *mujahidin* target non-Muslim or innocent people', there are reports that speak of Lashkar fighters being involved in the killing of several Hindu villagers in Jammu, Kashmir and in neighbouring Himachal Pradesh.

STOP CROSS-BORDER TERRORISM: RUSSIA TELLS PAK

Belying Pakistan's expectations that it will apply 'pressure' on India over Jammu and Kashmir, Russia on Thursday not only came out in full support of the steps taken by New Delhi to combat international terrorism in the state, but also asked Islamabad to stop cross-border infiltration of terrorists and dismantle their infrastructure. "The Russian Federation supported the steps taken by India in the Indian state of Jammu and Kashmir in combating international terrorism," said a joint statement issued at the conclusion of Prime Minister Atal Bihari Vajpayee's three-day visit to Moscow, during which he held extensive talks with President Vladimir Putin on the situation in South Asia, threat posed by terrorism to both countries and on a wide range of other issues.

Remarks attributed to Pakistan President Pervez Musharraf after his recent talks with Putin had generated speculation in Pakistan that the Russian leader would pressure Vajpayee to resume dialogue with Islamabad. Indian sources maintained that there was nothing in the Russian position as enunciated during the summit talks that could cause concern to New Delhi.

The 11-page joint statement, issued as Vajpayee emplaned for an overnight visit to the strategic Central Asian Republic of Tajikistan, leaves no doubt about the stand of Russia, which joined India in demanding that Islamabad implement its assurances to prevent cross-border terrorism. Appreciating Vajpayee's peace initiative and the accompanying measures for people-to-people contacts announced by India, Russia hoped that Pakistan would come out with a positive response to these initiatives, the statement said.

India, in turn, reiterated its support to the measures taken by Russia in Chechnya for the protection of Russia's territorial integrity and constitutional order, the statement said. A significant portion of the statement dealt with the situation in South Asia and Central Asia, Al Qaeda and Taliban.

The joint statement followed Wednesday's joint declaration by the two leaders aimed at dealing with global challenges and threats to world security and stability.

ROAD MAP FOR CONTROL OF TERRORISM IN INDIA

The growing menace of terrorism poses a formidable challenge to the civil society bringing civilization on the brink of disaster. It is needless to elucidate that loss of innocent lives in terrorist activities and trauma it has resulted in the society propelled me to write this chapter with complete focus on solution functionality, which to my understanding can curb terrorism to a great extent.

India being a very large country, with complex problems clouding socio economic fabric, multi pronged, and pluralistic approach will be instrumental in curbing terrorist attacks which are hitting head lines every other day.

ADMINISTRATIVE MEASURES

Luggage check by public transport operators: - It is impossible for police to check luggage round the clock 365 days. Police can only do brisk and discreet checking. In order to encourage the operators to check the luggage, luggage checking format with the provision of entering passenger's basic details and signature or thumb impression should be there. This information and possibility of taxi/Auto driver having a better look on the passenger can be ensured. A terrorist about to commit a crime is likely to exhibit certain distinctive psychological behaviour

- May show tensed up gait.

- Unusual generosity to driver
- High concentration
- May not be able make eye contact continuously if questioned.

In order to sustain above measures transport operators are to be given financial incentives which citizens will be interested to bear for safety. Incentives may be redeemable against filled in format with certain logical limit and may be adjusted with tax payable.

Technological Solution

A high speed scanner on certain stretch of the road should be able to detect explosives by virtue of its infrared signature. It is pertinent to mention that such scanner is already available in the world as created by Wugiang Yang of Manchester University. Infrared camera, rudder etc. are also the possibility for use which has the technical potential to detect explosives inside the vehicle.

Since billions of dollars are being spent in order to develop a full proof system, India should join in this venture along with the universities in India and abroad. We may also like to involve the Research organizations, interested talents across India. It is possible to create a platform in this connected world where people can share their expertise in co-ordination with the designated governmental agency that can support the sustainability of the research effort and be empowered to procure required gazettes/ explosives in a designated place in the select cities. Interested research groups can be connected by Internet/Video conferencing during a time, which will be convenient to most of the people.

Unfortunately terrorists seem to take the advantage of the connected world more often than the sane people.

Intelligence Network

Involve local people for gathering information regarding whatever is happening in the locality. A huge intelligence gathering across India within reward scheme for providing information can retard terrorist activities. If any terrorist is captured, it is important to understand his mind by psychoanalyst, Social psychologist by soft and empathetic approach rather getting into punitive third degree methodology right from beginning.

It is also important to maintain confidentiality after thorough dialogue with Media since every time details of investigation is known to everybody by national media, terrorist are getting smarter. Uses of wireless network, refraining from usage of mobile by terrorists are pointers to this fact.

Political Solution

A federal body involving top legal brains of the country, may be constituted for curbing terrorism from legal standpoint, whose recommendation after debate in parliament's upper house, may be constitutionally enacted as binding to all political parties and states. It must be remembered that counter terrorism measures should be enforced respecting international human rights obligations and the basic tenets of the Rule of Law, otherwise it will be self defeating.

MEDIUM TERM

Audio Visual Campaign

An all out audio visual campaign should be launched in order to counter the hate preaching by certain fundamentalist groups. It is important to study religious scriptures line by line in order to counter the misuse by certain misleading religious leader. Removing terrorism from the minds of people is more important than militarily fight terrorism. Broad minded religious leaders from all cross section of society should be requested to preach people for great cause of national harmony. The superior ingredient of religion can be translated into a motivation that will sanctify society".

Conference Room Solution

In the event of brewing conflict in the society, bring the leaders of opposing groups to the conference room. Otherwise even a small discord can aggravate to a great turmoil.

Rationing Negative News Reporting

It is important to ration negative news reporting in the media. Too much of negative news reporting round the clock is changing the social psychology irreversibly. It is important to highlight that many positive and innovative activities are taking place in society. Otherwise terrorists will bask on the sensionalism created in media.

National Forum

It is suggested to create a national forum with online participation of talents all across India not for only discussion but take decisions on issues of great national importance in consonance with Ministers and IAS officers and political leaders of different parties within the constitutional framework. Following Model may be suggested. Let us create a National Channel and involve talented media personalities from NDTV, Times Now, Headlines Today, CNN etc. evolving an enlightened society to curb the menace of terrorism.

Media brains can anchor the program with the focus on solution functionality rather than only capturing opinions or sterile intellectual exercise. Channel should allow detailed discussion involving an audience all across India either through physical presence or by video conferencing, Internet etc. Decisions should be taken on the channel itself and Ministers and IAS officers should prepare resolution on the spot itself and read out to nation. It may be noted many discussion in NDTV ushered in epoch making initiatives from Government especially in Indo –Pak relationship. Hence suggested model will be instrumental in encouraging many initiatives from Government for better tomorrow.

Invoke Liberal views in the society

Let us involve pious souls like Shri Ravi Shankar, Monks of Ramkrishna Mission and other religious institutions. To my understanding, some of the monks of Ramkrishna Mission are intellectual giants not only because of their knowledge of religious scriptures, but because of their amazing liberal views on social and political issues. Nation should be open to such great souls in our troubled times who can provide radically different solution acceptable to all conflicting parties.

Educational Campaign across country

Through out the world it is the education which is the ultimate solution for all social problems. Most of the social problems are arising out of people's ignorance. Hence Government should invest maximum amount in Education- more than any other sector. One can even do the deficit financing in this area, considering whatever the amount that will be spent today, its effect will be offset by the goods and service generated by the more educated people, as a result of the education drive. It requires no explanation that educated and enlightened individuals will definitely promote peace and harmony in the society.

Socio-Economic Solution

Oppression and wide spread neglect of human rights and denial of hope of better future for common people are the fertile ground for breeding terrorism. Social, economic and political disparities in a large scale engender conflicts within the State and beyond. Policy makers should ensure that a balance is maintained all across India. It is not important to have world class facilities only in select cities, it rather important that most of the people in India should be put on survival economy. Any meaningful endeavour to resolve conflicts and terrorism will have to ensure enjoyment the full range of Economic, Social and Cultural Rights by the citizens. Political leaders have to rise above narrow interest and limit the uneven economic development in India as much as possible. It may be argued that all out development in all villages in India will require astronomical amount and India may not have so much of resources. But on the contrary, amount required to curb social unrest and terrorism is not less either. At least let us share resource judiciously for the unfortunate section of the humanity. In that process, all of them may not live in prosperity but they will not starve either. Once we start contributing something for the nation with little honesty and sincerity, a miraculous result will follow- and that my belief.

Defusing religious extremism:- One major factor leading to terrorist activities for imposing so called religious or ideological intent needs to be defused by counter campaign which will convince people regarding the rationale of non violent approach against hatred policy of misguided fanatics. Society's condemnation to a climate of religious bigotry, which leads to discrimination, harassment and attacks on all those who are believers of other faiths, has to be very strong, otherwise indifference of the society to such acts will only encourage fundamentalism. Government must encourage, fund and protect NGO who will be focusing on defusing religious extremism.

2

Cross-Border Terrorism in India

Cross-border terrorism has emerged as a great threat to the security of India. Terrorism originating from across the border has slowly attempted to strangle the democracy and sovereignty of India.

By its nature, the term "terrorism" is bound up in political controversy. It is a concept with a very negative connotation. Because terrorism implies the killing and maiming of innocent people, no country wants to be accused of supporting terrorism or harbouring terrorist groups. At the same time, no country wants what it considers to be a legitimate use of force to be considered terrorism. An old saying goes, "One person's terrorist is another person's freedom fighter."

While there is no universal definition of terrorism, various experts point out that there are common elements to most terrorist acts. Acts of terrorism usually are committed by groups who do not possess the political power to change policies they view as intolerable. Middle Eastern terrorism intensified in the 1970s in response to defeats of Arab nations in wars with Israel over the Palestine issue. Convinced that further wars were futile, a number of countries, including Egypt, sought peace with Israel. This enraged groups within those countries dedicated to the defeat of Israel, who then turned to terrorism. Terrorists choose targets and actions to maximise the psychological effect on a society or government. Their goal is to create a situation in which a government will change its policies to avoid further bloodshed or disruption. For these reasons, terrorists often choose methods of mass destruction, such as bombings, and target transportation or crowded places to increase anxiety and fear.

The attacks on the World Trade Centre and the Pentagon in the USA on September 11, 2001 brought transnational terrorism to attention. This kind of terrorism is also known as cross-border terrorism. Cross-border terror groups do not confine themselves either territorially or ideologically to a particular country or region. They are global in orientation, readily moving funds, men and material from one place to another.

Groups like the Palestine nationalist groups and the Irish Republican Army (IRA) also crossed state borders to launch attacks, to smuggle arms and to seek refuge. The IRA got weapons from Libya and launched attacks across Britain; it also launched a one-off attack in Germany and plotted an assault on British forces in Gibraltar.

Palestinian 'terrorists' crossed into Israeli territory, or what they considered Palestinian territory, and sought refuge in states like Egypt and Syria. They hijacked aeroplanes across the world, took hostage Israeli contestants at the 1972 Olympics in Munich, and infamously hijacked an Italian cruise ship in 1985.

However, these groups were politically and organisationally tied to a particular territory. As international experts Ray Takeyh and Nikolas Gvosdev put it, these groups pursued largely 'irredentist aims' and built up their memberships 'from a specific population—even if they sought the sponsorship of a foreign patron for arms and logistical support'.

Today's cross-border groups view territory expediently, as a base from which they can organise their campaigns and plot their attacks. The new breed of Islamic terror groups are, according to Takeyh and Gvosdev, 'explicitly global'—in the sense that they have broadly anti-Western views rather than locally defined objectives, and their members hail from different states rather than from a distinct community with distinct interests.

Where the armed groups of old sought to build or remake nation states, today's cross-border terrorists feed off the demise of state authority. Where national liberation movements sought to redraw state boundaries, cross-border groups think nothing of moving from one failed state to another. Where the earlier violent groups focussed their energies on achieving limited local aims, even as they carried out international operations, today's terror groups talk about 'spreading jihad' around the globe.

Some analysts believe that it was Western intervention in, the third world, specifically the "humanitarian intervention' of the post-Cold War period, that encouraged the emergence of today's cross-border terrorists.

By undermining state authority and notions of sovereignty, humanitarian intervention created the space for the rise of non-state actors. And by internationalising local conflicts, Western intervention did much to encourage the flouting of traditional borders and the movement of armed groups between territories.

Through the process of weakening state authority and internationalising conflicts, Western intervention has given rise to a new kind of terrorist—terrorists who, as Pentagon officials put it, 'respect no borders, no boundaries and no state institutions', who feed off the absence of state authority and move across territories in the execution of their 'global' campaigns.

According to Dr. Thomas P.M. Barnett, a Professor at the Naval War College, US, the world may be divided into three areas, the core, the seam and the gap states, based on their level of globalization.

Core states are those thick with network connectivity, financial transactions, liberal media flows and collective security. States in this category feature stable governments, rising standards of living and more deaths by suicide than murder. Core states include North America, much of South America, the European Union, Russia, Japan, and Asia's emerging economies (most notably China and India), Australia, New Zealand and South Africa. Gap states are those where globalization is thinning or absent, plagued by politically repressive regimes, widespread poverty and disease, routine mass murder and most important—the chronic conflicts that incubate the next generation of global terrorists.

Seam states are those, lying between the Core and Gap, which are in transition to being fully globalized. Seam states include: Mexico, Brazil, South Africa, Morocco, Algeria, Greece, Turkey, Pakistan, Thailand, Malaysia, the Philippines and Indonesia.

The results of these efforts show an overwhelming concentration of activity in the regions of the world excluded from globalization's growing core. These areas are the Caribbean Rim, virtually all of Africa, the Balkans, the Caucasus, and Central Asia, the Middle East, Southwest Asia and much of Southeast Asia. Most of the nations in this area have demographics skewed very young and most are labelled, "low income" or "low middle income" by the World Bank (i.e., less than $3,000 annual per capita).

Osama Bin Laden and Al Qaeda sprang to life in Sudan and Afghanistan, which by any standards are two of the most disconnected countries in the world. A look at other places where US Special Forces have recently been deployed includes northwestern Pakistan, Somalia and Yemen which all fall in the same category. Dr. Barnett's message is: "A country's potential to warrant a US military response is inversely related to its globalization connectivity."

INSURGENCY IN INDIA'S NORTHEAST CROSS-BORDER LINKS AND STRATEGIC ALLIANCES

India's Northeast is one of South Asia's hottest trouble spots, not simply because the region has as many as 30 armed insurgent organizations 1 operating and fighting the Indian state, but because trans-border linkages that these groups have, and strategic alliances among them, have acted as force multipliers and have made the conflict dynamics all the more intricate. With demands of these insurgent groups ranging from secession to autonomy and the right to self-determination, and a plethora of ethnic groups clamouring for special rights and the protection of their distinct identity, the region is bound to be a turbulent one.

Moreover, the location of the eight northeastern Indian States itself is part of the reason why it has always been a hotbed of militancy with trans-border ramifications. This region of 263,000 square kilometres shares highly porous and sensitive frontiers with China in the North, Myanmar in the East, Bangladesh in the South West and Bhutan to the North West. The region's strategic location is underlined by the fact that it shares a 4,500 km-long international border with its four South Asian neighbours, but is connected to the Indian mainland by a tenuous 22 km-long land corridor passing through Siliguri in the eastern State of West Bengal, appropriately described as the 'Chicken's Neck.'

Battles at Home, Links Abroad

Trans-border linkages of Northeast Indian insurgent groups started developing within less than 10 years of the country's independence from the British yoke. The father of the Naga insurgency, Angami Zapu Phizo, chief of the rebel Naga National Council (NNC), had left the Naga Hills in 1956 to fight for an independent Naga homeland from foreign shores. He traveled through the then East Pakistan and Switzerland, to arrive, eventually, in London in 1960, and continued to pursue his dream from the British capital until his death in April 1990. His daughter Adinno Phizo, who has succeeded him as the NNC president, is still pushing that demand from her home in London.

In 1972, New Delhi declared the NNC an unlawful organization under the Unlawful Activities (Prevention) Act of 1967, and launched a massive counter-insurgency offensive. Cornered and faced with reverses, the insurgents agreed to hold peace talks with the Indian Government. This led to the signing of the controversial Shillong Accord on November 11, 1975, between a section of the NNC and its 'underground government,' the Naga Federal Government (NFG) and the Government of India. The signatories to this agreement accepted the Indian Constitution and agreed to surrender their weapons and join the Indian national mainstream.

A group of around 140 NNC cadres, however, repudiated the Shillong Accord and refused to surrender. They formed a new insurgent group called the National Socialist Council of Nagaland (NSCN) under the leadership of Thuingaleng Muivah, Isak Chisi Swu and S. S. Khaplang. The significant point to be noted is that this new group, formed in 1980, took shape and was launched from bases inside Myanmar. With the passage of time, the NSCN emerged as the most radical and powerful insurgent group fighting for the Naga cause. Clannish divisions among the Nagas (Konyaks and Tangkhuls) resulted in the split of the NSCN in 1988. The Konyaks took the lead in forming the NSCN-K (Khaplang) under the leadership of Khole Konyak and S. S. Khaplang. The faction, led mostly by the Tangkhuls under the leadership of Swu and Muivah, came to be known as the NSCN-IM (Isak-Muivah).

The NSCN, after its formation inside Myanmar and having established itself as a front-ranking insurgent group in India's Northeast, started providing arms training and other logistic support to outfits such as the United Liberation Front of Asom (ULFA), formed in April 1979 to fight for a 'sovereign, Socialist Assam.' The ULFA started sending its cadres for advanced 'military training' at the hands of the Kachin Independence Army (KIA), an anti-Yangon rebel group in Myanmar, from 1988 onwards. Surrendered or captured ULFA rebels, interviewed by this writer, have confirmed having received arms training at the hands of KIA instructors inside Myanmar. 7 American author Shelby Tucker writes about having met ULFA 'chairman' Arabinda Rajkhowa at the headquarters of the Kachin Independence Organization (KIO), political wing of the KIA, at Pajau Bum, during his trek across Myanmar around 1989. Former ULFA cadres say the group's 'commander-in-chief', Paresh Barua, too, was in Myanmar's Kachin hills around that time.

Such trips were among the first attempts by rebels from Assam to strengthen strategic alliances with militant groups located in India's South Asian neighbours like Myanmar. In 1985 itself, the ULFA opened shop in Bangladesh, setting up safe houses at Damai village in the Moulvi Bazaar district, bordering the Northeastern Indian State of Meghalaya. In 1990, the ULFA had its Pakistani contacts in place, and leaders like Munin Nobis (since surrendered) were instrumental in establishing the links. Nobis told this writer during extensive interviews in October 2002 that the Pakistanis facilitated the crossover of a number of ULFA leaders, including Paresh Barua, into Afghanistan through Pakistan's North West

Frontier Province. These visitors, assisted by the Pakistani Inter-Services Intelligence (ISI), met Gulbuddin Hekmatyar, a top Afghan Mujahideen leader of the time. Not surprisingly, ULFA cadres, who surrendered in the wake of the Bhutanese military assault on their camps in December 2003, talked of the presence of an Afghan-trained artillery expert in their Bhutan bases. By the end of 1990 and early 1991, the ULFA had set up well-entrenched bases inside Southern Bhutan, mainly in the district of Samdrup Jhongkar, bordering western Assam's Nalbari district.

The rebels' entry into the Himalayan Kingdom followed the first organized counter-insurgency operations that the Indian Army launched against the ULFA in Assam on the night of November 27-28, 1990, codenamed 'Operation Bajrang.' The Army offensive came in the wake of the ULFA creating a virtual reign of terror in the State, killing, kidnapping and extorting money from tea companies and others, and New Delhi's dismissal of the Asom Gana Parishad (AGP) Government of Chief Minister Prafulla Kumar Mahanta for its alleged failure in maintaining law and order. Unlike in Myanmar, where Indian insurgent groups like the ULFA had allies like the KIA, in Bhutan, they had none.

The Himalayan Kingdom was chosen by the ULFA, and later the National Democratic Front of Bodoland and the Kamtapur Liberation Organisation (KLO), 11 because Southern Bhutan, where it set up base, was not properly policed, was densely wooded and was located just across the border from Assam. Besides, Bhutan, had a small Army and limited capabilities in the beginning, and was reluctant to take on counter-insurgency measures against a group of heavily-armed rebels.

It consequently served as an excellent staging area for the Indian separatists, who could return to the safety of their camps in the Kingdom after carrying out violent strikes in Indian territory. Bhutan took 12 years to launch a military crackdown to oust the Indian separatists for reasons that are described later in this chapter. But, unlike Thimphu, which had admitted the presence of these foreign militants right from the beginning, Dhaka has always denied the fact that Indian insurgents were staying in, or operating from, Bangladesh.

Bangladesh: Partner in Terror?

On December 21, 1997, Bangladesh immigration and security officials arrested ULFA 'general secretary', Anup Chetia, from downtown Dhaka's North Adabor locality. The main charges against the Indian separatist leader were illegal entry into Bangladesh, possession of two forged Bangladeshi passports (Nos. 0964185 and 0227883), possession of an unauthorized satellite telephone and illegal possession of foreign currency of countries as diverse as the US, UK, Switzerland, Thailand, Philippines, Spain, Nepal, Bhutan, Belgium, Singapore and others. Two of Chetia's accomplices, Babul Sharma and Laxmi Prasad Goswami, were also arrested along with him the same day. Dhaka often seeks to cite this action by the Bangladeshi authorities against the ULFA leader to drive home its claim that the country would not permit Indian militants to operate from its soil.

The presence of Indian insurgents in safe havens in Bangladesh has never been in doubt, considering the volumes of hard intelligence inputs with New Delhi. In January 2004, New Delhi had handed over a detailed list of 194 Indian insurgent camps located inside Bangladesh. This was during the meeting of the Indian Border Security Force (BSF) and the Bangladesh Rifles (BDR) in New Delhi between January 6 and 9, 2004. If confirmation was needed, a spate of reports relating to multiple incidents on January 2, 2004, and Dhaka's subsequent responses, gave confirmation to India's long-standing complaint that its neighbour was being less than forthcoming on the issue.

On January 2, the BDR raided a hideout of the National Liberation Front of Tripura (NLFT) and captured six of its cadres and seized some weapons and a mobile telephone set. According to media reports originating from Bangladesh, the raided NLFT camp was located near Karisapunji village in the Habiganj district. The United News of Bangladesh identified those arrested as Kokek Tripura, Philip Debbarma, Manjak Debbarma, Bukhuk Debbarma, Satish Debbarma and Shoilen Debbarma.

In another incident on January 2, the All Tripura Tiger Force (ATTF) 'chief' Ranjit Debbarma's residence in Dhaka was attacked by rocket propelled grenades (RPG). Indian media reports said five ATTF cadres were killed in that attack and eight others, including Debbarma, were wounded.

Acccording to a section of the intelligence community, 14 the January 2 rocket attack occurred in the Shamoli building, apparently owned by a leading Bangladeshi political figure. The 'chiefs' of the ATTF and ULFA were reportedly staying in this highly secure building. After the rocket attack on the building's 2ndfloor, where the ATTF 'chief' was allegedly staying, the local police swung into action and detained almost everyone in the building. Some of those detained were supposed to have been Bangladeshi intelligence operatives. Four injured persons were taken to hospital. Later, the police released all those detained. These intelligence reports claim that top officials of the Directorate General of Forces Intelligence (DGFI) intervened to secure the release of these men. It is claimed that many of those arrested were ULFA cadres, and that this is the same incident that the local media reports in Dhaka had talked about, when they mentioned the arrest of 34 ULFA cadres. It is also claimed that members of a local mafia group called 'Seven Star' was behind the rocket attack. No independent confirmation of this incident was immediately available.

How did Dhaka respond to these media reports? While it preferred to remain silent on the reports relating to the raid and the arrest of six NLFT cadres as well as the bomb attack on the residence of the ATTF chief, Bangladesh came out with a formal denial of reports about the arrest of 34 ULFA militants from Dhaka. "We would like to categorically state that the reports (about the ULFA rebels' capture) are false, baseless and concocted and have been fabricated to strain the friendly relations between Bangladesh and India. No such incidents took place in the capital city of Dhaka," a Home Ministry Press Release issued in Dhaka on January 3 said. The Bangladesh Home Ministry statement added: "We would also like to reassert the well-known position of the Government of Bangladesh that Bangladesh has never allowed or assisted insurgent groups of any country for acts against that country and this policy was being pursued by the Government consistently and rigorously.

Within the changing global context of counter-terrorism and perspectives on South Asia, Bangladesh is certainly and increasingly on the back-foot, with its official position *vis-à-vis* Indian insurgent groups increasingly losing the cover of credible deniability. In addition to the volumes of evidence accumulated by Indian authorities, the case against Bangladesh is also gradually being independently validated. For instance, the location of the NLFT hideout that was reported in Bangladesh media as having been raided by the BDR on January 2, 2004 tallies with a location mentioned in the list of 194 Indian insurgent camps inside Bangladesh submitted by the BSF to its Bangladesh counterpart, the BDR, in January 2004. The Indian list stated that the NLFT had a transit camp at Thakurgaon under Chunarughat Police Station in the Habiganj District of Bangladesh. Again, the very fact that Dhaka did not deny the raid and subsequent capture of six NLFT cadres goes against its official position that there are neither camps nor any Indian insurgent cadres operating from Bangladeshi territory.

Denials aside, Bangladesh, by reliable accounts, may in fact be waking up to the need to rein in these foreign militants. This report in a leading English daily from Dhaka, makes interesting reading:

The Home Ministry at a high-level meeting with paramilitary BDR and intelligence agencies yesterday (January 4, 2004) asked them to step up border security and watch on Dhaka to stem infiltration of Indian terrorists. The Ministry officially denied discussion on steps to tackle infiltration of the operatives of the ULFA and other outfits, but meeting sources confirmed the agenda. They said Home Minister Altaf Hossain Chowdhury and State Minister Lutfozzaman Babar asked the DGFI and NSI (National Security Intelligence) agencies to keep an eye on suspicious people in hotels and rest houses in Dhaka. The ministers also asked the agencies to strengthen vigilance in the porous bordering areas of Cox's Bazaar, Bandarban, Rangamati, Khagrachhari and Sylhet.

There is some speculation that Dhaka may, in fact, have been stung by Bhutan's year-end crackdown in 2003 on anti-India separatist camps on its territory, a move for which the Royal

Government in Thimphu has received widespread appreciation from nations in the forefront of the global war on terror. But any action that Dhaka may be initiating, does not appear to have been triggered simply because another South Asian neighbour had shown the way by launching an assault on anti-India rebels in the Kingdom, or because New Delhi has been persistent in its claim that an increasing number of camps of Indian insurgents are located inside Bangladesh. It is, rather, the rising pressure of international opinion that is forcing a reassessment in Dhaka and could even be compelling it to launch a rather covert offensive against the Indian militants operating from Bangladesh.

The publication in part, on December 10, 2003, of a report on Bangladesh, prepared by the Canadian Security Intelligence Service (CSIS), and an advisory issued by the US State Department to its citizens and officials posted at or visiting Bangladesh, have been particularly embarrassing for Dhaka. The CSIS report prepared in December 2003, said that the Bangladesh Government was not taking enough measures to prevent the country from becoming a haven for Islamist terror groups in South Asia. The report expressed concern over the activities of terrorists suspected to be connected with Osama bin Laden's Al Qaeda network. The CSIS report added that Dhaka was not willing to crack down on terror, and expressed fear of dangers to Canadian aid workers in Bangladesh. Significantly, the report also said that there had been a number of serious terrorist attacks on cultural groups and recreational facilities in Bangladesh, but Prime Minister Khaleda Zia's Bangladesh Nationalist Party (BNP) had been blaming the main Opposition party (the Awami League of former Premier Sheikh Hasina Wajed) for such criminal activities as a matter of routine, rather than zeroing in on the real people or groups behind such acts of violence.

Dhaka rejected the observations made in the CSIS report and has been consistently denying that Bangladesh had become the latest hub of Islamist terror groups, including the Al Qaeda. The fact remains, however, that a local terrorist group, the Harkat-ul-Jehad-al-Islami Bangladesh (HuJI-BD), led by Shauqat Osman, with the avowed objective of establishing 'Islamic rule' in

Bangladesh, is indeed active in the country. Western media reports suggest this group has an estimated 15,000 cadres.

With increasing international attention focused on terrorist and insurgent activities in Bangladesh, Dhaka's past pretence is becoming progressively unsustainable. Nevertheless, the flow of insurgents from India to safe havens in Bangladesh continues. Indeed, with ULFA having lost its bases and once-secure staging areas inside Bhutan, it is expected to turn to two obvious alternate locations, Myanmar and Bangladesh. Yangon has reportedly turned on the heat on Indian insurgents in the country, leaving Bangladesh as the only place that rebels like those of the ULFA have to hold on to. This, too, may not be easy anymore. Dhaka might continue to push ahead with its stand that no Indian insurgents are located or operating from the country, but may eventually have to move as quietly as possible to neutralize these rebels and choke them off within its territory to escape a possibly foolproof indictment by the international community as a nation that has not done enough to combat terror.

It is the articulated views of Prime Minister Khaleda Zia's BNP on insurgent groups from Assam, for instance, that increases the level of concern in India. As Opposition leader in May 1998, within six months of Chetia's arrest, Zia had told this writer during an interview at the BNP headquarters in Dhaka that her party would like to regard the ULFA cadres as 'freedom fighters' just as the Mukti Bahini were freedom fighters. She had then also expressed her gratitude to the people of Assam and Meghalaya for sheltering the Mukti Bahini freedom fighters, indirectly implying that there was nothing wrong in some ULFA men taking shelter inside Bangladesh. That obviously may not be the BNP or Premier Zia's official position now, particularly after 9/11 when the world is engaged in a global war against terror.

It is in this context that some western media reports of the ULFA sending its representatives to attend a meeting of radical Islamist outfits, organized by the HUJI-BD, at a secret rendezvous in Bangladesh in the summer of 2002, arouse curiosity. The ULFA is not an Islamist outfit and is rather secular in the sense that its cadres are drawn from diverse groups and communities, cutting across religions. But what cannot be ignored is the possibility that ULFA would have to arrange for sanctuary for some of these Islamist militant leaders or cadres as a *quid pro quo* for its continued stay in Bangladesh, should the pressure against terror is to be increased by Dhaka. However, it would appear that the Bangladeshi Islamists would rather turn to the Rohingya rebels in adjoining Myanmar due to the fact that their chances of hiding in that terrain would be better than in India's Northeast, where the military is constantly on the insurgents' trail.

Bhutan: Taste of War

At the crack of dawn on December 15, 2003, Bhutanese monarch, Jigme Singye Wangchuck, unleashed his small military machine, comprising the Royal Bhutan Army (RBA) and the Royal Body Guards (RBG), to expel an excess of 3,000 heavily armed Indian separatists belonging to three different groups, the ULFA, NDFB and the KLO. Bhutan said the insurgents were operating from 30 camps inside the kingdom (ULFA had 13 camps, NDFB 12 and the KLO 5). Buddhist Bhutan had last gone to war against any foreign force 138 years ago when they fought the British. That was the Anglo-Bhutanese war of 1865 in which the Crown's Army defeated Bhutan's then Deb Raja or temporal head, Sonam Lhendup, and came to exercise much influence on Bhutan's affairs. That victory gave the British unhindered trans-Himalayan Middle-level ULFA and NDFB leaders who came for the meetings said they were unable to leave the kingdom immediately," Aum Neten Zangmo, Bhutan's Foreign Secretary, told this writer by telephone from Thimphu, the nation's capital. On the insurgents' response during the last round of talks, a Bhutanese Foreign Ministry statement had this to say:

> The ULFA said that it would be suicidal for their cause of independence of Assam to leave Bhutan while the NDFB said that even if they left their present camps, they would have to come back and establish camps in other parts of Bhutan...

The Foreign Secretary said even during most of the earlier 'exit talks' (talks to persuade the rebels to withdraw from the Kingdom), the insurgent groups were represented by middle-level leaders while the Royal Government was represented at the highest level, including that of the Prime Minister and Home Minister.

That was a difficult decision indeed for King Wangchuck to take. Firstly because, the battle capabilities of the RBA and the RBG (the Royal Body Guards is a force actually meant exclusively for protection of the Royal family) were totally untested. If anything, the Bhutanese Forces could have been absolutely rusty, not having had the occasion to fire a single shot except during their training sessions with the Indian Army, which runs a military training centre inside Bhutan. Secondly, a military crackdown could turn the insurgents against the Bhutanese state machinery or its citizens. This, in turn, would make access into the landlocked kingdom difficult as most of the roads into southern Bhutan, the insurgents' stronghold, pass through Indian territory, via the northeastern State of Assam and the eastern State of West Bengal. But, King Wangchuck could wait no more.

The timing of the assault certainly needs to be examined. The Bhutanese cite the mandate of the 81stsession of the National Assembly to the Royal Government to try and persuade the insurgents to leave the Kingdom 'one last time', or to expel them by using military force. However, that had been the National Assembly's directive for several years. This makes it pertinent to try and zero in on the possible trigger for the operations in December 2003, twelve years after the rebels had first entered Bhutan. Such an analysis would make it necessary to examine the significance of the relatively smaller and rag-tag group, the KLO, and its affiliations and linkages, more than those of the ULFA or the NDFB.

Both the Indian and Bhutanese security establishments were stung by news of the launching of the Bhutan Communist Party (Marxist-Leninist-Maoist) o n April 22, 2003, the 133rd birth anniversary of Lenin. Pamphlets widely circulated by this new group in the Bhutanese refugee camps in Nepal and in areas inside Bhutan itself, revealed that the new party's objective was to 'smash the monarchy' and establish a 'true and new democracy' in Bhutan. Both New Delhi and Thimphu were quick to put the KLO under the scanner. Security agencies soon came to the conclusion the KLO was active and had pockets of influence in the strategic North Bengal areas of West Bengal and could act as a bridge between the Maoists insurgents in Nepal and the newly emerging Maoist force in Bhutan. Besides, Indian intelligence agencies were aware of the fact that the KLO had provided sanctuary to fleeing Maoist cadres from Nepal, that the outfit had acted as a link between the Maoists and the radical left-wing activists in Bihar, and that it received help from the Maoists in setting up a number of explosive manufacturing units in North Bengal.

In the final analysis, Bhutan's emerging Maoist threat could have been the key factor in provoking the eventual Army action, although intense pressure from New Delhi to oust the Indian insurgents, as well as the threat the rebels' presence posed to Bhutan's own sovereignty and development, could be the other factors that may have made the King shake off his long-held ambivalence and act decisively.

THIMPHU'S ACTION: IMPACT IN SOUTH ASIA

The debate on whether the Bhutanese military carried out the anti-rebel offensive entirely on its own or whether the Indian Army's role, as claimed by New Delhi, was limited to providing nothing more than 'logistic support' and ammunition, is not very relevant. However, the fact remains that Bhutan carried out a military operation and managed to dismantle the well-entrenched bases of three Indian insurgent groups which were carrying out violent strikes against symbols of Indian Governmental authority as well as civilians with ease, and returning to the safety of their bases in the Himalayan kingdom by simply walking across the porous border.

Thimphu's military strike against the Indian insurgents did create an immediate impact in South Asia in so far as the war against terror was concerned. The following responses were clearly noticeable in the region:

Bangladesh reacted by saying it had sealed its borders with India to prevent Indian insurgents fleeing Bhutan or Myanmar from entering its territory.

The arrest of 34 ULFA cadres in and around Dhaka and the rocket attack on the ATTF chief's apartment in downtown Dhaka were some post-Bhutan offensive developments that cannot be ignored.

The Bangladesh Home Ministry, as mentioned earlier, decided to crack down on Indian militants, and to keep such operations secret, obviously due to Dhaka's official stand that no Indian insurgents were operating from that country.

There were strong indications of Myanmar already tightening its noose on Indian insurgent groups like the NSCN-K and the ULFA, which have bases in the country.

New Delhi seized the initiative and used the forum of the South Asian Association for Regional Cooperation (SAARC), which was holding its 12th Summit in Islamabad in the first week of January 2004, to call upon nations in the region to actively clamp down on terror. Pakistan could not have missed this strong statement by India to fight terrorism in South Asia as well as globally. The then Prime Minister, Atal Behari Vajpayee, addressing the Summit, said:

I would like to draw attention to the courageous action taken by His Majesty the King of Bhutan and his government against insurgent groups which were trying to use Bhutanese territory to launch terrorist activities in India. It is an outstanding example of sensitivity to the security concerns of a neighbour which is at the same time in the direct long-term security interest of Bhutan itself.

Earlier, on January 1, 2004, the then Indian Foreign Minister, Yashwant Sinha, had urged the SAARC countries to emulate Bhutan in flushing out insurgents from their soil. New Delhi's remarks and Bhutanese Prime Minister Jigme Thinley's strong plea for the adoption and effective implementation of the protocol on terrorism during the Summit were points that did not go unnoticed. In an indirect reference to Pakistan's role, Thinley, during his address at the Summit, said that the attempt to assassinate Pakistan President Pervez Musharraf was a rude reminder of the need to root out terrorism.

Post 9/11 and, thereafter, post-military offensive by Bhutan, India's neighbours and all those engaged in the global war against terror, had started speaking in a similar language, that terrorism needed to be curbed with a firm hand. During the offensive, in a dramatic move, ULFA 'chairman', Arabinda Rajkhowa, appealed to the Chinese leadership on December 25, 2003,32 to provide safe passage to the insurgents from Bhutan for temporary shelter in China. Rajkhowa in his fax communication to the Chinese leadership said: "We have come under massive attack of Indo-Bhutan joint forces and our combatants have been forced to retreat up to the Sino-Bhutan border due to all out air and artillery campaigns..." Beijing was quick to turn down the ULFA plea and cautioned that it had alerted its frontier forces to prevent any intrusion of Indian militants. A Chinese Embassy spokesperson in New Delhi said the Chinese Frontier Forces were quite capable of preventing the entry of Indian insurgents into their country and that they were closely monitoring the development of the situation.

It is not that China or sources in China have always maintained a distance from Indian separatists. Indian insurgents had not only visited China in the past for help, but had received assistance from sources within the country. NSCN-IM 'general secretary', Thuingaleng Muivah, is on record as having said that Naga insurgents had, in the early days, obtained arms from China and Pakistan. Of course, Muivah's claims do not match Indian media reports in 2000, that talked of a Chinese 'agency' supplying machine guns and AK-47 rifles to insurgent groups in India's Northeast. A crossed cheque of half-a-million dollars encashed by a Chinese firm in Beijing revealed the source from where the NSCN-IM was getting arms. News reports talked of NSCN-IM arms procurer, Anthony Shimray, having flown from Bangkok to Beijing in September 2000 and holding talks with the 'Chinese agency' in Kunming. The report may or may not be correct, but it is undeniable that China has always been looked upon by several Northeast Indian insurgent groups as its ideological source.

While New Delhi may have received sufficient co-operation from Bhutan and Myanmar in combating the separatists, it is yet to get what it would like to from, say Thailand. Pakistan, of course, is a different story altogether. To illustrate: In a major joint Indo-Myanmar anti-insurgency drive in April 1995, the Indian and Myanmarese Armies launched a pincer attack on a group of some 200 Indian insurgents, codenamed 'Operation Golden Bird,' along the border with Mizoram. Up to 60 ULFA and other Northeast Indian insurgents were killed and several others arrested during the 44-day offensive. The insurgents were returning to their bases in India after procuring a huge consignment of arms from Bangladesh. This military co-operation has been generally continuing between the two nations despite some ups and downs in recent years.

Thailand, too, has been a favourite location of some of the top Northeast Indian insurgent leaders. New Delhi has, for long, been persuading Bangkok to disallow insurgents from the Northeast using Thailand as a sanctuary for striking arms deals and holding strategy sessions. In the mid-nineties, the Royal Thai Navy seized an illegal arms shipment of the People's Liberation Army (PLA) of Manipur. Ten men were arrested after their 16-metre vessel was intercepted by a Navy patrol boat following a chase in the Andaman Sea off the southern Thai seaport of Ranong. The arrested persons, suspected to be PLA cadres, were found holding Bangladeshi passports. Among the two tons of weapons seized by the Thai Navy were two RPG launchers, 20 American assault rifles, two recoilless guns, four M-79 grenades launchers and more than 10,000 rounds of assorted ammunition. It was for the first time that the Thai authorities swooped down on Northeast Indian insurgents, including the ULFA and both factions of the NSCN, who had been using this particular sea route to ferry military hardware to their bases.

However, this appears to have been a one-off action. Since then, New Delhi has not been receiving much help from Bangkok. For instance, on January 19, 2000, Thai authorities arrested Muivah from the Bangkok International Airport. But it is unlikely that the Thai authorities acted against him because of New Delhi's persuasion. According to p ublished reports, Muivah was arrested apparently on the basis of information that he was travelling on a false South Korean passport and that he was actually a North

Korean agent on a mission to blow up the South Korean embassy in Bangkok. Media reports have also said that Muivah and the NSCN-IM chairman, Isak Chisi Swu, have been living in Bangkok for more than 20 years now, own apartments and have business interests in the Thai capital.

Rebel Groupings as Force Multipliers

Events on the insurgency front in India's Northeast have shown that rebel groups have often succeeded in neutralizing the reverses faced by them by entering into deals with other insurgent groups, and these alliances act as force multipliers. Insurgent politics in the region registered a very important development in year 2000—the signing of a deal for joint operations by the ULFA and United National Liberation Front (UNLF), a Manipuri insurgent group whose primary area of operation was Manipur's Jiribam Valley and neighbouring Assam's Cachar district. A UNLF statement on July 29, 2000, disclosed the agreement between that group and the ULFA for the first time. Significantly, the statement came less than a fortnight after the UNLF claimed responsibility for the July 16, 2000, killing of three soldiers in the Cachar district of Assam. Given the admission about the agreement, the ULFA could well have provided logistic support to the UNLF in carrying out that ambush.

The UNLF, formed on November 24, 1964, under the leadership of Areambam Samarendra Singh to establish an independent socialist Manipur, has a rather frightening history, in so far as its one-time allies are concerned. At its inception, the outfit shared a close 'political relationship' with the then East Pakistani regime, and in 1969 underwent military training in that country. The group is also said to have backed the Pakistani Army during the Bangladesh liberation war in 1971. Not just depending on Pakistan, the UNLF moved closer to China with a team headed by N. Bisheswar Singh proceeding to Lhasa in 1975 to ask for Beijing's assistance. Now headed by Rajkumar Meghen alias Sana Yaima, the UNLF is also close to the NSCN-K and has training camps in Myanmar and Bangladesh. It is linkages such as these and the potential for immense trans-border movement by cadres of these groups that has made the ULFA-UNLF pact so significant. The ULFA would like to describe the agreement as a 'fraternal bond sealed to fulfil certain tactical goals.' It may not have been a purely bilateral pact, but could have emanated from the loose pan-Mongoloid coalition called the Indo-Burma Revolutionary Front (IBRF) forged in May 1990, of which both the ULFA and UNLF were a part. Formed to wage a 'united struggle for the independence of Indo-Burma', the IBRF itself was a failure, primarily because it was too much of a problem for its leaders to hold on to a coalition of insurgent outfits that claimed to represent diverse tribes and communities.

What then was the need for the ULFA to tie up with the UNLF in 2000 or vice-versa? The ULFA's main fighting machine, until the Bhutanese crackdown in December 2003, was located in Bhutan. For several years before the crackdown, the ULFA had been under pressure from Thimphu to pull out of the Kingdom. Bhutan's Home Minister, Lyonpo Thinley Gyamtsho, confirmed at that time that, by December 31, 2001, the ULFA had indeed closed down four camps as per an agreement of June 2001. By 2001, the ULFA had started feeling the heat and perhaps realized that they would have to leave Bhutan sooner or later.

Under the circumstances, the ULFA perhaps was eyeing the UNLF's bases and training facilities in Myanmar and Bangladesh. A denial from Dhaka notwithstanding, it is a fact that Bangladesh has been a favourite hiding place for the ULFA leaders. The ULFA knew that, in the event of a possible assault on its camps inside Bhutan, the group would have to have an alternative destination to head for, and that would obviously be either Bangladesh or Myanmar, or both. The pact with the UNLF was, therefore, an absolute must for the ULFA, as 'hiding places' apart, some concrete training bases in Bangladesh and Myanmar would be necessary.

At one stage, some of the ULFA arms consignments were even traced to the Khmer Rouge in Cambodia, a deal brokered in 1993 by General Bo Mya's Karen National Union (KNU), an anti-Yangon guerrilla group. That deal was apparently clinched by ULFA's self-styled foreign secretary, Shasha Choudhury, who visited the KNU base at Manerplaw, on the Thailand-Myanmar border. As surveillance increased, rendering weapons smuggling more difficult, the ULFA might then have pinned its hopes on the UNLF to serve as a conduit for shipment of military hardware from Myanmar rebels.

The UNLF's equations with the Junta in Myanmar also appears to have been extraordinary, at least around year 2000, a fact which the ULFA may have taken note of while forging a deal with it. In December 2001, as many as 192 UNLF cadres, including some top leaders, were 'arrested' by the Myanmarese Army. Interestingly, all of them were set free by February 14, 2002, in four phases. The entire episode is still shrouded in mystery, particularly because Yangon had been almost simultaneously promising Indian leaders of support in checking cross-border insurgency. Does this mean that the UNLF has some sort of an understanding with the Junta in Myanmar, or a section of it? Answers are difficult to find, but theories abound, particularly because New Delhi was, from the mid-nineties onwards, supposed to have improved relations with Yangon considerably.

There is no scope for complacency in so far as the Indian authorities are concerned. This is because groups such as the NSCN-IM, even while engaging in peace negotiations with New Delhi, supported the 48-hour general strike in Assam and elsewhere in the region called on December 20-21, 2003 by the ULFA, NDFB and KLO in protest against the 'brutal operations' and 'human rights violations' he military inside Bhutan to oust the Indian separatists. The conflict dynamics as well as complex rebel equations combine to keep India's Northeast on the boil.

TERROR AND THE INDIAN MUJAHIDEEN

There is something disquieting in what Ashish Khetan has written and said recently on terror in India (in The Hindu and on Tehelka.tv), and centrally within it, the Indian Mujahideen. More so, because it comes from one of the most credible journalist's today, who has done some commendable work over the years. A journalist I personally respect. But there are several reasons which compel this response. And yet, this is not just a response, but also an attempt to elucidate the many complex processes within which 'terror' is located today, and the way the discourse has transformed, and has implications for a people's negotiated relationship with their state.

Over the last one year, through Gulail.com, Ashish Khetan has exposed several cases which have been fabricated against individuals and groups, all of them Muslims. This expose, through the revelation of classified Interrogation Reports in the public realm-using the police's own documents to challenge their own story-has been, till now, the most brilliant and effective way to challenge the cases, which many, suspected to be fabricated from the very start. And this expose was, and remains, a brave and mammoth task requiring extensive contacts, sources, and credibility, as anyone working in the fiercely guarded territories of national security and 'terror' would know.

It is this body of work that constitutes the historical background and legitimating authority of his recent op-ed in The Hindu on terror in India, and forms its silent and silencing basis. And yet, the work itself is neither the point of the chapter, nor forms the basis of what Mr. Khetan is trying to say, while the chapter exists primarily in the realm of speculation and an authoritative *khutba* meant for the country's muslims. The larger argument in the opinion piece-the first one in which Mr. Khetan has made sense of his one year long research on terror cases in India-is not based on facts, beyond the jurisdiction of journalistic inquiry, unwarranted, un-necessary, laced with presumptions, and even possibly incorrect. But what makes it dangerous, so much so that the chapter seemingly overturns the very idea that Mr. Khetan has been challenging in the past, is the way it is implicated, and plays to, an extremely communal politics and narrative within which terror today has been a central rallying point. The ideological framework within which the fabricated terror cases have been expounded-neither supported by facts, nor seeking in any way to serve the struggle for human rights of the citizen-, sits comfortably with particular political agendas today. Let's take it piece by piece.

I am compelled to state that I do not write here as a Muslim. I am neither trying to contest a narrative of terror that has been associated with Muslims, nor am I speaking from the location of a Muslim in whatever else I am trying to say. I write here, today, as a citizen contesting and challenging the infringement of human rights of its citizens by the state-whether minorities or tribals, or any of those peoples, communities, religious groups who have been expendable in the state's slow and gradual weakening of democratic institutions. All in a political game of power and control over peoples and dissent.

Mr. Khetan's central argument is this: the Indian Mujahideen is a reality, a terrible spectre responsible for many of the blasts that have taken place in the last decade, and that Muslims should come to terms with it, develop a political understanding, move out of narrow narratives of victimization, stop defending all and any who have been accused of terrorism, and demand that all should be brought to justice-including the IM who are Muslims. Tactfully arranged within it is a secondary argument: that before the IM was busted in 2008, many innocent Muslims were wrongly prosecuted-as he has shown-and that the police and the judiciary has been complicit in producing and convicting them, making a mockery of the criminal justice system.

The stakes are high. To claim that the IM exists and that it is responsible for the many bomb blasts has huge implications, something that will be discussed later. But it is a claim that cannot be lightly made. What proof is offered behind the claim? None. Only Mr. Khetan's own reading and privileged access to Interrogation Reports(IR), none of which he deigns to share with his readers. Ironically, the only Interrogation Reports that have been revealed are those which have helped prove that the cases against some have been fabricated. It is based on this credibility that Mr Khetan argues that the Interrogation reports reveal a sinister reality of the IM that we as a people, or rather, muslims, have to come to terms with. But there appears to be a misplaced sense of value put on the Interrogation Reports', as well as limited understanding of how they can help prove that the accused in the 7/11 blast, or the others that Mr Khetan has revealed, were innocent.

There are three questions that need to be asked here:

1. Whether such a claim can be made based on IRs

2. Mr Khetan's authority or legitimacy to make such a claim
3. The possible, factual incorrectness of the claim.

The IRs are classified documents and are not meant to be shared publicly. They are prepared by the police for their own use. Though, that in no way raises its credibility, it does make them crucial if these internal reports stand in stark contradiction to another official case made by the same agency on the same matter. At the same time, IRs in themselves are of no evidentiary value in any court of law, nor do they have any inherent truth value as they could be lacking in any material basis as the information obtained by the police could be through the use of third degree and the person may be compelled to state what the agency *wants* to hear rather than the truth. Even in the realm of the commonsensical, the IRs are just that-reports prepared by the police of a suspect's interrogation, with no value whatsoever but as investigative leads. Since Mr. Khetan does not reveal the source and content of these IRs, one has to largely and only accept his word about there being anything in the IR's about the IM, if at all.

However, it is inconsequetial if there is anything in the IR's about the IM or not. The credibility of the previous work by Mr. Khetan, stems not from any inherent truth value of the IR's, but from something entirely different-the fact that these reports, prepared by the police themselves, *were contradictory* to the official case. And hence, a crucial part of the defence case against the official prosecution. The plea for the innocence of those prosecuted by the revelation of the IRs, has nothing to do with whether the IRs are true or not, but rests on contradictory evidence being available and the conscious and deliberate suppression of the same by the police. To put it simply while it is the job of the court to weigh the evidence and make a value judgment as to the truth or otherwise of the prosecution's case, the prosecution itself cannot act knowing that its case is false. In these cases, the IRs revealed that not only did the prosecution itself not believe in its own case, it infact had reason to believe that it was false. The good faith of the prosecution was hence absent and the prosecution was proved to have acted in bad faith. The IRs, in themselves are in no way any proof of the guilt of Sadiq sheikh or any others who have been clubbed together with the overarching term of the Indian Mujahideen. It would be enlightening to look at what Justice A.M Thipsey of the Bombay High Court who dealt with this issue in the 7/11 case had to say regarding this very point.

Much before the revelation by Mr. Khetan, the defence council of the 13 accused in the 7/11 train blast case wanted to tender as part of the evidence the confession of Sadiq Sheikh who claimed to have done the blast. The prosecution objected to the confession being tendered as evidence in this case by arguing, among other things, that the confession if admitted here would be:

"inconsistent with the guilt of the accused in this case...[and that]it would prejudice the accused in that case(Crime Branch IM case-MCOCA Special case no.4 of 2009) and would not afford them the chance." (Pg 37.)

The trial Court accepted the prosecution's argument. When the defense took it to the High court, Justice A.M. Thipsey setting aside the order explicitly pointed out:

" It is not possible to accept the view of the learned judge. In the first place, the appellants had not claimed-and could not have claimed that the confessions of those accused 'were true'. They were not expecting to 'prove' those confessions against those accused. What they were saying is that someone else has confessed of having committed the offense with which they are charged...and it is the court that decides whether the fact of a confession having been made is true and also whether the facts stated in the confession are true. Confessions are treated as circumstantial evidence of the truth of the facts stated therein and it is the court that decides whether the facts stated in a confession are to be believed or not in a given case. It is a matter of evaluation of evidence to be done by the court after it is tendered."

It is important to note that a confession is immeasurably more valuable when compared to an Interrogation report. It can be tendered as evidence in court. Despite this, as the High court points out and rightly so, that even then there is no presumption to their inherent truth value, and, it is the job of the court of law to evaluate if they do and can be believed and relief upon. For, the court remains the final arbitrator of guilt or innocence.

How is it possible, then, to proclaim the guilt of the IM based on Interrogation reports, even when the cases of Sadiq Sheikh and the rest, under the rubric of the IM, are still sub-judice? Can a claim be made even on the basis of certain facts which journalistic research might have brought to light, when those facts are yet to be tested in court?

Mr Khetan offers us neither proofs nor explanations. What is offered instead is a narrative of how 5 people-Sadiq Sheikh, Mujahid Saleem, Asif and Amir Reza Khan, and Riaz Bhatkal-fired by ideas of Jihad and retributive justice, bankrolled by forces across the border, went about bombing places one after the other.

The preposterousness of the claim, in the sheer absence of any proof offered, even when all these cases are sub-judice, do not warrant a rebuttal. If anything, it warrants the forceful disciplining of the clause of 'contempt of court'-for the sheer damage that the claim could possible wreck for all the cases that are presently under trial at a time when the 'collective conscience of the people' has assumed legal weight.

And yet, as the narrative has been expounded by Mr. Khetan, I shall take it seriously within the bounds of this chapter, as, unfortunately the entire fabric of the discourse of terror has been created by such unsubstantiated and baseless allegations. Allegations which have assumed the status of commonsense-and through repetition-gained legitimacy and have become the "truth". And it needs to be said that this narrative is thoroughly contested-factually.

For the last one year, as a Research Fellow at the Tata Institute of Social Sciences, I have been researching on terror cases across the 4 cities-Hyderabad, Mumbai, Bangalore and Kolkata. Over this period, I have gone through all relevant documents-legal and otherwise-, met lawyers (both prosecution and defense) as well as accused and their families, of almost all the cases of bomb blasts and attacks in these four cities.

This research has encompassed the criminal and social history of two of the 5 people that Mr. Khetan authoritatively mentions as the original member who started the Indian Mujahideen-Mujahid

Saleem, and Asif Reza Khan. And the picture that emerges is completely different from what Mr Khetan has attributed to them without proofs or explanations.

Mujahid Saleem: A study of the 4 bomb blast cases of Hyderabad (*forthcoming in EPW*), as well as my meeting with the lawyer associated with his encounter case, his friends, as well as his father Aleem Islahi (whose provocative writing on Jihad and Babri Masjid is the sudden and only explanation offered by Mr. Khetan of Mujahid's crime) makes a story worth telling.

But, it is Maulana Naseeruddin, a cleric who has been a friend of Aleem Islahi as well as his son, whose story of prosecution is directly linked to that of Mujahid. The families of both Maulana Naseeruddin and Aleem Islahi live next to each other in Saidabad- a densely populated Muslim pocket of Hyderabad. Maulana Naseeruddin was first arrested in 1992 when he organized public prayer for the 'martyrship' of the Babri Masjid. He was arrested along with 62 other young men under TADA. Since then Maulana Naseeruddin has been accused in several cases of terror in Hyderabad, including the famous case of the murder of the Haren Pandya. Last year Maulana Naseeruddin, after spending almost 2 decades in prison, was acquitted of *all* charges in*all* the cases. A minor case is still pending against him. In 2004, when Naseerudin was first accused in the Haren Pandya murder case, there were protests and people had gathered when the Gujarat contingent came to arrest him. The Gujarat contingent was led by IPS officer Narendra Amin who is presently an accused in the Ishrat Jahan fake encounter case. Mujahid Saleem, then a 20 year old boy, was standing the closest to Naseeruddin, protesting with the others. He was shot at point blank range by Narendra Amin. At the time of his death, there was not a single case against him.

Md Rayeesuddin, a friend of Mujahid, was also there that day. He is the prime witness in the case of encounter against Narendra Amin. The case is presently lying dormant. Since the time time Md Rayeesuddin listed as a witness, he has been arrested and interrogated, in every single case of bomb blast in Hyderabad. He was Accused no 16 in the case no 198/2007, one of the 4 Mecca Masjid Blast cases. In that case, his name was included in the chargesheet after he refused to step down as a witness. Even after receiving compensation for the false framing, he has been picked up and tortured after the recent 2013 Dilsukhnagar blast. Ironically, previously listed in the chargesheet as a member of Huji, Rayeesuddin was picked up and interrogated even as the police claimed that it was the Indian Mujahideen. He still refuses to step down as a witness in the day-light encounter of his friend Mujahid Saleem.

Aleem Islahi: The mere holding of an opinion, irrespective of its nature, does not constitute crime, unless an overtly violent act has been done. Though it is difficult to understand the link with the opinions of Aleem Islahi with the guilt of his son Mujahid, it remains a fact that Aleem Islahi has not been accused in a single case of crime or terror in Hyderabad. His name was in the FIR in case no 198/2007, it was however not included in the chargesheet.

Asif Reza Khan: Asif Reza Khan, a resident of Kolkata, was 22 years old when he was first arrested in 1994 under TADA. A student at Aligarh Muslim University then, Asif had just finished his graduation from the well known Maulana Azad College in Calcutta. At AMU, Asif had Kashmiri friends with whom he lived in the hostel. The arrest was among the hundreds of arrests of Muslims across the country for alleged 'Jihadi' links and disruptive activities pertaining to Kashmir. Also arrested under TADA at the same time was ShahidAzmi-the lawyer who was later killed defending those who were falsely accused in terror cases.

Asif Reza and Shahid Azmi spent 5 years in Delhi's Tihar Jail. Released in 1999, after the Supreme Court acquitted them of all charges, both Asif and Shahid, like most others who were released, were re-arrested in several cases, especially in the many hi-profile cases of kidnapping of businessman in the country. After their release, all three of them-Shahid and Asif and Aftab-were accused in the kidnapping of Partha Roy Burman, the 'Khadim's' shoe baron from Kolkata. Shahid and Asif were taken in custody and interrogated. Asif was also accused in the kidnapping of a Gujarat diamond merchant, Bhaskar Parekh.

In 2001, immidietly after SIMI was banned, the Gujarat police took Asif into police custody, and took him to Rajkot where they shot him on December 7 -one and half months before the American Centre attack. The police said, officially, that Asif, a member of SIMI, in a bid to escape, fired upon them by snatching the AK-47 of one of the policemen. They shot him in retaliation. None of the policemen were hurt.

The entire case of the Calcutta attack is built on the assumption that Asif Reza Khan was a terrorist with links with 'Jihadi organisations'. An assumption which is not substantiated by any proof or corroboration.

According to the official case, the American Centre attack which was a ride by shooting of the guards stationed outside the United States Information Service which lasted 40s, was carried out by friends of Asif (one of the two shooters was Sadiq Sheikh according to the police) who wanted to avenge his death. Strangely, the attack took place in Kolkata, even though Asif was killed in Gujarat, as Asif was initially in custody of the Kolkata police according to a confession in the case. Out of the total of 9 accused, 7 were sentence to death by the trial court. The High court acquitted two of them and reduced the punishment of 3 others to 5 years of imprisonment. Two of the accused who presently stand between the complete collapse of the case, face the death penalty in a case which is laced with irregularities, and where the possibility of fabricated evidence cannot be ruled out, as I have concluded after studying the records of the case and speaking to people concerned.. The appeal by the two accused against their convictions is up for hearing in the Supreme Court the next month, where the entire narrative of Asif as well as the attacks by his friends, including Sadiq Sheikh, will be put to test. Strangely, in this case where the accused have veered between two judicial extremes-from death penalty to acquittal-Sadiq Sheikh, the prime accused who was shown as absconding till 2008, is yet to be tried even though the final appeal of the other two who only have minor conspiratorial roles is being heard.

The reality of the IM is sub-judice in many courts of the country with the allegations against them yet to be evaluated and appraised by examination to the level of evidence. For, along with allegations, are also irregularities, severe contestations and allegation of possible fabrication as well as violence-as the legal and extra legal stories of two out of the five named by Mr. Khetan reveal. And this, here, is the crucial point: this is not a contestation of facts. The above facts about the individuals who have been condemned unheard by Mr. Khetan, have not been narrated here to proclaim the innocence of Asif Reza Khan or Mujahid Saleem, but rather, to reveal the falsity of the innuendos which form the basis of Mr. Khetan's proclamation of their guilt.

This chapter is also not a proclamation of the innocence of the Indian Mujahideen. What is intended here is to raise a crucial question: On what basis can the Indian Mujahideen be declared as a reality responsible for many blasts across the country – without evidence-when the matter is sub-judice and also deeply riven with contestation and stories of state violence?

Purely on the basis of a personal, closeted reading of Interrogation reports whose validity is less reliable than the facts pointed out above or the testimonies of all those who are willing to testify in court against it?

IMPLICATIONS, TERROR AND PEOPLE'S RIGHTS

Terror today is neither limited to cases of bomb blasts and attacks and questions of justice therein, nor is it about the guilt or innocence of individual/individuals and groups. Terror-whether in the jungles or urban centres, or in the iniquitousness of security cameras-today, is a narrative. A narrative informing a politics, informing relations between the state and its citizens, informing our very ideas of lives negotiated as a people.

And it is this political centrality of terror as a narrative that has made cases of attacks and bomb blasts-the episteme of that narrative-not mere question of crime and justice alone. Put together, terror has taken a heavy toll on lives of the people. And yet, this number is insignificant if compared to, lets say, deaths due to hunger, poverty, diseases, or even traffic accidents. However, the centrality of this narrative today is undisputed-inexplicably. For, there is something in this narrative that offers enormous potential for the state and the powers that be, to assume an authoritarian, overriding, exception-making, dissent-quelling, posture, which commands unquestionable powers and obedience-all in the name of security of the state and its people. What this narrative allows is the people's collective acquiescence in the withdrawal of their own rights, or other's rights and permits the creation of a security state which seemingly only exists to protect people from each other.

Let's take the direct association or causal relationship between the two central terror attacks when this narrative of terror, as well as one of Muslims as terrorist, was being born-the parliament and the Kolkata attacks and the passing of POTA three months later-an act whose extraordinary provisions have been proved to have been used against the minorities for a communal politics.

Or, let's say, in the enormous ability of the narrative of terror to declare an unspoken state of exception. The most powerful example being the Mecca Masjid blast case, where the very evocation of the name, a blast, levied a state of exception on the city's Muslims so powerfully that the police could round up 200 Muslims after the blast, even when the place bombed was the community's own mosque and the people killed were the Muslims themselves. And no questions were asked.

These narratives of terror-that Muslims are jihadists spreading terror, or on the other hand, Muslims believe that all Muslims are innocent and ask for justice only for them (as also assumed in Mr. Khetan's asticle)-have been the basis of politics, political mobilization over the last decade. And this is the most crucial point here. That these narratives and its ideological counterpart-the question of security-have been the central rallying point of decade long politics, and the terror cases their site, the building block.

Hence, the falling apart of any case, is not an isolated incidence of wrong prosecution, but rather the collapse of a narrative which puts to question the very basis of the politics and the ideological formulation which has manifested itself into history post 2001. These are the fissures that help us expose the myth that is being narrated to through our governments, media and war machines. It needs to be said that Mr Khetan's previous contribution-the publishing of Swamy Aseemanand's confession, as well as the expose of the case, has helped dent this narrative. Yet, in the present formulation Mr Khetan has first tried to prove that some individuals are innocent, and then, used that credibility, to add weight to an extremely communal narrative-completely unsupported by evidence. This sleight of hand is subversive of the very struggle for rights and justice in its raising, or lending force, to the terrible spectre of the Indian Mujahideen-a new narrative to be used by both communal and authoritarian forces.

By implicating the Indian Mujahideen after giving SIMI a clean chit, Mr. Khetan seeks to demolish the argument built by an entire body of evidence of fabrication of cases against Muslims by the state-by stating that this is not a case of political targeting of a community, but of mistaken identity. A corollary of the argument : that the state has not acted communo-politically and targeted Muslims, and hence not implicated in the fabrication, but as much a victim of the fabrication as those wrongly accused by it. Mr. Khetan also seeks to subvert the other challenges to the state's blatant violation of human rights of its citizens-as the new data of fabrication proves-, the real spectre of Hindu terror especially after the Asseemanand confession, and most importantly the imputations that the state acted communally and in bad faith. And here comes the most lethal and dangerous aspect of Mr. Khetan's argument: it reinforces the belief that though not all Muslims are terrorists, all terrorists are indeed Muslims.

3

Pakistan Decries India's Admission of Involvement in Cross-border Terrorism

The adviser to the prime minister on national security and foreign affairs, Sartaj Aziz, expressed serious concern over the statement made by Indian Defence Minister Manohar Parrikar that India will use terrorism to counter terrorism from other countries. This statement, Aziz said, only confirms Islamabad's apprehensions about India's involvement in terrorism in Pakistan.

"It must be the first time that a minister of an elected government openly advocates use of terrorism in another country on the pretext of preventing terrorism from that country or its non-state actors," said the national security adviser.

Pakistan sincerely pursues a policy of good neighbourly relations with India, maintained Aziz. "Terrorism is our common enemy and it is vital for the two countries to work together to defeat this menace, from which Pakistan has suffered much more than almost any other country," he asserted.

"The statement of Indian defence minister is open and blatant admission and declaration of sponsoring terrorism," Defence Minister Khawaja Asif said in an official statement issued late on Saturday. Asif said Indian defence minister specifically mentioned that regulation will not be used to quell terrorist activities and terrorism will be promoted instead.

"This is the worst kind of declaration by a state functionary of cabinet level which confirms that India is sponsoring terrorism against its neighbours in the name of preventing terrorist activities," Asif said. Earlier, Indian Defence Minister Manohar Parrikar, in a shocking and radical statement, has asserted that terrorists have to be neutralised only through terrorists.

"India will take proactive steps to prevent a 26/11 type attack," Press Trust of India quoted him saying. Commenting on the shocking utterances of the Indian Defence Minister, a defence analyst said the statement was appalling and beyond comprehension.

Speaking at an event in New Delhi, the minister used the Hindi phrase "kante se kanta nikalna" (removing a thorn with a thorn) and wondered why Indian soldiers should be used to neutralise terrorists. The proactive steps, he said, could include pressure tactics. "We have to neutralise terrorists through terrorists only. Why can't we do it? We should do it. Why does my soldier have to do it?" he said and added that the issue could not be discussed beyond this.

"There are certain things that I obviously cannot discuss here. But if there is any country, planning something against my country, we will definitely take some pro-active steps," he said. The defence analyst lamented that the menace of terrorism could not be defeated by promoting state-sponsored terrorism.

India, he added, was carving out a disastrous strategy as it would never help in rooting out terrorism, which was a global issue threatening all states. The international community should take notice of this irresponsible statement, which was reflecting a sick mindset, he stressed.

CROSS BORDER TERRORISM SPONSORED BY PAK ARMY AND SUGGESTED INDIAN RESPONSE

Six decades after its independence Pakistan continues to search for a durable and credible identity. Pakistan's rulers constantly strive to show how Pakistan is equal to, if not better than India in all respects. The complex psychology of the Pakistani ruling elite is dominated by the military. Even after more than three and a half decades, the role in the creation of Bangladesh continues to rankle, with the Pak Army in search of 'revenge' for its humiliating defeat in 1971. The mindset of the Pak Army is a cocktail of arrogance and brashness, at times bordering on cockiness, which becomes even more potent with the addition of a measure of a fundamentalism.

The Pak Army sees itself as the dominant power in Pakistan & has always enjoyed a larger than life status in socio-political fabric of the country. Democratic regimes have not survived and people represented institutions remain weak in Pakistan. It is difficult to comment authoritatively on whether it is the weak political leadership which is responsible for the democratic failures or the overpowering army which has led to military coups in Pakistan. However, what is certain is this, whenever the position of Pak Army has got threatened they have managed to come back into focus as 'saviours' of the nation by destabilising the Indo-Pak relations.

The Pak Army's single minded pursuit of its proxy war for over a decade clearly indicates its long-term game planned to destabilize India by keeping the pot boiling in Kashmir, keeping the Indian Army and other security forces embroiled in counter insurgency operations and, more recently, to extend the area of engagement to other parts of India through wanton acts of terrorism in or around high value targets. In short the Pak Army's strategy is to bleed India through a thousand cuts. For Pak Army it is a win-win situation as there is an element of deniability about its involvement. The Pakistani Generals, are convinced that their bleed-India strategy is a low-cost, high pay off option for Pakistan and, therefore, they are loathe to give it up.

WHAT GIVES PAK ARMY CONFIDENCE TO WAGE COVERT WAR?

A brutal confidence underlies Pakistan's continuing commitment to a strategy of waging war by proxy. This confidence is founded on two pillars. The first is the belief in the Pakistan Army's ability to crush any insurgency if it really decides to do so. This conviction was expressed most clearly in General Pervez Musharraf's statement in 2005 to the insurgents in Balochistan that he would "sort them out" and that "they won't know what hit them". The second source of confidence is Pakistan's nuclear weapons. Many in Pakistan's army and political leadership believe that these weapons protect Pakistan from the outside world. Indian restraint during both the 1999 Kargil War and during the 2001-2002 OP PARAKRAM after the militant attack on India's Parliament, is an evidence of the power of Pakistan's nuclear card. This was evident again after the Mumbai attacks on 26 Nov 2008.

Many—if not all—of the militant groups active in J&K have enjoyed the specific patronage of the Pakistani state intelligence and military agencies to prosecute Islamabad's interests in India.

This dissertation seeks to carry out a study of the conduct of cross border terrorism by Pak Army, estimate its future contours & suggest suitable responses.

METHODOLOGY

To identify & analyse role of Pak Army in creating dissonance in Indo- Pak relations by sponsoring cross border terrorism against India. To suggest India's response to counter this threat.

Hypothesis

With power now in hands of civilian establishment the Pak Army is finding itself in a vulnerable position and is gradually losing its commanding status. To regain their image as 'guardian angels' of the country they are resorting to destabilising Indo-Pak relations by triggering violent terror incidents.

The Pak Army attributes all such incidents as being carried out by 'non-state' actors and 'freedom fighters', while the truth is that Pak Army along with ISI is directly involved in promoting cross border terrorism.

Justification of the Study

Pak Army continues unabated in its quest to destabilise India through covert means. The investigations into the recent attacks in Mumbai have also revealed a clear link between the Pak Army and the non- state actors and yet the true propagators (read ISI) of the violence are yet to be brought to book. The more India talks in front of the whole world about it, the more denials come from Pakistan, in the light of these facts, it is essential that India must take concrete steps to counter Pak Army support to terrorists who wage covert war against India & also unveil its true colours to the world community.

Scope

The focus of this study is on Pak Army's use of radical Islamic Fundamentalism & terrorism as a military strategy to create dissonance in Indo-Pak relations. The emphasis is on role of Pak Army in the recent Mumbai attacks. The study further analyses the likely contours of future covert war methods and concludes by suggesting various options with India to counter the new emerging threat. The dissertation does not cover Pak Army role in raising the 'Taliban' and it's so called ongoing war against terrorism and only concentrate on the events and actions that destabilise Indo- Pak relations.

Method of Data Collection

The source of this dissertation has been the books, periodicals and articles available in the library of Defence Services Staff College. The web sites of IDSA, USI, and several other Indian dailies on the Internet also have been a great help. The bibliography is appended at the end of the text.

UNDERSTANDING TERRORISM

"In an interconnected world, the defeat of international terrorism - and most importantly, the prevention of these terrorist organizations from obtaining weapons of mass destruction — will require the cooperation of many nations. We must always reserve the right to strike unilaterally at terrorists wherever they may exist. But we should know that our success in doing so is enhanced by engaging our allies so that we receive the crucial diplomatic, military, intelligence, and financial support that can lighten our load and add legitimacy to our actions. This means talking to our friends and, at times, even our enemies."

Defining Terrorism

Virtually any especially abhorrent act of violence perceived as directed against society—whether it involves the activities of antigovernment dissidents or governments themselves, organized-crime syndicates, common criminals, rioting mobs, people engaged in militant protest, individual psychotics, or lone extortionists—is often labeled "terrorism."

Terrorism, in the most widely accepted contemporary usage of the term, is fundamentally and inherently political. It is also ineluctably about power: the pursuit of power, the acquisition of power, and the use of power to achieve political change. Terrorism is thus violence—or, equally important, the threat of violence—used and directed in pursuit of, or in service of, apolitical aim.

State Sponsored Terrorism

One of the most authoritative studies by Daniel Byman, a leading scholar on terrorism defines state sponsorship as "a government's intentional assistance to a terrorist group to help it use violence, bolster its political activities, or sustain [its] organization." His research identifies six areas in which states provide support to terrorists—training and operations; money, arms, and logistics; diplomatic backing; organizational assistance; ideological direction; and (perhaps most importantly) sanctuary. Byman argues that terrorist groups which receive significant amounts of state support are far more difficult to counter and destroy than those which do not.

However, it is also important to note that there are several types of state sponsorship of terrorism: "strong supporters" are states with both the desire and the capacity to support terrorist groups; "weak supporters" are those with the desire but not the capacity to offer significant support; "lukewarm supporters" are those that offer rhetorical but little actual tangible support; and "antagonistic supporters" are those that actually seek to control or even weaken the terrorist groups they appear to be supporting.

Another category Byman examines is passive support, whereby states "deliberately turn a blind eye to the activities of terrorists in their countries but do not provide direct assistance." A state's tolerance of or passivity toward a terrorist group's activities, he argues, is often as important to their success as any deliberate assistance they receive. Open and active state sponsorship of terrorism is rare, and it has decreased since the end of the Cold War. Yet this lack of open support does not necessarily diminish the important role that states play in fostering or hindering terrorism.

At times, the greatest contribution a state can make to a terrorist's cause is by not policing a border, turning a blind eye to fundraising, or even Combating the Sources and Facilitators of Terrorism tolerating terrorist efforts to build their organizations, conduct operations, and survive. Passive support for terrorism can contribute to a terrorist group's success in several ways. It often allows a group to raise money, acquire arms, plan operations, and enjoy a respite from the counterattacks of the government it opposes. Passive support may also involve spreading an ideology that assists a terrorist group in its efforts to recruit new members.

Benefits to State Sponsored Terrorists

For the terrorist, the benefits of state sponsorship were even greater. Such a relationship appreciably enhanced the capabilities and operational capacity of otherwise limited terrorist groups, placing at their disposal the resources of an established nation-state's entire diplomatic, military, and intelligence apparatus and thus greatly facilitating planning and intelligence. The logistical support provided by states assured the terrorists of otherwise unobtainable luxuries, such as the use of diplomatic pouches for the transport of weapons and explosives, false identification in the form of genuine passports, and the use of embassies and other diplomatic facilities as safe houses or staging bases. State sponsorship also afforded terrorists greater training opportunities; thus some groups were transformed into entities more akin to elite commando units than to the stereotypical conspiratorial cell of anarchists wielding Molotov cocktails or radicals manufacturing crude pipe bombs. Finally, terrorists were often paid handsomely for their services, turning hitherto financially destitute entities into well-endowed organizations with investment profiles and healthy balance sheets.

The Four Stages of Terrorism

The terrorist tactics though essentially focuses on creating terror through violence has evolved over a period of time.

1980s-1990s: Era of backyard Islamicist Struggles

During this time the focus was on overthrowing specific regions, like the non democratic governments of Algeria and Egypt, or fighting countries seen to be occupying Muslim lands like Israel and India.

(a) Spectacular Example. Assassination of Anwar Sadat of Egypt in 1981 was probably the most famous terrorist act of this period.

(b) Preferred Tactics. Mimicking the methods of secular left wing and nationalist terrorist groups like the Palestinian Fatah or the Irish Republican Army. This generally involved hijacking of aircraft, assassination of political and kidnapping of foreigners. Few of these attacks had much of a ripple outside the region that they took place. These acts were largely seen as a local law and order issue rather than an international menace.

1990s- 2001: Rise of Spectacular Jihad

This period saw the arrival of Osama Bin Laden and the Egyptian Ayman al Zawahri on the scene. These men argued that local islamicist struggles need to combine force so they can replicate soviet defeat in Afghanistan.

(a) Successful Attack. 9/11, the world's most lethal and media-friendly terrorist attack. It was preceded by attacks on US warships and embassies in Africa and Persian gulf.

(b) Preferred Tactics. 9/11 stamps suicide bombing as the preferred jihadi tactic but also raised the bar on how spectacular the attack must be From roughly 2002 onwards there was a huge surge in suicide bombings across the world, spreading into places like Kashmir, Chechnya and so on where they had previously been rare.

2001-2007: Maturing of Local Guerrilla Terrorism

Losing its Afghan base al Qaeda turned to local jihad affiliates to keep up the momentum of attack. Transit attacks in Madrid and London took place. But US invasion of Iraq and Afghanistan provided a new outlet for jihadi wrath. Abu Musab al Zarqawi replaced Bin Laden as the terrorist of the moment.

(a) Successful Attack. The entire campaign against US military in Iraq which soured the US public to the war and lead to a consensus on the need for the US to withdraw from Iraq as soon as possible.

(b) Preferred Tactics. In Europe it was bomb in the bus or terror on the train. In Iraq it is a more straight forward guerilla style war with roadside explosives devices, suicide bombers. Zarqawi introduced shocking media footage such as the execution video of Daniel Pearl.

2008: Possible start of Global Terrorism

Suicide Bombing hurts al Qaeda Sentiment among mainstream Islam. Surveys have shown declining support for such tactics since 2005 onwards. Further it is getting increasingly ineffective against new security methods and in terms of winning media attention.

(a) Tactical Experiment. The use of small bands of suicide fighters, trained like professional soldiers, who simultaneously strike local and global targets. Mumbai is now being seen as the most intricately coordinated and most successful islamicist terrorist attack since 9/11. This could well be the dawn of new era of such terrorism.

CROSS BORDER TERRORISM : AN ALTERNATIVE MILITARY STRATEGY

"In the South Asian context, talks on conventional military confidence building cannot be divorced from terrorism. The route of the escalatory process is militancy."

The Pakistani military leadership believes the terrorist threat is an incentive to India to come to the negotiating table; without it India will simply ignore Pakistan's calls for a resolution of the issue. Terrorism also poisons Hindu-Muslim relations and weakens the foundations of India's secularism. It affects the image of India as an investment destination, which would explain the terror attacks in cities like Bangalore and Mumbai. It panders to extremist lobbies within Pakistan whose declared ambition is to break up India from within. The repeated attacks on Hindu religious places is intended to provoke a communal backlash against the Muslims, in the expectation that this will engender greater Muslim alienation, leading eventually to the tearing up of the social fabric of India.

Terrorism has become an institution in Pakistan and has widespread support. Its army and intelligence services consider it a strategic weapon. After each terrorist strike, the Pakistani government cleverly dodges international pressure by temporarily clamping down on terrorism until the focus shifts away. It never completely eliminates this menace.

Post Mumbai, Ironic as it may seem the Pakistan Army has gained in an important way. The crisis has gone some way in building bridges between the militant groups and the Pakistan military. Their historical relationship, which had broken down in several ways, is on the mend. Taliban groups in the tribal areas battling Pakistani security forces offered ceasefires so that troops could devote all their energies on what was built up as a coming war on the eastern front. They even offered to fight alongside the troops against India.

Cost to Pakistan to Support Cross Border Terrorism

Pakistan officially accepts that it is providing diplomatic, political and moral support to Kashmiri militants. However, it is now internationally accepted that the Pakistan army and the ISI Directorate are providing military training, weapons, military equipment, ammunition and explosives to the militants, besides financial support. The ISI spends approximately Rs 5 Crore per month for its proxy war campaign. The Pakistan Army also actively assists the militants to infiltrate into j&K by engaging Indian posts on the LC along the routes of infiltration with artillery and small arms fireand provides a large number of officers to lead the militants.

The Pak 'Terror' Machine

How did the present day terror infrastructure originate? The answer this question can be found in the Soviet invasion of Afghanistan in 1979. The invasion provided Pakistan Army an opportunity to reconstruct its professional image which had considerably tarnished as a consequence of 1971 war and dismemberment of Pakistan. In 1981, when the Reagan administration agreed to support the Afghan Mujahideen and US military assistance to Pakistan began to filter in. It helped the military to build its professional image.

The planning and coordination of Afghan resistance movement was done in close collaboration with US intelligence agencies and the Inter Service Intelligence (ISI) of Pakistan. While supporting, training and organizing the various Afghan Guerrilla Bands the ISI built its reputation and skills as a professional organisation. In the process, the ISI enhanced its intelligence and surveillance capabilities.

The Zia regime at that time also availed this opportunity to embark on a program to modernize the armed forces of Pakistan. The regime was able to strike a deal with Reagan administration for the procurement of sophisticated F-16 fighter planes. It was also able to procure some artillery and armoured equipment for the army. Consequently the Afghan war and US military aid did facilitate the moderenisation of the Pakistan military. This helped the Military to bolster its professional image.

Neither the Americans, stung and exhausted after the wars of the CIA and the armed forces in Vietnam, Laos and Cambodia, nor the Saudis, who hate to get involved in fighting anywhere, wanted to commit their own forces. So they let Pakistan's ISI do the donkey work. The ISI, controlled directly by President Zia al-Haq and influenced on the ground by affluent Arab organizations close to the Muslim Brothers and Pakistan's Islamist groups, ran the war against the Russians. Many billions of dollars to fund it came from the United States, the Saudi treasury, and finally as the conflict was winding down, from the resources of financiers like the Saudi construction tycoon Osama bin Laden, who effectively privatized global terrorism in the 1990s.

The fundamentalist groups which were trained initially for Afghan war were indoctrinated to believe that it is their religious duty to kill unbelievers and their supporters wherever they are found. Funded by the ISI and religion- based political parties of Pakistan, they are armed with sophisticated weaponery. It is well known that the ISI had surreptitiously siphoned off up to 40-50 % of the weapons supplied by the CIA for use by the Afghan Mujahideen against Russia. These weapons have eventually found their way into J&K. It is not as well known that towards the end of Afghan resistance against Russian occupation, 'mullah warlords' had taken over the cultivation and processing of poppy along the Pakistan-Afghanistan border. Since then, the illicit trade in narcotics has been generating hefty profits. These are being ploughed into fuelling terrorism in J&K and in supporting the Taliban in Afghanistan. This vicious politician-mulla-ISI-army racket suited the ruling elite in Pakistan and is a major cause of continuing war in Afghanistan and terrorism in Kashmir.

The sketch below shows the movement of CIA/ISI trained guerrillas out of Afghanistan after driving out Soviet Union from Afghanistan.

Islamic Fundamentalism & Pak Army

From the early days, the secular apolitical army that the British left behind deviated in Pakistan from the basic tenets of professionalism and began to intervene in politics and governance aided by the bureaucratic class (later to be simply used by the army) and the incompetence of the political elites. The army defined the parameters of national policy and the means by which it was to be pursued even when it was not in direct control of state. It also began from the very beginning to rely on clandestine covert war, executed through multiple means and tactics, while following up with traditional professional military forces for a coup de grace when it wanted.

When General Zia ul Haq came to power he did not take too long to reveal his religious political outlook. He was brisk in replacing the Jinnah's motto of Pakistan Army- Unity, Faith & Discipline with Faith, Piety & Holy War (Jihad). In his opening speech, after the take over he, extended two reasons for military intervention. Firstly the country was on threshold of a civil war. Secondly Islam had not been effectively put into practice in Pakistani society. Zia ul Haq after assuming power lent his support and affinity with the Pakistan National Alliance (PNA) protest movement. PNA was an alliance of nine parties to throw out Zulfikar Ali Bhutto and they promised to bring back Islamic laws. "I must say that the spirit of Islam, demonstrated during the recent movement was commendable. It proves that Pakistan, which was created in the name of Islam, will continue to survive only if it sticks to Islam. That is why I consider the introduction of Islamic system as an essential pre-requisite for the country."

The army has seen itself for the last three decades or more as the defender of not only of the physical frontiers but also of ideological frontiers of the state, conceptualized on the foundations of exclusivity of religion. It has inevitably been increasingly 'islamised' which at one level enhanced internal cohesion and motivation to fight and at another created a spectre of potential discord within the army. In 1976, the Pakistan army had amended its secular motto to include the term 'jihad' in it. All the eight groups of irregular resistance fighters that it equipped and trained for the war in Afghanistan during the 1980s were called 'Mujahideen'- those who carry out jihad. The military-dominated state has used jihad, which is intrinsic to faith and ethics in Islam, to advance its strategic, economic, and political ends. Such a shrewd strategic vision, backed by political denial and policies of economic exclusion, violates elementary Islamic principles of equity and justice. The army has capitalised on the jehadi industry to further ensconce itself in the power structure.

Role of ISI

The Inter Services Intelligence (ISI) of Pakistan and the inter services public relations are officially under the ministry of defence.

In reality, the ISI functions under direct control of Pak Army and its Chief is answerable to the military leaders. The ISI does not report to the civilian authority, even when there is a democratically elected government. The ISI enjoys a unique status in the infrastructure of the Pakistani establishment. It is not an ordinary intelligence apparatus of the state. It has emerged as a fulcrum of Islamic jihadist operations of the state of Pakistan and jihadist tanzeems created by the state.

The ISI devoted two full wings of its establishment for carrying out operations inside India. The joint intelligence miscellaneous (JIM) and the joint intelligence north (JIN) are reported to be responsible for directing the Indian operations of the ISI. Whole other wings of the ISI are known to play supportive roles. The JIX often came to the notice of the Indian agencies for coordinating special operations inside India. The Pakistan IB, unlike Indian IB, is not totally barred from conducting operations in selected foreign countries. For Indian targets they are allowed to conduct certain shallow penetration trans-border operations as well as assigned high commission based operations.

The Lashkar-e-Taiba (LeT) and ISI

The Lashkar's nexus with the ISI is well established. "LeT had worked in close coordination with the ISI, which also provided support to launch the militants across the border" Dr. Khalid Mehmood Soomroo of the Jamiat-e-Islam asks: "Is there a single militant training centre in Pakistan which can operate without the consent of the Pakistan army?" The are numerous training camps in Pakistan-occupied Kashmir (POK). Zahab and Roy mention three, the principal one being Um al-Qura at Muzaffarabad. Five hundred mujahids are trained here every month. Moreover, India has been victimized by a host of militant groups based in and supported by Pakistan for decades. With the possible exception of the militant groups associated with Jamaat-Islami, the so-called Kashmir tanzeems have been raised, nurtured, assisted, and trained by the ISI. As such, these groups are not strictly non state actors but rather extensions of the state intelligence apparatus, albeit with some degree of plausible deniability.

Groups that were previously limited to the Kashmir expanded into the Indian hinterland following the 1998 nuclear tests. Notable attacks included the 2000 LeT attack on the Red Fort, the 2001 Jaish-e-Muhamad (JeM) attack on the Indian parliament, the 2006 LeT Mumbai rail system attack, and numerous other attacks by LeT or JeM throughout India. In addition, in 2000, LeT introduced the fidayeen (high-risk suicide commando) operation in Kashmir and has since used it throughout India.

LeT is still considered to be an important asset in Pakistan's quest to secure its regional objectives and because it, unlike the proliferating morass of Deobandi groups, has never targeted the state.

Civil-Military Power Relationship in Pakistan

As a ruler Zia left Pakistan turbulent and rife with sectarian and ethnic tensions. Political parties were weak and divided. In such a divided polity the military was not merely the hegemonic, but also the only institution that had grown, expanded and emerged as the arbitrator in defining power relations among various contending power groups. Having established its hegemony in political system the military was poised to search for redefining its role in the post Zia era. Military Hegemony has emerged as the most dominant and durable character of Pakistan's political system. Hegemony was achieved through four process

(a) Promotion of the "corporate interests" of military.

(b) Political exclusion i.e. exclusion of political leaders, political parties and urban middle class.

(c) Political control, i.e. control of the press and labour.

(d) Political inclusion, i.e. co-optation and consolidation of bureaucratic elites, financial industrial groups and feudal classes.

Govt and Pak Army Today

Fast forward to the present and today as a result of the tumultuous political developments in Pakistan during 2007-08 leading to the historic 2008 elections, the Pak Army is under pressure but has not lost its power. It may go back to its old ways when the situation calms down. Pakistan is still far from having a genuinely democratic government that wields effective power. A tug-of-war is underway. It is not ruled out that spate of terrorist acts and destructive activities against India are intended to show up the ineffectiveness of the Pakistan's civilian government and create suspicions in India about its bonafide's, and the way for the Pak Army to reassert itself openly in Pakistan's political arena

While Musharraf's departure has reduced the visible level of involvement of the Pakistan Army in affairs of state, it has by no means reduced its stature as a major domestic force and one of the key pillars of governance in the country. It can safely be expected that the weakness and instability of the political coalition will bestow greater significance on the domestic role of the Pakistan Army and could even see the coalition in Islamabad acceding to all "requests" of the Pakistan Army. The chance that any reluctance on the part of the elected politicians to digress from the path desired by the Pakistan Army may lead to yet another military coup in Pakistan is likely to prominently in the thinking of the elected leaders and could well force them to acquiesce to the desires of the Pakistan Army. In some ways, this would highlight a paradox that has continued to in Pakistani politics - the departure of a strong albeit despised military ruler from the corridors of power has once again presented the all-powerful Pakistan Army with yet another opportunity for calling the shots in Islamabad. The power and influence that the Pakistan Army continues to enjoy became fairly evident when Prime Minister Gillani's government had to revoke an order placing the powerful ISI under the Ministry of Interior within six hours of its issuance, primarily due to pressure from the Army.

PAK ARMY SPONSORED CROSS BORDER TERRORISM

The Pak Army is now inextricably involved in exporting terrorism to India. A cosy relationship has developed at the functional level between the local army commanders, the drug mafia, the politicians, the bureaucrats, the police, and the mullahs who supply young recruits as cannon fodder for the so called jihad in Kashmir. It suits everyone's vested interests to keep the pot boiling. The vigorous advocacy of jihad provides a share in spoils of the narcotics booty. Power and pelf make a potent cocktail; this heady mixture is an extremely motivating incentive for institutionalizing the perpetuation of a proxy war against India. Hence, no matter what incentives India offers, there is likely to be no let up in the ongoing hostilities.

Pak Sponsored Terrorism in J&K

The ISI had initiated the Proxy war in J&K in 1989-90. This campaign can be categorized in three main phases

(a) The Azadi Phase (1990-1995). The ISI had raised, trained and equipped the JKLF to initiate terrorism in the Valley. The JKLF based its struggle on the slogans of Azadi. By 1993, the JKLF had taken serious losses. It tried to find safe sanctuaries in the remote areas of Doda and Kishtwar to survive. However, by 1995 the JKLF was wiped out. In 1996, Assembly and Lok Sabha Elections were held in J&K which restored political legitimacy to the state.

(b) The Jihadi Phase (1996-2005). Pakistan now dumped the JKLF for it did not trust its agenda of Azadi. It had in the meanwhile raised a whole set of Jihadi Tanzeems like the Hizbul Mujahideen (HM), Harkut ul Ansar and Harkat ul Jihad-e-Islami (HUJI) and pushed them into the Valley in a major way to launch struggle for the accession of Kashmir to Pakistan. The ISI felt that the Kashmiri cadres could not stand up to the Indian Army and hence sent in a large number of Afghan, Pakistani and other Foreign Terrorists from its Afghan Jihad Corpus. It tried to widen the arc of instability to South of the Pir Panjal and under its Operation Balakote, it tried to spread jihadi insurgency in the districts of Rajouri, Poonch and Udhampur. Concerted counter-terrorist operations, however, inflicted serious levels of attrition on the HM and allied Tanzeems. Pakistan now sent in the LeT and JeM. Their training camps had been moved out of POK to the Afghanistan/Pakistan border but with the overthrow of the Taliban these were brought back to POK. All these Tanzeems had suffered serious attrition as India raised more Rashtriya Rifles (RR) formations and increased force levels to counter the new Tanzeems and the widening of the arc of terrorism in J&K. Then came the Kargil intrusions These intrusions were designed to internationalize the Kashmir issue as a nuclear flash point and take the pressure off the Tanzeems by drawing the Indian Army away towards the LC and the border. This gave the Tanzeems a reprieve in the hinterland and a chance to revive their sagging fortunes. Counter-terrorist Operations were re-intensified and heavy losses inflicted on the terrorist ranks in the years 2000 and 2001. By 2002 a positive degree of control had been achieved and, free and fair Assembly Elections were held in J&K.

(c) The Third Phase: Though very heavy attrition had been inflicted on terrorist Tanzeems, the constant Pak Army endeavour was to send in terrorist replacements and regenerate their force levels in J&K. To end this regeneration syndrome it was decided to build the LC Fence at huge cost. It proved to be a key turning point in J&K. The creation of the Fence in J&K in 2004/05 had not just entailed the erection of a physical obstacle but also an electronic wall of sorts. It had been Pak Army's constant endeavour to continue to push in terrorists each year in summer to make up for the attrition inflicted by the Indian Army as also turn over its Tanzeem cadres for rest and relief. The erection of the Fence and the widespread use of Night Vision devices severely curtailed Pakistan's ability to infiltrate or exfiltrate terrorists or provide any meaningful degree of logistics support. A distinct drop was encountered in the availability of ammunition and this had lowered terrorist morale.

(d) The Intifida Phase. Realising that the terrorist battle had been largely lost, the ISI tried to respond in several ways The Pakistani Army staged firing incidents on the LC to provide fire cover for renewed attempts at infiltration. It thereby did its best to break the ceasefire that had held since 2003. The intention was possibly to divert attention from President Musharraf's serious problems as also to possibly create excuses in the east to slow down or call off its campaign against the Taliban in FATA and NWFP, west of the Indus.

Terror Training camps

There are around 40-50 terror training camps in Pakistan. The number has gone down may be because the terrorists have become careful, Instead of being spread out, they are focusing on running fewer camps across a smaller area. There are apparently three kinds of camps: those for recruitment, training and launching attacks. The recruitment camps (marked in red in the sketch below) in PoK exist between Muzaffarabad and Lahore and training here lasts 30-35 days. From here, the brainwashed young men are sent to learn about guns and grenades, navigation and radio telephony.

Most instructors are from Pak Army or ex-servicemen. ISI officials control the camps and come to inspect progress of training. After completion of training the terrorists are moved to launch pads (Marked in yellow) to be launched across the IB/LC. The launching pads have 10-30 terrorists including handlers and instructors. These can be dismantled in no time as most of the infrastructure is mobile.

TERROR SPONSORED IN REST OF INDIA

ISI is promoting local organizations which seem to draw their angst from purely local causes and have a highly localized narrative. ISI Support to Indian Mujahideen (IM). The IM is an offshoot of the Students Islamic movement of India (SIMI). A series of training camps were held in various forest locations in India where Pakistani trained activists imparted training to the IM cadres in the manufacture Improvised Explosive Devices (IEDs) from locally available material like Ammonium Nitrate (used in fertilizers) and Hydrogen Peroxide for mass casualty actions.

Though not as powerful as Service RDX or Plastic Explosives, these, when used in multiple strikes, could create mayhem and panic. Non use of RDX or Plastic Explosives obviated the need for logistics support networks from across the border and ensured deniability for the ISI.

A number of camps were held in the year 2007/08, which included camps held at Hubli, Dharwad, Jungles of kerala and Pawagarh jungles near Vadodra. Instead of camps run by Jihadi Tanzeems in Afghanistan or POK, these camps are being organized in remote jungles within Indian territory. The entire enterprise is far more sophisticated and professional and in text book covert action style, ensures deniability by using local agents and localized narratives. Tracing their antecedents and support back to the ISI is increasingly difficult because the logistical footprint of AK-47s, RDX and Plastic Explosives or other sophisticated equipment is simply not there. What is even more significant is that there are no electronic signatures. These new set of terrorists do not use citizen band radio sets, or even cellular phones but make sophisticated use of the Internet or just face to face communications. The lessons learnt by al Qaeda in the last few years are fully evident in the new modus operandi of the IM. We are now dealing with a new phase of Jihadi terrorism in India. It has not happened overnight but was for one year in the making. The ISI has fully ingested its lessons of the earlier campaigns in J&K and the rest of India. What we are now witnessing is the effectiveness of the changed tactics. The former Jihadi triumphalism has now been replaced by a far more sophisticated professionalism.

ISI has also been reported to operate training camps near the border of Bangladesh where members of separatist groups of the North Eastern states, such as the United Liberation Front Of Assam (ULFA) are trained with military equipment and terrorist activities. These camps also include training for groups including the National Security Council of Nagaland [NSCN], People's Liberation Army [PLA], and North East Students Organization [NESO].

Mumbai : India's 9/11

Why Mumbai? Pakistan based terrorists see India as a part of the "Crusader-Zionist-Hindu" alliance, and therefore the enemy of Islam. LeT has declared that its objective is not merely liberating Kashmir but breaking up India. More pragmatically, a terrorist attack on India can exacerbate antagonisms between India's Hindu and Muslim communities and provoke Hindu reprisals that, in turn, divide India and facilitate recruiting by Islamist extremists.

The terrorist's attacks have increased tensions between India and Pakistan, which could have been part of terrorist's strategic objectives. The prospect of another armed confrontation with India or India's conducting attacks on suspected terrorist training bases in Pakistan, will provoke and strengthen Pakistani hardliners. That, in turn, will take the pressure off the terrorists based in Pakistan by forcing a redeployment of Pakistani forces from the frontier tribal areas to the border with India.

How was 26/11 Different?

The attack was sequential and highly mobile. Multiple teams attacked several locations at once combining armed assaults, carjackings, drive by shootings, prefabricated IEDs, targeted killings(policemen and selected foreigners), building takeovers and barricade and hostage situations.

These tactics were a break from the now common suicide bombings associated with jihadist groups. What was new here was a combination of various tactics. It was a complicated, multipart operation. By dispersing into separate teams and moving from target to target, the terrorists were able to sow confusion and create the impression of a greater number of attackers. The explosive devices that would go off after the terrorists departed heightened the confusion. The multiple attacks at different locations prevented the authorities from developing an overall assessment of the situation. Media reports consistently overestimated what we now know to be the actual size of the force. The small size of individual attack teams-two to four men- limited their capability in any firefight with the security forces. Upon confronting any serious return fire, as they eventually did at the train station, for example, they broke off contact and moved onto another target.

Involvement of Pak Army

Ajmal Kasab the only terrorist captured alive by the police revealed that he underwent 21 days of physical training and Darshe-Quran (Quran recital) at a LeT camp at Muridke in Punjab in Pakistan in 2007. This training programme was called Daura-e-Shufa (Era of Simplicity). He was then sent to Manzera in PoK for another 21-day training programme called Markaz-e-Tayyeba (Centre of the Pure). He was taught how to use automatic rifles, including AK-47s andM-16s, and pistols. On completing his arms training, he had to undergo two months of khidmat (service) training - as a cook in the camp kitchen.

The courses were very intensive and gruelling and not all recruits made the cut. Ajmal did and was then sent to another LeT camp in the Cherapadi region of Muzaffarabad in PoK in Jun-Jul 2008. For the next two-and-a-half months he received advanced training from ustads (teachers) in fiiring AK 47, Rocket Launchers and Mortars and was also taught how to use GPS systems and Marine Compass. Having 'qualified' Ajmal and his cohorts were taught to operate maritime vessels. His handlers now considered him a finished product. He proceeded to Azizabad in Karachi where he and nine others were briefed about their deadly mission.

The group of ten started in a medium-sized boat from an isolated creek in Azizabad on Nov 23. Three or four nautical miles into the sea, they boarded al Hussaini, a larger, sea faring vessel. They were given a bag each, which contained eight grenades, one TT pistol with one or two magazines, an AK 44 with three double magazines, a gas lighter, a dry fruit packet weighing 500 gms, loose ammunition, one mobile phone with an Indian SIM card and a walkie talkie.

Each of them was also given fake ID cards. By 12.30 to 1.00 pm they were within reach of Mumbai, but the instructions were to launch the operations only after night fall. So, they slowed down and waited for the sun to set. At 6.30 pm, the group of ten boarded a rubber speed boat, fitted with a new Yamaha engine and came ashore in India's financial capital at 8.30 pm.

The training the group received on handling of sophisticated equipment including maritime vessels, the intelligence they were fed about the targets, and logistic support they received all point to direct involvement of ISI/Military agencies.

ISI Involvement In Terror Strike at Mumbai

There are strong indications that Pak ISI Colonel Mehmud Hasan had allegedly played a role in assisting the LeT plot, the Mumbai attacks, according to a senior Intelligence Bureau (IB) officer. Hasan, was involved in rustling up logistics required for the Mumbai attack. Among the things he arranged were retired armed forces and ISI personnel, who trained the Lashkars suicide attackers. Hasan, a serving officer, works with an ISI division named Joint Intelligence Miscellaneous (JIM). Hassan, had been tasked to interface with 'jihadi' tanzeems that operate in India to aid and guide their operations'.

According to the senior IB officer the LeT would not have dared to orchestrate its Mumbai attacks without the approval of their mentors in the ISI. They knew the ramifications would be great. Intelligence sources revealed that another ISI division named "X" had allegedly 'played a role in fine tuning the attack plans.' Indian enforcement and intelligence have come across the names of a few other ISI officers who allegedly aided the LeT in carrying out the audacious, clinical attacks having the "precision of a commando operation".

Mumbai crime Branch's Additional Commissioner of Police Devan Bharti has said that Kasab confirmed that retired personnel from ISI and the Pakistani armed forces would attend the training camps and especially hold taqreers (discussions) on how to handle tactical situations in such terror attack.

FUTURE CONTOURS & SUGGESTED RESPONSES

What Next ?

The attackers' purpose, as indicated by the testimony of the surviving terrorist, was to kill as many people as possible. However, there is some uncertainty that slaughter alone was the sole purpose of the operation's planners. If we compare the 2008 Mumbai attack with the 2006 Mumbai train attack, in which seven bombs killed 209 people, or the 1993 Mumbai attack. In which 257 persons died in 13 bomb blasts across the city, it would seem that bombs would have been more effective if body count were the sole criterion.

Indiscriminate bombings, as in the London and Madrid bombings, have been criticized, even by some jihadists, as contrary to an Islamic code of warfare. So it is possible that by relying on shooters, the 2008 attack would appear to be more selective, even though the vast majority of those killed in Mumbai were ordinary Indians gunned down at random. This pretension of selectivity was underscored by the terrorists' purported search for Americans and Britons, by the brutal murders at the Chabad Centre, and by what appear to have been considered decisions to kill certain hostages. The massacre at the Chabad centre had its own logic. According to transcripts of phone calls between the terrorists and their handlers during the attack, terrorists at the Chabad centre were instructed to kill their Jewish hostages in order to "spoil relations between India and Israel." It also enabled the attackers to eventually engage the police and soldiers in what their supporters could portray as a heroic last stand.

Security may have been another factor. Based on the pattern of previous terrorist attacks, Indian authorities were focused on truck bombs at hotels. Rail security focused on trying to keep bombs off trains, not armed assailants out of train stations. An armed assault might also have been more attractive than suicide bombings to the attackers themselves. Once they opened fire, their fate was sealed, but the prolonged nature of the operation enabled them to engage in a sustained slaughter where they could see the results. Still martyrs in their own minds, they could also think of themselves as being more like warriors than mere button-pushing suicide bombers. Putting aside the drive-by shootings, the train station and the two hotels provided the opportunity for achieving a high body count. The Leopold Café and the hotels were dramatic venues for the attack—providing the "emotional value" sought by terrorists.

They may call the next several years the 'Era of Mumbai Terror', an increasing number of counter terrorism specialists say the nature of the attack is clearly different from the South Asian norm and possibly even by global measure. And because it was so successful- a score of armed men holding an entire country to ransom for three days- it may become a model for the next wave of jihadi fighters. Colonel Jonathan Fighel of Israeli international institute for counter- terrorism is among those who has pointed out that the Mumbai attacks are 'unusual not only for India, but also on the International scale.'

The sub-continental norm has been a series of explosions undertaken simultaneously by radical Islamic organisations aiming to kill 'masses of people' this was an all out offensive, with clear military hallmarks.'

The military nature of the attack is striking. Indian commandos have been interviewed as saying it was like fighting regular soldiers, whose training was not unlike Indian Army, and contrary to the common perception, the militants largely avoided the taking of hostages or using civilians a shield. The innocents were either executed or got caught in the cross fire. The attack indicates that LeT, probably with the assistance of al Qaeda, have shifted to quality over quantity. US intelligence sources say they rate the Mumbai attack as being more sophisticated and logistically complex than even 9/11.

Slam Bang terrorism may make way for a special forces variety. Why would jihadi - master blasters feel the need to try a new tactic? The reason is that their cause is in the grip of its own global meltdown. The movements main fighting force, al Qaeda in Mesopotamia, is in retreat - ironically because of attacks by infuriated Arab Sunni tribal groups. The enemies that Osama Bin Laden has often declared to be his number ones- the US, Israel and Britan- haven't had their hair seriously ruffled now for several years. al Qaeda affiliates in Saudi Arabia, SE Asia and the Caucasus are sub-prime and falling.

Future Contours

Given that one of the possible reasons for the 26/11 outrage was to divert the Pakistani military from its counter insurgency engagement in FATA and NWFP to its eastern border, the possibility of a similar attack in the future remains. This could be state inspired, at least partially and covertly, or could have autonomous origin in terrorist strategy against both India and the Global War On Terror (GWOT). Therefore, the possibility cannot be ruled out.

The Mumbai attack demonstrates that jihadist organizations based in Pakistan given the requisite support are able to plan and launch ambitious terrorist operations, at least in neighbouring countries such as India. Put in the context of previous terrorist attacks in India by Pakistani-based or local jihadist groups, it suggests a continuing, perhaps escalating, terrorist campaign in South Asia. Beyond India, the Mumbai attack reveals a strategic terrorist culture that thoughtfully identified strategic goals and ways to achieve them and that analyzed counter- terrorist measures and developed ways to obviate them to produce a 9/11-quality attack.

The attack put into actual practice LeT's previous rhetoric about making the Kashmir dispute part of the international jihad. In so doing, LeT has emerged, not as a subsidiary of al Qaeda, but as an independent constellation in the global jihad galaxy. Indeed, with al Qaeda central operational capabilities reduced, the Mumbai attack makes LeT a global contender on its own.

The masterminds of the Mumbai terrorist attack displayed sophisticated strategic thinking in their choice of targets and tactics. The attack appears to have been designed to achieve an array of political objectives. This indicates a level of strategic thought—a strategic culture— that makes this terrorist foe particularly dangerous.

Given that the terrorists seek to maximize the psychological impact of the attacks, we can expect that future attacks will aim at both large-scale casualties and symbolic targets. The jihadists have stated, and the Mumbai attack demonstrates, the determination of the terrorists to seek high body counts, go after iconic targets, and cause economic damage. The masterminds designed the Mumbai attack to do what authorities were not expecting. There were no truck bombs or people attempting to smuggle bombs onto trains, as in previous attacks. Since attacks against high-profile soft targets are relatively easy and cheap to mount, such institutions will remain targets of future attacks. The protection of those targets presents particularly difficult challenges. Many of India's older symbolic buildings were not built with security considerations in mind or are in exposed locations.

One of the most important lessons of this attack is the continuing importance of an earlier operational form: the firearms assault. While the counterterrorism world has been focused almost exclusively on explosives, this attack demonstrates that firearms assault, while not as deadly as mass-casualty bombings, can be an effective tactic in creating prolonged chaos in an urban setting.

Cyber Terrorism

Two types of offensive actions are key components of the insurgency doctrine: armed conflict and mass mobilization. It is clear that the insurgents use IEDs/suicide attacks as their main instrument to conduct armed conflict. It is just as clear that they have learned how to mobilize and conduct conflict-related cognitive activities using cyber capabilities.

Insurgent cyber mobilization capabilities are designed to conduct psychological warfare activities, to propagandize insurgent successes and counter coalition allegations, and to recruit, finance, and train more fighters. Insurgents designate public affairs specialists to be their spokespersons and establish video production centers to promote their cause.

From a psychological perspective, two of the greatest fears of modern times are combined in the term "cyber terrorism." The fear of random, violent victimization blends well with the distrust and outright fear of computer technology. An unknown threat is perceived as more threatening than a known threat. Although cyber terrorism does not entail a direct threat of violence, its psychological impact on anxious societies can be as powerful as the threat of terrorist bombs.

The most sophisticated have been Web sites of various radical Pakistani organizations such as LeT, HUM, Harakat al-Ansar (Movement of the Partisans). Although the majority of the Pakistani-based groups have had relatively anemic and poorly designed sites (e.g., Hizb ul Mujahideen (HM), Harakat al-Ansar), LeT is an exception. Its Web designers are not only proficient but also capable of posting content in multiple languages—English, Arabic, and Urdu. Audio links on the site provide connections to Radio al-Jihad and Mercaz al-Dawa. Fund-raising is a prominent feature on the Web for Lashkar and other groups, with banking details and instructions provided for direct deposits into the group's account. An entreaty on the site described how the group's holy warriors were engaged in fighting the "oppressive Hindu Army in the snow covered valleys, mountains and jungles of Kashmir. These Mujadhideen best deserve your charity." The site is visceral in its enmity towards what its authors defined as Islam's triumvirate of most-hated opponents: India, the United States, and Israel.

CBRN Terrorism

A new age of technology has produced a threat of non-state & state sponsored actors with international networks that have access to weapons of mass destruction—chemical, biological, radioactive, and nuclear (CBRN)—sometimes based in failing or failed states like Pakistan. The CBRN threat in the hands of terrorists poses new challenges to the concept of national security. Terrorism confronts the state with a different set of challenges; the worst-case scenario for any government would be the acquisition of nuclear material by a terrorist group with a demonstrated history of conducting suicide bombing. The potential situation in which such a group obtains materials to conduct a suicide bombing attack using weapons of mass destruction (WMD), but cannot be discovered in time due to lack of coordination among government agencies, adds a sense of urgency to attempts to improve interagency coordination. For instance, the U.S.-German cooperation, worked together to identify and seize a ship bound for Libya in 2003 that contained banned nuclear materials, believed to be destined for a terrorist organization.

The poisonous anthrax letter campaign post 9/11 by a still undetermined perpetrator ushered in a new era of catastrophic terrorist warfare. There are also reports in the media about training by al Qaeda operatives in chemical and biological warfare, as well as the group's interest in acquiring radiological and nuclear weapons. These are strong indicators of their intention and potential capability to carry out catastrophic warfare involving chemical, biological, radiological, and nuclear weapons and devices against their adversaries which include our country.

Indian Responses

While India understands the costs of military action, from its point of view there are also costs to not responding. Since 2001, India has suffered a number of militant attacks that have involved in varying degrees Pakistan-based and indigenous militants. Given the origins of the various attacks perpetrated on its soil, India exhibited exceeding restraint in the aftermath of the 2006 LeT attack on Mumbai's local trains. Pakistan has likely concluded from the events since the December 2001 attack on the Indian parliament complex and prior, that India is unable or unwilling to mount a serious effort to punish and deter Pakistan for these attacks. Accordingly, from India's vantage point, to not respond would signal a lack of Indian resolve or capability.

26/11 gave a sense of déjà vu in the sense of being in a way a repeat of the 13 Dec 2001 attack on the Parliament. India's response on the previous occasion was military mobilisation as part of an exercise in coercive diplomacy.

The outcome was in drawing out a commitment from Pakistan not to allow its territory to be used for terrorist purposes directed against India. Since then, there has been the resumption of the peace process, ceasefire along the Line of Control and a drawdown in Pakistani sponsorship of terrorism in Kashmir, best evidenced by peaceful elections there. However, that terrorist infrastructure remains intact in Pakistan was starkly revealed in the well prepared and orchestrated terrorist outrage perpetrated at Mumbai. This gave rise to considerable speculation of Indian exercise of the military option in response. While this option was kept open, India instead relied on diplomacy for targeting Pakistan, to bring pressure on Pakistan to take appropriate action against terrorist organisations.

However, India has possibly reached the limit of its tolerance levels. Internal politics may compel adoption of a hard-line in face of future testing of its resolve. India's military preparations for a set of response options would likely be in place as a result of the lessons learnt from this crisis and would be in a position to execute a response strategy in a short warning scenario. Lastly, having tried mobilisation in Dec 2001 and diplomacy in Dec 2008, and with both being found wanting, there would be a requirement for adopting other options, not excluding the military option.

Instruments Available to Deal with State Sponsored Terrorism

Nations usually employ several means to coerce state sponsors: political pressure, economic sanctions, and military force. As an alternative (or, more rarely, a complement), states may try to engage sponsors of terrorism. Each of these instruments has its flaws.

Engagement. Victims of terrorism may try to engage a sponsor, offering concessions in order to reduce the likelihood of further terrorism. Regardless of the morality of "giving in to terrorists," such engagement is often based on a ruthless strategic judgment: by conceding on what a government may deem as a minor issue, it can free itself from the scourge of terrorism. In past India has adopted this strategy in resolving the J&K dispute but time and again Pakistan has not kept its side of promise. Engagement also suffers from a drawback, i.e the victim state is open to blackmail and is perceived as weak.

Despite these many problems, engagement is at times necessary as long as it is part of a broader effort that involves coercive forms of pressure. Engagement, by itself, tends to make the problem of terrorism worse. However, coercion without any promise that the pressure will relent is not really coercion in the true sense: there must be an incentive to stop the support for terrorism, and the promise of engagement is thus often necessary.

Political Pressure. State efforts to halt support for terrorism almost always involve some form of political pressure. The US state sponsor list's "name and shame" power is one means of getting state sponsors to abandon their support for terrorism. As Edmund Hull, the former acting Coordinator for Counterterrorism contended about regimes on the list, "Most of these governments are extremely uncomfortable with the stigma that comes attached to being accused of sponsoring terrorism, and they will over time seek ways to escape that stigma." Another common form of pressure is an official demarche meant to discourage a particular act in support of a terrorist group. At times, states may attempt to make a rival regime an international pariah, shunned by its neighbors and the world.

Isolation may also prove ineffective or difficult to establish because of the supporting state's importance for a host of other issues not related to terrorism. For example Pakistan is seen as an important ally of US in GWOT. So efforts by India to isolate Pakistan are only partial success. However, political isolation offers several advantages for policymakers over other options. Most important, it is low cost: it demands few sacrifices and carries few risks. In addition, political isolation is almost always part and parcel of a larger coercive campaign involving economic and military measures. Political pressure can be seen as a first step, or a reinforcing measure, for other forms of coercion.

Economic Pressure. Economic pressure is another common means of trying to persuade sponsors to stop supporting terrorism. States can limit trade, withdraw investment, punish foreign companies, and otherwise use economic means to convince other countries not to support terrorism. Economic pressure can be unilateral, multilateral, or, more rarely, comprehensive., Unilateral sanctions are the most common and are often initiated by the stronger, victim state. India has restricted trade with Pakistan. Economic pressure may also affect elite or popular support for a regime, another theoretical potential point of leverage. A regime that fails to deliver economically might be voted out of power or lose the support of key interest groups keeping it in power. Sanctions, however, have several profound limits on their effectiveness. Studies of sanctions have determined that, in general, they succeeded only 17 percent of the time when imposed unilaterally and only slightly more when imposed multilaterally. The humanitarian impact of sanctions is another major drawback, both due to the inherent suffering they cause among innocents and because this suffering makes it harder to sustain them.

The Use of Force. When political and economic pressure does not lead to promising results, states often use their military forces to respond to terrorism. At the most extreme levels, this may involve invading another country and trying to change its government by force. A recent example is the 2001 U.S. invasion of Afghanistan, where the United States worked with local Afghan allies to overthrow the ruling Taliban because of its support for al Qaeda. The United States bombed Libya in 1986 because of Libya's use of terrorism; in 1993, the United States struck Iraq in response to its attempted assassination of former President George H.W. Bush; and in 1998, the United States attacked Afghanistan and Sudan after al Qaeda bombed U.S. embassies in Kenya and Tanzania.

Military Option as a Response to Pak Sponsored Terrorism

India has demonstrated restraint and maturity in wake of both the Parliament and the Mumbai attacks. It has not allowed the calibration of its policy to be hijacked by war hysteria.

From political aims flow military objectives and strategy. Political aims range from minimal to expansive. In the context of response options these would be formed internally by political pressures, media hype, public outrage and capabilities; and externally by availability of international support and an assessment of Pakistani reaction. Along an ascending order the aims could range from exacting revenge to making Pakistan comply. The former would imply acute limitation in military strategy restricted to 'demonstration strikes' on terrorist infrastructure, while the latter means strategic compellence amounting to Limited War.

Operationalising the Strategy

Military means would require to be tightly controlled in light of limited political ends. Self-regulation internal to the military would be a necessity. Likewise the media would require to be appropriately managed in order that media fanned public passions do not adversely impact policy. Use of multiple voices and diplomacy through media should be abjured. The opposition would require to be taken on board so that a consensus is presented not only internally but also to the outside world. Maximisation of diplomatic effort should be done simultaneously as the military instrument is only meant to complement these resources. At all times, all channels to Pakistan be kept open to include direct diplomatic, through friendly countries and intermediaries as special envoys, back channel and hotlines.

A strategic dialogue needs to be initiated with Pakistan so as to convey Indian resolve and limited intent in wake of a possible future terrorist outrage. This would in the event defuse Pakistani over-reaction, permitting termination of the conflict at the lowest escalatory levels. Higher escalatory levels of a Limited War should be avoided at all costs. However, these need be resorted to only in case of usurpation of power in Pakistan by right wing extremists and in coalition with the international community, preferably with the approval of the UN Security Council. The timeline of response at the lowest level should be earliest. The firebreak between each level should be such, so as to allow diplomatic gains to be made and assessed.

The main limitation of the military option is the implication of its inherently escalatory potential for political aims. It is likely that military coercion would serve to prompt Pakistani nationalism, resulting its cohering at least temporarily, behind its military. Such a constellation would push India to further exertion or stand down. Exerting high levels of pressure could prompt the undesirable outcome of rightist forces taking over the state in alliance with fundamentalist elements in society. Pakistani fragility, though taken as being over projected by Pakistan for the purposes of blackmailing the international community, should be taken with seriousness as Pakistanis themselves see their 'failed state' status as an existential threat. Since India would prefer to see Pakistan on even keel, the utility of the military option is only for posturing to supplement diplomacy. Resorting to it, however, would be only in an extreme circumstance since India would not like to be deflected from its socio-economic trajectory by the action of a set of terrorists aimed at this very reaction.

CONCLUSION

"When I say that terrorism is war against civilization, I may be met by the objection that terrorists are often idealists pursuing worthy ultimate aims — national or regional independence, and so forth. I do not accept this argument. I cannot agree that a terrorist can ever be an idealist, or that the objects sought can ever justify terrorism. The impact of terrorism, not merely on individual nations, but on humanity as a whole, is intrinsically evil, necessarily evil and wholly evil."

Power Equations Between Civil & Military

The Mumbai attacks have thrown up stark reality of two opposing power centres in Pakistan and the tensions between them. If the July attempt by the Pakistan People's Party (PPP) government to rein in the country's Inter-Services Intelligence (ISI) ended with the government retiring hurt, the Mumbai attacks pitched both sides in a fresh battle. In the first round, the government gave a repeat of its July performance and said that it would send the ISI chief to New Delhi for talks. But it had to issue a "correction" on that soon.

Thus, Pakistan's civilian government does not control the Military's (or ISI's) policies toward militant groups operating in and from Pakistan. Most analysts of Pakistan now believe that Pakistan's best hope is to slowly civilianize and incrementally exert civilian control over the military and intelligence agencies, but few are optimistic that this can or will occur.

The challenge for India, and the international community is how to selectively put pressure on the military and intelligence agencies in the near term without destabilizing Pakistan's fragile civilian government. The reality of the power equation in Pakistan is that the Army is the most organised and powerful party around. And although the present military leadership would prefer to stay out of the lime light after nine years of Musharraf's high profile rule, it still calls the shots where Pakistan's regional policy is concerned.

Given this reality, it is difficult to see how terrorist groups like the LeT and the JeM can be reined in. Both have received official blessings and support in the past. Even if formal links with the ISI have been severed, training camps are difficult to shut down permanently, given the sympathy these groups enjoy in sections of the military, the police and the judiciary.

Since Zia's poisonous rule in the 1980s, extremism has seeped into every level of the bureaucracy. Many Pakistanis are in denial about the extent to which their country has been infected by this plague. Under these circumstances the arrest of an individual like Zaki-ur-Rehman Lakhvi, a commander in the LeT is meaningless. In the past, top terror suspects like Masood Azhar of the JeM and Hafiz Sayeed of the LeT have been scooped up in the wake of terrorist outrages, only to be released a few weeks later.

It needs to be recognized that the real problem between India and Pakistan is the Pakistan's rogue army. The Punjabi dominated Pak Army, that is the foremost among Pakistan's several elites, such as the mullahs and maliks, has a vested interest in destabilizing India through covert means. It will never allow Kashmir issue to be amicably settled.

As there would then be no justification for Pakistan to maintain a 450,000 strong force. The only language that Pak Army junta is likely to understand is that of reciprocal violence-directed not against civilians inside POK but against Pak Army deployed on LC. The time has come to review India's Kashmir strategy and institute stronger steps to neutralize Pak Army sponsored cross border terrorism. The government needs to follow active two pronged approach to finding a lasting solution to the Kashmir problem. While it must persist in smoking the peace pipe with all the genuine representatives of the Kashmiri people to find a political solution and win the battle of hearts and minds, it must simultaneously adopt pro-active measures to reach across the country's borders with Pakistan to eradicate the menace of trans-border terrorism from its roots and turn the screws on the Pak army.

One major reason of the army is unwilling to completely sever its links with extremists is that it fears an alliance between India & Afghanistan that would see Pakistan encircled. Having an army of proxy warriors is an insurance policy military planners are reluctant to surrender. Years ago, a Pak Army general said ' by supporting the mujahideen in Kashmir, we have tied down at least four Indian divisions there. What could be a more cost effective strategy."

Future

Pakistan may be facing the most crucial moment of its existence. But its policymakers even now seem unwilling to recognise fully the dangers and are reluctant to confront them. The struggle becomes more difficult with each delay, deception and ruse. To confront the threat truly, the first challenge is for Pakistanis to agree that they want to live in a modern, democratic and plural society. To achieve this goal, Pakistanis must face and overcome the jihadi movement. Put simply, to meet the Islamist challenge effectively, the Pakistani state must finally accept and fully exercise its responsibility to maintain peace, provide justice, foster democracy and participation, and make available in an equitable manner the resources necessary for economic and social development.

The limited gains made so far in wake of 26/11, of getting Pakistani compliance with Indian requirements indicate that next time around there would be greater pressure for adopting a hard line, to include the military option. The discussion here has revealed this to be of limited utility. There is, therefore, a need to think through the need for India to engage with Pakistan meaningfully as has been envisaged in the Shimla and the Lahore Agreements.

The only credible way for Islamabad to gain the presumption of innocence when acts of terror occur in India is to continuously crack down on those who support such operations from safe havens on Pakistani soil. These steps have been repeatedly promised in the past, with half-hearted or ephemeral implementation. As a consequence, Pakistan's professions of innocence continue to be suspect. Nor can plausible deniability be gained by outsourcing terror to cells based in Bangladesh or Nepal, if shadowy links remain to groups or handlers in Pakistan. Pakistan's best defence is to go on the offense against Islamic extremists.

INDIA SAYS COMMITTED TO PEACE BUT WILL RESPOND TO FIRING BY PAKISTAN

Six days after an apparent thaw in ties brought about by talks between prime ministers Narendra Modi and Nawaz Sharif, India warned Pakistan of a "forceful and effective response" as it protested ceasefire violations along the Line of Control and international border — but kept the door open for talks.

Islamabad, in turn, summoned Indian high commissioner TCA Raghavan on Thursday to protest what it termed "airspace violations and unabated ceasefire provocations", a day after it claimed to have shot down an 'Indian' drone. New Delhi denied the charge.

"We remain committed to steps that ensure peace and tranquility along our border. However, there should be no doubt that any unprovoked firing from the Pakistani side would meet with an effective and forceful response from our forces," foreign secretary Subrahmanyam Jaishankar said. Pakistan's foreign office too clarified that it remained committed to the joint statement issued by India and Pakistan in the Russian city of Ufa under which the NSAs of the two sides will meet soon.

The media briefing by Jaishankar came after a high-level meeting between foreign minister Sushma Swaraj, home minister Rajnath Singh, defence minister Manohar Parrikar and national security adviser Ajit Doval, and intense parleys between the two neighbours. Days after the meeting between Modi and his Pakistani counterpart Sharif in Russia's Ufa, tension between the countries has escalated with both sides blaming each other for repeated ceasefire violations and heavy firing along the border. There have been at least six violations of the 2003 ceasefire by Pakistan in the past four days.

The recent escalation in border violence over the last two days has claimed a life in Jammu while Pakistan has said five of its civilians have also been killed. The latest finger-pointing has led to the view within official circles that the Pakistani army may be upping the ante because the crucial 'K' word was not mentioned in the Ufa joint statement.

Responding to photographs released by Pakistan of the 'Indian' drone it claimed to have shot down, the foreign secretary said, "The picture of the drone shows it's not of Indian design or available in the Indian armed forces' inventory. It appears to be of Chinese design." "At the moment, the issue for us is stabilising the border," Jaishankar said, even as Pakistan insisted the "spy drone" belonged to India and it entered that country's airspace violating international law and its territorial integrity.

Observing that nature of unprovoked firing by Pakistan was "serious", Jaishankar said there were series of consultations between officials of the two sides. Asked if India will go ahead with its engagement as was decided in Ufa, Jaishankar said, "I think my statement made it very clear. If the intention or the inclination is to strengthen peace and tranquillity on the border and do the meetings that we have agreed to do, we remain committed to that."

"If on the other hand there is unprovoked firing and there is infiltration and cross-border terrorism then, obviously the situation is different. So that choice is not ours." Jaishankar evaded questions on whether the cross-border firing will affect talks between the two countries and PM Modi's proposed visit to Islamabad in 2016.

Before Jaishankar's tough talk, India had chosen to exercise restraint when three days after the Ufa meeting, Sharif aide Sartaj Aziz said there could be no talks unless Kashmir was on the agenda. India had then ascribed his comments to "domestic compulsions". Thursday's briefing by the foreign secretary came after several phone calls following the escalation in border violence. "The national security adviser spoke to the Pakistan envoy twice yesterday (Wednesday) and once today (Thursday) on the border situation," Jaishankar said, also confirming reports that Pakistani high commissioner Abdul Basit was clearly briefed about India's stand. Basit had reportedly told Doval that India had initiated the firing.

Indian authorities dismissed this charge, saying soldiers had been forced to take counter-measures after an escalation by Pakistani border troops on Thursday. The latest border skirmish started two days before PM Modi's scheduled visit to Jammu on Friday. Pakistan providing cover fire to militants infiltrating into Kashmir ahead of important visits is not uncommon.

4

Cross-border Terrorism in Indian Kashmir

Responding to comments made by Pakistan High Commissioner in India Abdul Basit, the official spokesperson for India's Ministry of External Affairs (MEA) Vikas Swarup said on Friday that they will be taking up cross-border terrorism in Indian Kashmir during the national security adviser talks scheduled for late august. "The only struggle in Jammu and Kashmir is against Pakistani sponsored terrorism," Swarup alleged in a tweet on Friday evening. Swarup was responding to a question posed on micro-blogging website Twitter.

"This will be the subject of the upcoming NSA level talks," Swarup added, hinting at the agenda for the August 23-24 talks in New Delhi. Earlier in the day, Pakistan's High Commissioner in New Delhi Abdul Basit had said that Pakistan would not abandon Kashmiris in their legitimate struggle for freedom.

"No matter how much time their legitimate struggle takes, Pakistan will never abandon Kashmiris and their cause." Pakistan's national security adviser Sartaj Aziz had confirmed on Thursday that he will visit New Delhi on August 23 for bilateral talks.

Noting how his visit was "not a breakthrough" for the composite dialogue and all the issues but, Aziz hoped that it would at least provide and an "ice breaking on some issues... and let's hope it will lead to further more comprehensive dialogue on the other issues between the two countries."

INDIA, PAKISTAN, AND THE QUESTION OF KASHMIR

NUCLEAR-ARMED regional rivals India and Pakistan pulled back from the brink of war in mid-June. With more than a million troops massed on their mutual border, politicians and generals on both sides had traded threats for weeks, each claiming that they would not hesitate to use the "nuclear option." The results of even a brief nuclear exchange would be horrific. In just the first hour, according to a U.S. military estimate, 15 million people would be left dead or injured.

After a flurry of diplomatic activity, the crisis was averted as both governments began a process of de-escalation. With some arm-twisting from the U.S., the Pakistani government announced that it would act to stop the infiltration of militants across the border into India. The Indian government, in turn, was pressured into acknowledging the validity of this assurance from Pakistani "President General" Pervez Musharraf. Soon after, the Indian navy pulled back its warships, and India appointed a new ambassador to Pakistan.

This is only a temporary reprieve. India's mobilization of 800,000 troops is the largest peacetime military buildup anywhere since the Second World War, and the situation at the border remains tense.

U.S. "war on terror" fuels the crisis

With the war in Afghanistan, the U.S. entered Central and South Asia in full force, and has now established military outposts in both Pakistan and Afghanistan–in addition to existing ones in former Soviet Central Asian republics such as Uzbekistan and Turkmenistan. The U.S. now portrays CIA and Pentagon officials as vital to the security and stability of the region, and the State Department pointed to the recent de-escalation of military tensions as a diplomatic victory.

The U.S. military presence, however, may have also unleashed forces beyond its control. In the first place, it has backed the Islamist organizations into a corner. The Islamists have been driven to provoke a fight with India in the hopes that it will break the Pakistani military from its current collaborative relationship with the United States.

Secondly, the U.S. search for allies in its "war on terror" has exacerbated regional rivalries as both India and Pakistan try to forge a new partnership with U.S. power. Pakistan won the first round, as the U.S. turned to it as an ally in the war against Afghanistan. But friendship with the U.S. comes at a price, and the Pakistani government had to agree to crack down on Islamist organizations operating within its borders and within its own military. In a series of well-publicized moves, the Musharraf government banned a number of militant groups, arresting more than two thousand individuals.

Musharraf's crackdown has been selective. The largest Islamist party, the Jamaat-i-Islami (JI)–which has longstanding roots in the army's officer corps–has received the softest treatment, as its leaders tend to get released soon after they are arrested. In January, the JI's top leader returned the favor by supporting the crackdown on other Islamist organizations. Later, Musharraf gave a public endorsment to the JI's armed group in Kashmir, the Hizbul Mujahideen (HM). The HM is the only significant pro-Pakistan force in Indian-occupied Kashmir that includes members of local origin–and thus would be exempt from the ban on "cross-border terror."

Musharraf's strategy, in other words, has been twofold: on the one hand, to appease India, the U.S., and secularists at home with his crackdown on some of the most sectarian Islamist groups, and, on the other, to gain favor with Pakistan's most important Islamists in order to consolidate his own power base.

In a bid to draw Musharraf into a fight with India and thereby weaken his ability to carry out the crackdown, a handful of Islamic militants launched an attack on the Indian parliament on December 13 last year. The Indian government, led by the Hindu nationalist Bharatiya Janatha Party (BJP), treated this attack as "India's September 11" and began whipping up war hysteria, emulating recent U.S. tactics and rhetoric.

But the BJP's warmongering and its "antiterrorism" rhetoric are in part a desperate attempt to deflect attention away from a crisis of legitimacy. In March, it suffered a huge defeat in state-level elections, losing control of the most populous state, Uttar Pradesh, with its large Hindu majority.

At the same time, the true horror of Hindu nationalism was exposed in the state of Gujarat, the only state where the BJP is still in government. Hindu zealots belonging to a group called Shiv Sena and to the fascist Rashtriya Swayamsevak Sangh (RSS)–with which the ruling BJP has fraternal ties–literally set the state on fire. They massacred more than 900 Muslims and displaced some 120,000 in an anti-Muslim pogrom. The chief minister of the state, Narendra Modi (an RSS man himself), gave the fascists the go-ahead, while the BJP-led government in New Delhi sat on its hands.

The BJP pushed through a series of repressive measures, the Prevention of Terrorism Act (POTA), in an extraordinary joint session of the Indian parliament on March 26. Taking its cue from the USA PATRIOT Act, POTA allows the government a free hand in dealing with "terrorist" groups. Under POTA, suspects can be detained for up to six months without being charged. Then Home Minister L.K. Advani–a Hindu nationalist hardliner who has since been raised to the position of deputy prime minister–justified the passage of POTA by stating that "state-sponsored cross-border terrorism is a kind of war and not just a law and order problem." In other words, the BJP is trying to leverage the "war on terror" to justify domestic repression and to gain U.S. blessing for its crackdown on militancy in the state of Jammu and Kashmir.

Since the U.S. began last fall to demand that Musharraf take a stand against Islamists in Pakistan, Indian prime minister Atal Bihari Vajpayee has felt free to press similar demands. Shortly after Islamic militants attacked an Indian Army base in Jammu on May 14, the Indian military began a massive troop mobilization in the state, and tensions escalated to the brink of war. For the BJP, this was a perfect opportunity to show the U.S. that it has a right to wage its own "war on terrorism."

Soon after, the U.S. publicly acknowledged that "cross-border terrorism" in Kashmir was a problem and began pressuring the Pakistani government to halt the flow of Islamic militants into Indian-occupied Jammu and Kashmir.

The Hindu right-wingers in India were emboldened to push for more. Taking its cue from the Israeli intransigence with respect to Palestinian leader Yasser Arafat, the Indian government now claims that while the infiltration of its borders declined in the immediate aftermath of the crisis, it has begun to increase again. Indian External Affairs minister Yashwant Sinha stated recently: "Quite clearly, we are looking not only at assurances of Pakistan that infiltration from across the borders of terrorists will be permanently stopped. We are looking for visible and credible signs of that action."

The Kashmir question

The immediate flashpoint for the crisis, of course, is the so-called "disputed territory" of Jammu and Kashmir (J&K). India and Pakistan have fought three wars over J&K, including a small-scale war led on the Pakistani side by Musharraf himself, in the mountains of Kargil in 1999. Musharraf, who was then army chief to civilian prime minister Nawaz Sharif, deposed Sharif later in the year when Sharif began to distance himself from the Kargil adventure under U.S. pressure–and threatened to fire Musharraf.

Despite the longstanding nature of the dispute, the Indian government has tried, especially in the aftermath of September 11, to present the Kashmir conflict as a problem with "Islamic terrorists" infiltrating its borders from Pakistan. The recent U.S. acknowledgement of "cross-border terrorism" as the main problem in Kashmir was thus a diplomatic victory for India's rulers. In the coming months, India will seek to capitalize on U.S. support for its "antiterror" position, and the most fanatical nationalists in the government no doubt see a war with Pakistan as the only way of settling the dispute once and for all.

But behind the talk of "disputed territory" and "terrorism" lies a gruesome history of state oppression and brutality. At the time of independence from British rule, J&K was one of 565 princely states that were to be given the option of acceding to either India or Pakistan. In 1948 Maharaja Hari Singh, the decrepit ruler of J&K, acceded to India in return for an assurance by Indian Prime Minister Jawaharlal Nehru that a referendum would soon be held to determine the "will of the people." The referendum never came.

Since then, the Indian military has occupied the Muslim-majority province of Kashmir, putting down every attempt at self-assertion by the Kashmiri people by rigging elections, importing Hindus from other states to serve as top administrators, imprisoning Kashmiri leaders, and terrorizing the population.

In 1989, following a rigged election, a mass national liberation movement erupted in Kashmir, to which the Indian army responded with brute force. The movement, initially led by the secular, pro-independence Jammu and Kashmir Liberation Front (JKLF), rejected both Indian and Pakistani rule and called for a single secular state in all of historic J&K. The sheer scale of repression by the Indian state–50,000—80,000 Kashmiris have died in the last decade alone–severely weakened the mass movement by 1994. Subsequently, pro-Pakistan Islamist groups have been engaged in skirmishes with the Indian armed forces, which numbered 700,000 in J&K before this year's border buildup. Most of these groups have little or no support from a population that is both war-weary and skeptical of Pakistan.

India's insistence that the conflict over Kashmir is a bilateral issue to be settled by India and Pakistan with no "third party" interference–and no input from Kashmiris on their own behalf–is designed to maintain the status quo, since the ultimate arbiter in a bilateral dispute would be India's superior military might.

But the Indian government has also tried to construct the appearance of fairness in its treatment of the Kashmir problem. Thus it plans to hold "free and fair" elections in the state in September of this year, and has invited "anybody from anywhere in the world," including the international media, to observe the election. But the fact that no outsiders will have the status of "election observers" significantly dilutes their power. Earlier this year, Indian forces arrested Syed Ali Shah Geelani, the head of the All-Party Hurriyat Conference (APHC), a coalition of various political organizations in J&K, as well as Yasin Malik of the JKLF, using the cover of POTA. This has revealed both the Indian government's arrogance and its brazen hypocrisy over political freedom in J&K.

On the Pakistani side, Kashmir has long been a rallying point for all sections of the ruling class, from the landlord-dominated political elite to the military dictators to the right-wing Islamic clergy. Musharraf owes his current position to a coup conducted when Nawaz Sharif proved insufficiently militant about Kashmir. The rulers' strategy, like India's, gives the appearance of concern for the "will of the people" of Kashmir, as they have constantly upheld the demand for a referendum in the region. However, the so-called referendum that they propose, and that the Indian government refuses to accept, would force the Kashmiris to choose between India and Pakistan with no third option of independence–the demand that stood at the centre of the Kashmiri upsurge of 1989—94.

Today, Musharraf is caught in a precarious and defensive position. In danger of being perceived as too friendly to the U.S. by Islamists at home–who taunt him with the nickname "Busharraf"–he needs to prove that he is not a stooge of the U.S. government. He has to give the appearance of being reluctant to go along, not only with U.S. dictates but also with India's demands. To do this, he has done his own share of saber rattling–including conducting nuclear missile tests in the middle of the crisis.

As the International Socialist Review went to press, reports were re-emerging–after being discredited when U.S. Defense Secretary Donald Rumsfeld first raised them in mid-June–of the presence of al Qaeda forces in the fraction of Kashmir that is occupied by Pakistan. True or not, the newest reports have likely been planted in the media by the Indian and U.S. governments. India seeks to undermine Musharraf's credibility, and the U.S. seeks legitimacy for extending its war on terror. al Qaeda's alleged presence in Pakistani Kashmir allowed Rumsfeld to float the idea of deploying U.S. troops in previously unthinkable South Asian locations–as the "war on terror" has already licensed the U.S. to do in Central Asia.

HARDENING OF THE RIGHT-WINGERS

If the Islamists have been driven to adopt a more confrontational attitude in Pakistan and in Kashmir, in India the Hindu fascists have been significantly emboldened. The RSS, which heads the fascist umbrella group known as the Sangh Parivar, took the lead in calling for a nuclear attack on Pakistan. Meanwhile, the RSS and the Vishwa Hindu Parishad–another group in the Sangh–put forward demands for J&K to be split into separate states along communal (i.e., religious) lines. The RSS also called for Kashmiri assembly elections to be held under "President's rule"–direct rule from Delhi–and for rescinding Article 370 of the Indian constitution, a long-dormant clause that promises limited autonomy to J&K.

The RSS's political faction, the BJP, has historically supported this position, and the recent elevation of L.K. Advani, an RSS stalwart, to the position of deputy prime minister, marks a shift in elite politics to the right. However, the RSS has always had a rocky relationship with the BJP. In order to achieve electoral success, the BJP has had to water down the project of "Hindutva," the fascist vision of creating a Hindu state in India. In the 1993 elections, after Advani and the BJP had led the demolition of the Babri mosque by thousands of fascist goons, the BJP lost 20—80 percent of the seats that it won around the country in the previous elections. A majority of the Indian population clearly did not accept the Hindu nationalist vision. A study conducted shortly after found that only 22 percent of the population actually supported the demolition of the mosque. This led the BJP to tone down its rhetoric in the 1996 elections, much to the chagrin of the RSS.

Today, after facing major losses in state elections in March and after being exposed for its complicity in the Gujarat massacres, the Hindutva agenda of the BJP has again been set back, and it is not entirely free to implement a fascist program. Thus, Advani and the BJP had to reject the RSS's resolution for splitting up Kashmir on religious lines.

This situation could change rapidly, however, given the absence of any significant opposition to the Sangh Parivar's agenda in mainstream politics. Indian Marxist Aijaz Ahmad recently raised an alarm in Frontline magazine:

Today India faces the classic situation of a pre-fascist upheaval. What used to be the political centre has collapsed, with the [formerly dominant] Congress [Party] reduced to a parliamentary minority and all the rest so splintered as to be assimilated as small ineffectual groupings into support for the fascist project.

Can the left rise to the challenge?

More importantly, the organizations of the Indian left have been hamstrung in their ability to take on the BJP effectively because of their own internal weaknesses. In numerical terms, the Indian left is quite large, with two mass Communist Parties (the CPI and the CPI-M), a handful of smaller revolutionary organizations such as the CPI-ML, and reformist organizations like the People's Union of Civil Liberties (PUCL). As shown by the mass protests that erupted in the wake of the BJP's 1998 nuclear tests, there is a tremendous potential for opposing the militarism of the present government. Politically, however, these organizations have responded in a confusing way to the current crisis.

As long as the BJP and its allies relied solely on "Hindutva" for their mobilizations, the left responded vigorously, attacking the anti-democratic, fascist politics the former represented. But the BJP learned quickly from its past mistakes, toned down its Hindutva-related demands, and began to elaborate a bolder imperialist image, taking a hard-line stance against Kashmiri militants and "cross-border terrorism" in the name of "national unity and security" and adopting a belligerent attitude towards Pakistan.

Here, large sections of the left have stumbled, accepting as they do the essentially nationalist premise that control over Kashmir is crucial to India's "unity" and "integrity." While many on the left have loudly opposed the Indian military occupation and human rights abuses in Kashmir, they barely pay lip-service to the cause of self-determination. When they do, they often make concessions to Indian nationalism, so that the question of independence for

Kashmir is rarely even mentioned. As a result of its failure to respond forthrightly to the single most extreme instance of Indian state oppression of Muslims–the real "Kashmir question"–the Indian left has been hamstrung in its efforts to present a credible alternative to the Sangh Parivar's communal agenda, which includes both belligerence toward Pakistan and the scapegoating of Muslims at home.

The Indian left can only counter the BJP and its fascist allies today by categorically rejecting the nationalist premises behind the latest adventures. This would mean an unequivocal defense of the right of Kashmiri self-determination, to the point of secession. A bold and aggressive policy of winning support for Kashmiri self-determination would also play an important part in breaking down the barriers between Hindus and Muslims within the Indian working class. This is the only way to undermine the fascism of the Sangh and of its political agents in the BJP.

Supporting genuine self-determination for Kashmir, including the option of independence, is also crucial to building Pakistan's left from its current state of extreme weakness. The left needs to help workers break from the cardinal principle of the Pakistani state–the idea that Pakistan exists to defend all Muslims regardless of class. Pakistan's vast inequality exposes the hollowness of this principle, but so does the sectarian basis of what counts as "Muslim." The Ahmadiya minority has been excluded from legal consideration as Muslims for some twenty years, and the state routinely tolerates attacks by zealots of the Sunni majority upon Shia Muslims. Most Kashmiri Muslims belong to the the Sufi wing of Shia Islam, which helps account for why joining Pakistan is unattractive to so many Kashmiris. Leftists in Pakistan need to emphasize these points to promote working class (as opposed to religious) identification with the Kashmiri struggle and to open the question of a common front with Indian Hindu workers–both against war and against the rulers of both states.

No long-lasting solution to the crisis facing South Asia exists outside this framework. The rulers of both India and Pakistan have shown that they are willing to go to monstrous extremes to achieve their goals. But the working classes of both countries have nothing to gain either from living under current levels of military spending or from a communalism that threatens to drag the entire region down the road to nuclear holocaust. By championing the right to self-determination of the Kashmiris, Indian and Pakistani workers can show the way forward to a different future.

PAKISTAN ADMINISTERED KASHMIR

Azad Kashmir

Claim of religious discrimination and restricting religious freedom in Azad Kashmir have been made against Pakistan. It is also accused of systemic suppression of free speech and demonstrations against the government. The United Nations Commission on Human Rights reported that a number of Islamist militant groups, A number of Islamist militant groups including al-Qaeda, operate from bases in Pakistani-administered Kashmir with the tacit permission of Pakistani intelligence And there have been several allegations of human rights abuse.

In 2006, Human rights watch (organization) accused Pakistani intelligence agency ISI and the military of systemic torture with the purpose of "punishing" errant politicians, political activists and journalists in Azad Kashmir. A report titled "Kashmir: Present Situation and Future Prospects", which was submitted to the European Parliament by Emma Nicholson, Baroness Nicholson of Winterbourne, was critical of the lack of human rights, justice, democracy, and Kashmiri representation in the Pakistan National Assembly. According to the Human Rights Commission of Pakistan, Pakistan's Inter Services Intelligence operates in Pakistan-administered Kashmir and is accused of involvement in extensive surveillance, arbitrary arrests, torture, and murder. The 2008 report by the United Nations High Commissioner for Refugees determined that Pakistan-administered Kashmir was 'Not free'. According to Shaukat Ali, chairman of the International Kashmir Alliance, "On one hand Pakistan claims to be the champion of the right of self-determination of the Kashmiri people, but she has denied the same rights under its controlled parts of Kashmir and Gilgit-Baltistan".

Kashmir herald, a News and Analysis Reporting agency reoprted that on 28 May 1999, the Supreme Court of Pakistan delivered a stinging broadside of Islamabad's oppressive, undemocratic and colonial subjugation of the Northern Areas of Pakistan Occupied Kashmir, including denial to fundamental rights, illegal detention with limited access to justice.". After 2011 elections, The Azad Kashmir (also called PoK or 'Pakistan Occupied Kashmir') Prime Minister Sardar Attique Ahmad Khan stated that there were mistakes in the voters list which have raised questions about the credibility of the elections.

It was reported that politically "PoK" (aka Azad Kashmir) is a "replica of Pakistan": Basic Democracy of Ayub Khan and Gen. Zia's Martial Law. In December 1993 the blasphemy laws of Pakistan were extended to the POK. They are ruled directly through a chief executive Lt. Gen. Mohammed Shafiq, appointed by Islamabad with a 26-member Northern Areas Council.

The regime in Muzaffarabad (capital of Azad Kashmir or POK) is one set up by Pakistan in territory it has occupied not acquired by law.

The United Nations Commission on Human Rights reports that the status of women in Pakistani-administered Kashmir is similar to that of women in Pakistan. Women are not granted equal rights under the law, and their educational opportunities and choice of marriage partner remain "circumscribed" in Pakistan-administered kashmir. Domestic violence, forced marriage, and other forms of abuse continue to be issues of concern. In May 2007, the United Nations and other aid agencies temporarily suspended their work after suspected Islamists mounted an arson attack on the home of two aid workers; the organizations had received warnings against hiring women. However, honour killings and rape occur less frequently than in other areas of Pakistan.

Gilgit-Baltistan

The main demand of the people of Gilgit-Baltistan is a constitutional status to the region as a fifth province of Pakistan. However, Pakistan claims that Gilgit-Baltistan cannot be given constitutional status due to Pakistan's commitment to the 1948 UN resolution. In 2007, International Crisis Group stated that "Almost six decades after Pakistan's independence, the constitutional status of the Federally Administered Northern Areas (Gilgit and Baltistan), once part of the former princely state of Jammu and Kashmir and now under Pakistani control, remains undetermined, with political autonomy a distant dream. The region's inhabitants are embittered by Islamabad's unwillingness to devolve powers in real terms to its elected representatives, and a nationalist movement, which seeks independence, is gaining ground.

The rise of sectarian extremism is an alarming consequence of this denial of basic political rights". A two-day conference on Gilgit-Baltistan was held on 8–9 April 2008 at the European Parliament in Brussels under the auspices of the International Kashmir Alliance. Several members of the European Parliament expressed concern over the human rights violation in Gilgit-Baltistan and urged the government of Pakistan to establish democratic institutions and rule of law in the area.

In 2009, the Pakistan government implemented an autonomy package for Gilgit-Baltistan which entails rights similar to those of Pakistan's other provinces. Gilgit-Baltistan thus gains province-like status without actually being conferred such a status constitutionally. The direct rule by Islamabad is replaced by an elected legislative assembly and its chief minister.

There has been criticism and opposition to this move in Pakistan, India, and Pakistan administrated Kashmir. The move has been dubbed as an eyewash to hide the real mechanics of power, which allegedly are under the direct control of the Pakistani federal government. The package was opposed by Pakistani Kashmiri politicians who claimed that the integration of Gilgit-Baltistan into Pakistan would undermine their case for the independence of Kashmir from India. 300 activists from Kashmiri groups protested during the first Gilgit-Baltistan legislative assembly elections, with some carrying banners reading "Pakistan's expansionist designs in Gilgit-Baltistan are unacceptable"

In December 2009, activists of nationalist Kashmiri groups staged a protest in Muzaffarabad to condemn the alleged rigging of elections and killing of a 18-year old student.

Map Issues

As with other disputed territories, each government issues maps depicting their claims in Kashmir territory, regardless of actual control. Due to India's Criminal Law Amendment Act, 1961, it is illegal in India to exclude all or part of Kashmir in a map (or to publish any map that differs from those of the Survey of India). It is illegal in Pakistan not to include the state of Jammu and Kashmir as disputed territory, as permitted by the United Nations.

Non-participants often use the Line of Control and the Line of Actual Control as the depicted boundaries, as is done in the CIA World Factbook, and the region is often marked out in hashmarks, although the Indian government strictly opposes such practices. When Microsoft released a map in Windows 95 and MapPoint 2002, a controversy was raised because it did not show all of Kashmir as part of India as per the Indian claim. All the neutral and Pakistani companies claim to follow the UN's map and over 90% of all maps containing the territory of Kashmir show it as disputed territory.

The boundaries, names, and designations used on the map prepared by the United Nations do not imply official endorsement or acceptance by the United Nations, the Commonwealth Secretariat, or the publishers concerning the legal status of any country, territory or area, or of its authorities, or concerning the delimitation of its frontiers or boundaries. There is no intention to define the status of Jammu and/or Kashmir, which has not yet been agreed upon by the parties. A dotted line represents the Line of Control agreed upon by the Republic of India and the Government of Pakistan since 1972. Both parties have not yet agreed upon the final status of the region, and nothing significant has been implemented since the peace process began in 2004.

The Government of Pakistan maintains unprovisionally and unconditionally that the informal accession of Jammu and Kashmir to Pakistan or to the Republic of India remains to be decided by UN plebiscite. It accepts the UN's map of the territory. The Government of India states that "the external artificial boundaries of India, especially concerning the Kashmir region under its jurisdiction created by a foreign body are neither correct nor authenticated".

Recent Developments

India continues to assert their sovereignty or rights over the entire region of Kashmir, while Pakistan maintains that it is a disputed territory. Pakistan argues that the status quo cannot be considered as a solution. Pakistan insists on a UN-sponsored plebiscite. Unofficially, the Pakistani leadership has indicated that they would be willing to accept alternatives such as a demilitarized Kashmir, if sovereignty of Azad Kashmir was to be extended over the Kashmir valley, or the "Chenab" formula, by which India would retain parts of Kashmir on its side of the Chenab river, and Pakistan the other side – effectively re-partitioning Kashmir on communal lines.

The problem is that the population of the Pakistan-administered portion of Kashmir is for the most part ethnically, linguistically, and culturally different from the Valley of Kashmir, a part of Indian-administered Kashmir.

A partition on the Chenab formula is opposed by some Kashmiri politicians, though some, such as Sajjad Lone, have suggested that the non-Muslim part of Jammu and Kashmir be separated from Kashmir and handed to India. Some political analysts say that the Pakistan state policy shift and mellowing of its aggressive stance may have to do with its total failure in the Kargil War and the subsequent 9/11 attacks.

These events put pressure on Pakistan to alter its position on terrorism. Many neutral parties to the dispute have noted that the UN resolution on Kashmir is no longer relevant. The European Union has viewed that the plebiscite is not in Kashmiris' interest. The report notes that the UN conditions for such a plebiscite have not been, and can no longer be, met by Pakistan. The Hurriyat Conference observed in 2003 that a "plebiscite no longer an option". Besides the popular factions that support either parties, there is a third faction which supports independence and withdrawal of both India and Pakistan. These have been the respective stands of the parties for long, and there have been no significant changes over the years. As a result, all efforts to solve the conflict have been futile so far. In a 2001 report titled "Pakistan's Role in the Kashmir Insurgency" from the American RAND Corporation, the think tank noted that "the nature of the Kashmir conflict has been transformed from what was originally a secular, locally based struggle (conducted via the Jammu Kashmir Liberation Front – JKLF) to one that is now largely carried out by foreign militants and rationalized in pan-Islamic religious terms." Most of the militant organizations are composed of foreign mercenaries, mostly from the Pakistani Punjab. In 2010, with the support of its intelligence agencies, Pakistan has again been 'boosting' Kashmir militants, and recruitment of mujahideen in the Pakistani state of Punjab has increased. In 2011, the FBI revealed that Pakistan's spy agency ISI paid millions of dollars into a United States-based non-governmental organization to influence politicians and opinion-makers on the Kashmir issue and arrested Syed Ghulam Nabi Fai.

The Freedom in the World 2006 report categorized Indian-administered Kashmir as "partly free", and Pakistan-administered Kashmir, as well as the country of Pakistan, as "not free". India claims that contrary to popular belief, a large proportion of the Jammu and Kashmir populace wishes to remain with India. A MORI survey found that within Indian-administered Kashmir, 61% of respondents said they felt they would be better off as Indian citizens, with 33% saying that they did not know, and the remaining 6% favouring Pakistani citizenship. However, this support for India was mainly in Ladakh and Jammu regions, not the Kashmir Valley, as only 9% of the respondents from the Kashmir Valley said that they would be better off with India. According to a 2007 poll conducted by the Centre for the Study of Developing Societies in New Delhi, 87% of respondents in the Kashmir Valley prefer independence over union with India or Pakistan. However, a survey by the Chatham House in both Indian and Pakistani administered Kashmir found that support of independence was at 43% and 44% respectively.

The 2005 Kashmir earthquake, which killed over 80,000 people, led to India and Pakistan finalizing negotiations for the opening of a road for disaster relief through Kashmir.

Efforts to End the Crisis

The 9/11 attacks on the United States resulted in the U.S. government wanting to restrain militancy in the world, including Pakistan. They urged Islamabad to cease infiltrations, which continue to this day, by Islamist militants into Indian-administered Kashmir. In December 2001, a terrorist attack on the Indian Parliament linked to Pakistan, resulted in war threats, massive deployment, and international fears of a nuclear war in the subcontinent. After intensive diplomatic efforts by other countries, India and Pakistan began to withdraw troops from the international border on 10 June 2002, and negotiations began again. Effective 26 November 2003, India and Pakistan agreed to maintain a ceasefire along the undisputed international border, the disputed Line of Control, and the Siachen glacier. This is the first such "total ceasefire" declared by both powers in nearly 15 years. In February 2004, Pakistan increased pressure on Pakistanis fighting in Indian-administered Kashmir to adhere to the ceasefire. The neighbours launched several other mutual confidence-building measures. Restarting the bus service between the Indian- and Pakistani-administered Kashmir has helped defuse the tensions between the countries. Both India and Pakistan have decided to cooperate on economic fronts. On 5 December 2006, Pakistani President Pervez Musharraf told an Indian TV channel that Pakistan would give up its claim on Kashmir if India accepted some of his peace proposals, including a phased withdrawal of troops, self-governance for locals, no changes in the borders of Kashmir, and a joint supervision mechanism involving India, Pakistan, and Kashmir. Musharraf stated that he was ready to give up the United Nations' resolutions regarding Kashmir.

2008 Militant Attacks

In the week of 10 March 2008, 17 people were wounded when a blast hit the region's only highway overpass located near the Civil Secretariat—the seat of government of Indian-controlled Kashmir—and the region's high court. A gun battle between security forces and militants fighting against Indian rule left five people dead and two others injured on 23 March 2008. The battle began when security forces raided a house on the outskirts of the capital city of Srinagar, housing militants. The Indian Army has been carrying out cordon-and-search operations against militants in Indian-administered Kashmir since the violence broke out in 1989. While the authorities say 43,000 persons have been killed in the violence, various rights groups and non-governmental organizations have put the figure at twice that number.

According to the Government of India Home Ministry, 2008 was the year with the lowest civilian casualties in 20 years, with 89 deaths, compared to a high of 1,413 in 1996. 85 security personnel died in 2008 compared to 613 in 2001, while 102 militants were killed. The human rights situation improved, with only one custodial death, and no custodial disappearances. Many analysts say Pakistan's preoccupation with jihadis within its own borders explains the relative calm.

2008 Kashmir Protests

Massive demonstrations occurred after plans by the Indian-administered Jammu and Kashmir state government to transfer 100 acres (0.40 km^2) of land to a trust which runs the Hindu Amarnath shrine in the Muslim-majority Kashmir valley. This land was to be used to build a shelter to house Hindu pilgrims temporarily during their annual pilgrimage to the Amarnath temple.

Indian security forces and the Indian army responded quickly to keep order. More than 40 unarmed protesters were killed and at least 300 were detained. The largest protests saw more than a half million people waving Pakistani flags and crying for freedom at a rally on 18 August, according to *Time magazine*. Pro-independence Kashmir leader Mirwaiz Umar Farooqwarned that the peaceful uprising could lead to an upsurge in violence if India's heavy-handed crackdown on protests was not restrained. The United Nations expressed concern on India's response to peaceful protests and urged investigations be launched against Indian security personnel who had taken part in the crackdown.

Separatists and workers of a political party were believed to be behind stone-pelting incidents, which led to retaliatory fire by the police. An autorickshaw laden with stones meant for distribution was seized by the police in March 2009. Following the unrest in 2008, secessionist movements got a boost.

2008 Kashmir Elections

State elections were held in Indian-held Kashmir in seven phases, starting 17 November and finishing on 24 December 2008. In spite of calls by separatists for a boycott, an unusually high turnout of almost 50% was recorded. The National Conference party, which was founded by Sheikh Abdullah and is regarded as pro-India, emerged with a majority of the seats. On 30 December, the Congress Party and the National Conference agreed to form a coalition government, with Omar Abdullah as Chief Minister. On 5 January 2009, Abdullah was sworn in as the eleventh Chief Minister of Jammu and Kashmir.

In March 2009, Abdullah stated that only 800 militants were active in the state and out of these only 30% were Kashmiris.

2009 Kashmir Protests

In 2009, protests started over the alleged rape and murder of two young women in Shopian in South Kashmir. Suspicion pointed towards the police as the perpetrators. A judicial enquiry by a retired High Court confirmed the suspicion, but a CBI enquiry reversed their conclusion. It gave a fresh impetus to the popular agitation against India. Significantly, the unity between the separatist parties was lacking this time.

2010 Kashmir Unrest

The 2010 Kashmir unrest were a series of protests in the Muslim majority Kashmir Valley in Jammu & Kashmir which started in June 2010. These protests occurred in 'Quit Jammu Kashmir Movement' launched by Hurriyat Conference led by Syed Ali Shah Geelani and Mirwaiz Umar Farooq, who had called for the complete demilitarization of Jammu and Kashmir. The All Parties Hurriyat Conference made this call to protest, citing human rights abuses by Indian troops. Protesters shouting pro-independence slogans, defied curfew, attacked security forces with stones and burnt police vehicles and government buildings. The Jammu and Kashmir Police and Indian Para-military forces fired live ammunition on the protesters, resulting in 112 deaths, including many teenagers. The protests subsided after the Indian government announced a package of measures aimed at defusing the tensions in September 2010.

US President Obama on the Conflict

In an interview with Joe Klein of *Time* magazine in October 2008, Barack Obama expressed his intention to try to work with India and Pakistan to resolve the crisis. He said he had talked to Bill Clinton about it, as Clinton has experience being a mediator. In an editorial in *The Washington Times*, Selig S Harrison, director of the Asia Programme at the Centre for International Policy and a senior scholar of the Woodrow Wilson International, called it Obama's first foreign policy mistake. In an editorial, *The Australian* called Obama's idea to appoint a presidential negotiator "a very stupid and dangerous move indeed". In an editorial in *Forbes*, Reihan Salam, associate editor for *The Atlantic*, noted "The smartest thing President Obama could do on Kashmir is probably nothing. We have to hope that India and Pakistan can work out their differences on Kashmir on their own". *The Boston Globe* called the idea of appointing Bill Clinton as an envoy to Kashmir "a mistake". President Obama appointed Richard Holbrooke as special envoy to Pakistan and Afghanistan. President Asif Ali Zardari hoped that Holbrooke would help mediate to resolve the Kashmir issue. Subsequently Kashmir was removed from the mandate of Holbrooke. "Eliminating... Kashmir from his job description... is seen as a significant diplomatic concession to India that reflects increasingly warm ties between the country and the United States," *The Washington Post* noted in a report. Brajesh Mishra, India's former national security adviser, was quoted in the same report as saying that "No matter what government is in place, India is not going to relinquish control of Jammu and Kashmir". "That is written in stone and cannot be changed." According to *The Financial Times*, India has warned Obama that he risks "barking up the wrong tree" if he seeks to broker a settlement between Pakistan and India over Kashmir.

In July 2009, U.S. Assistant Secretary of State Robert O. Blake, Jr. stated that the United States had no plans of appointing any special envoy to settle the dispute, calling it an issue which needs to be sorted out bilaterally by India and Pakistan. According to *Dawn* this will be interpreted in Pakistan as an endorsement of India's position on Kashmir that no outside power has any role in this dispute.

CHINA'S KASHMIR POLICY

Since November 2003, India and Pakistan have effectively maintained a ceasefire along the Line of Control separating their respectively controlled segments of Kashmir. Meanwhile, New Delhi and Islamabad have renewed their efforts to arrive at long-term solutions to this intractable conflict that has dragged the two neighbors to war three times since the 1947 partition. Despite incessant, albeit much reduced violence and incidents, peace has so far prevailed. The latest thaw is manifested in summit meetings between the two countries' top leaders and regular official consultation, proposed and actual troop pullback, and agreement on missile launch notification. During his recent visit to the Siachen Glacier, where the Indian and Pakistani troops have stood eyeball-to-eyeball on the highest battleground in the world for over two decades, Indian Prime Minister Manmohan Singh called for turning the glacier into a "mountain of peace," which reportedly has received endorsement from the Indian military.

Beijing has welcomed these positive developments, and considers Indo-Pakistani rapprochement a major step toward regional peace and stability. Rarely stated though, are the implications of either the continued impasse or a possible resolution of the Kashmir for China's own security interests. How does China view the Kashmir conflict, and to what extent do its positions on the issue reflect broader Chinese foreign policy toward South Asia and its relationships with India and Pakistan respectively? This brief seeks to address these questions by examining the change and continuity of Beijing's policy toward the Kashmir dispute and explaining the underlying rationales behind it, with a focus on the more recent developments.

Understanding China's Policy

China's declared positions on the Kashmir issue have evolved through four distinct phases. In the 1950s, Beijing upheld a more or less neutral position on the Kashmir issue. The 1960s and 1970s saw China shift its position toward public support of Pakistan's views on the issue as Sino-Indian relations deteriorated. Since the early 1980s, however, with China and India moving toward normalization of bilateral relations, Beijing returned to a position of neutrality even as it sought to balance between the need to satisfy Pakistan's demands for support and the growing interest in developing a better relationship with India. By the early 1990s, China's position became unequivocal that the Kashmir issue is a bilateral matter to be solved by India and Pakistan through peaceful means.

China's Kashmir policy must be understood within the broader contexts of its South Asia policy in general and where this policy fits in Beijing's global strategies, and its bilateral relationships with India and Pakistan in particular. While in the past, Beijing supported Islamabad's positions on the Kashmir issue to demonstrate solidarity with an "all weather" ally during periods of Sino-Indian estrangement and hostility, normalization with New Delhi has necessitated the adoption of a policy of neutrality to avoid unnecessarily alienating India and running the risk of entrapment. Indeed, as both India and Pakistan have acquired nuclear weapons capabilities, China has become extremely worried that any escalation of conflicts over Kashmir could precipitate a nuclear exchange, with horrifying consequences.

Beijing is very interested in the reduction of tension over Kashmir and therefore is particularly encouraged by recent developments, such as the ceasefire along the line of control, the defense secretary meeting on the Siachen Glacier demilitarization, the resumption of civilian flight and the opening of the bus service through Kashmir, discussion on reducing military presence along the line of control, and military confidence building measures including the agreement on missile launch notification. A recent article in People's Daily on August 11 describes the ongoing Indo-Pakistani talks as "warm and constructive" and noted that New

Delhi and Islamabad are beginning to tackle issues of substance, including measures to reduce tension and avoid military conflicts in areas along the line of control.

Chinese analysts suggest that both India and Pakistan have a lot to gain from the current rapprochement. Prolonged tension and fighting over Kashmir has exacted severe tolls in human and material terms for both countries. For instance, maintaining supplies to the Indian troops stationed on the Siachen Glacier costs New Delhi $1 million a day. Since fighting began in 1984, some 2,500 Indian and 1,300 Pakistani troops have died over the years, not so much in direct combat but as a result of the treacherous weather and terrain conditions. Managing the Kashmir issue has become a critical consideration in New Delhi's efforts to realize its great power potentials by channelling more resources to economic development. For Pakistan, the conflict consumes even more resources. The post-September 11 regional security environment and the U.S.-led global war on terrorism also exert external pressure for Pakistan to deal with cross-border terrorist activities.

Beijing is also interested in the evolving negotiations over Kashmir due to its own entanglement, which is largely a result of the October 1963 Sino-Pakistani Border Agreement. India claims the Chinese-controlled Aksai Chin of approximately 35,000 square kilometers as part of the territory in Ladaakh, Kashmir. While a remote possibility, a resolution of the Kashmir dispute between New Delhi and Islamabad could re-open the sovereignty issue left over in the 1963 Sino-Pakistani border agreement.

Looking Ahead

Yet due to the intractable nature of the Kashmir conflict and the still widely divergent positions held by the two sides, any imminent resolution remains elusive. Indeed, resolving the Kashmir dispute may be a most challenging diplomatic undertaking since the original conflict has evolved over the years from a purely India-Pakistan contention for jurisdiction to one that increasingly involves an independent movement within Kashmir, interwoven ethnic and religious strife and conflicts, and an increasingly fertile ground for cross-border terrorist activities. Nonetheless, Beijing hopes that the current thaw between New Delhi and Islamabad will continue. Peace and stability on the sub-continent would advance Chinese interests of further improving relations with India. Indeed, over the last few years, the bilateral relationship has registered significant progress, with regular high-level visits, booming trade, continuing border negotiation, joint military exercises, and closer cooperation on intelligence sharing to fight terrorism.

Beijing has also sought to nudge Islamabad toward seeking a peaceful solution to the Kashmir issue. China, however, continues to value its traditional ties with Pakistan, which is seen less as a counter to India and rather more as an important factor in Beijing's fight against ethnic separatist movements in its northwestern territories.

Beijing has growing interests in seeing a stable South Asia and is seeking a better relationship with India. That explains Beijing's more unequivocal position on the Kashmir issue, which in turn is firmly grounded in the belief that the only realistic way to resolve the Kashmir conflict is through peaceful negotiation between India and Pakistan. As Islamabad's trusted friend, Beijing could and should use its influence to convince Pakistan that it is also in their own interest to resolve the issue peacefully.

THE KARGIL WAR AND ITS COLLISION ON INDO-PAK RELATIONS

The euphoria that followed the February Lahore Declarations by India and Pakistan abruptly dissipated when nearly 1500 Pakistan-backed Muslim militants known miles into the India-held Kargil region of North Kashmir. The militants who were mostly Afghanis together with Pakistani regulars, occupied more than 30 well-fortified positions located atop the most inhospitable frigidly cold ridges, at 16,000 and 18,000 feet above sea level, in the Great Himalayan range facing Dras, Kargil, Batalik, and the Mushko Valley sectors stretching covering over 30 miles. Indian army patrols, between May 8 and 15 detected and came in contact with the militants and on May 26, India launched air attacks known as Operation Vijay (victory) against the bunkers from which the intruders had been firing upon the Indian troops below the ridges. On May 27, two MIG aircrafts were shot down. One pilot was taken prisoner of war (POW) and the other killed. On May 28, a MI-17 helicopter was shot down and the four-man crew killed. As the battle raged on between May 31 and June 11, Indian troops were able to clear up some pockets of resistance and to cut off the supply lines to the intruders by outflanking them. They also launched a major offensive in the Kargil Drass sector accompanied by air strikes on June 6, in order to protect the only highway linking Srinagar to Leh in Ladakh region from Pakistani threat. On June 10, Pakistan returned seven severely mutilated bodies of soldiers to New Delhi outraging India. In the face of India's fury, on June 12, Pakistan's foreign Minister Sartaj Aziz visited New Delhi to talk to Jaswant Singh. But the talks failed. India identified Pakistan as an aggressor that had violated the LOC, while Aziz surprisingly questioned the validity of the line, which was based on the 1972 Simla Agreement signed by both countries. He also called for a joint working group to help settle India's claim of the Kargil, which Singh angrily rejected. Before he visited New Delhi, Aziz had visited China, a Pakistan ally, China, seeking its support, but was coming visit to China was designed to garner. This was especially important to India, since it was the first time Singh visited China after the Pokhram II nuclear tests.

As the battle turned bloodier and more intense, the Clinton administration intervened to help defuse the crisis. In the second week of June, Bruce Reidel, Special Assistant to President Clinton, in a briefing at the Foreign Press Centre, asserted the inviolability of the LOC by stating the following: "we think the Line of Control has demarcated the area over the years. The two parties have not previously had significant differences about where the LOC is," and the "forces which have crossed the line should withdraw to where they came from." He noted that the President in his recent letters to both Prime Ministers had stressed that point. On June 15, in separate telephonic conversations, Mr. Clinton told Sharif to withdraw the infiltrators from across the LOC, and Vajpayee that he appreciated his display of restraint in the conflict. To Pakistan's further sense of isolation, the G-8 members, at their annual meeting in Cologne, Germany, June 19-20, came out strongly in support of India's contention that the Kargil crisis was precipitated by mercenaries backed by Pakistani troops. Mr. Brajesh Mishra, the Principal Secretary to Vajpayee, who had taken Vajpayee's letter to Mr. Clinton at the G-8 in Cologne, also took the opportunity to explain the situation to the rest of the G-8 leaders. Following that meeting, a communiqué was issued on June 20 by the G-8, which condemned in unequivocal terms the violation of the LOC and dubbed Pakistan's military action as "irresponsible" in its attempt to change the status quo at the LOC, and called on it to end the intrusion. The communiqué also urged the two countries to resolve the Kashmir dispute with "dialogue". This position was also supported by China. by Gen. Anthony Zinni, Commander-in-Chief of the US Central command. The delegation also included Gibson Lampher, the Deputy Assistant Secretary of State for South Asia, and Karl F. Inderfurth. On behalf of the President Zinni asked Sharif to withdraw the troops from across the LOC and Lampher traveled to New Delhi to brief Brajesh Mishra on the details of their visit to Pakistan. On June 28, a day after Zinni's visit, Sharif rushed to Beijing to seek Chinese diplomatic support of the conflict. The Chinese, however, told him that he could not count on their support, and he cut short his six-day visit and returned home disappointed. Meanwhile, on June 20, Indian troops, after a fierce battle and the loss of 50 lives, recaptured Tololing Rill in the Drass sector, and on July 4, recaptured Tiger Hill, which is considered to be the most strategic point in Drass sector as it overlooks the Srinagar-Leh highway.

As the Indian troops steadily recaptured one hill or ridge after another, and Pakistan's isolation in the world community increased (only Saudi Arabia and the United Emirates supported Pakistan), it desperately sought a face-saving formula to extricate itself from its miscalculated adventure. For instance on June 27, former Foreign Secretary Niaz Naik, a person known to be close to Sharif as well as to the Americans, secretly went to New Delhi, met with Vajpayee and his Principal Secretary Mishra, and slipped back to Pakistan.

Although Pakistan's foreign office insisted that it was "Naik's private visit and had nothing to do with Pakistan's foreign policy," it was speculated that he presented a set of "face-saving" proposals to Sharif that would allow Pakistan to escape from the Kargil imbroglio as gracefully as possible. On July 3, Sharif requested a meeting with Clinton on "an urgent basis" and met with him on July 4, in Washington.

to withdraw the intruders. The statement indicated that the forces needed to be returned to the Pakistani side. This was followed by the White House statement which stated that the President shared with Sharif the view that the current fighting "contains the seeds of wider conflict" and that "it was vital for the peace of South Asia that the LOC in Kashmir be respected by both parties in accordance with their 1972 Simla accord," and that "bilateral dialogue begun in Lahore in February provides the best approach for resolving all issues dividing India and Pakistan, including Kashmir," and that the President would take a "personal interest in encouraging an expeditious resumption and intensification of those bilateral efforts once the sanctity of the LOC has been fully restored." Mr. Clinton also indicated that he would visit South Asia soon. As the meeting with Sharif progressed, Mr. Clinton frequently called Mr. Vajpayee in order to "keep him fully appraised of the discussion," as the latter had declined the invitation to go to Washington. On July 12, the Congress also turned up the heat on Islamabad when it passed House Resolution 227 "expressing the sense of the Congress in opposition to the Government of Pakistan's support for armed incursion into Jammu and Kashmir, India." Further declaring that Pakistan was culpable in sending armed insurgents into the Indian territory, while stressing that India and Pakistan "resolve all of their differences within the framework of the Simla agreement in order to preserve peace and security in South Asia." It also suggested that the administration block loans to Pakistan from international financial institutions.

Following this agreement, beginning on July 11, the infiltrators began retreating from Kargil as India set July 16 as the deadline for the total withdrawal. On July 12, in Clinton as well as his request to the intruders to withdraw from Indian Territory. He also defended his Kargil policy as something designed to draw the attention of the international community to Kashmir issue. In the war, more than 400 Indian soldiers, 679 intruders, and 30 Pakistani regulars were killed excluding those who were wounded. Sharif's agreement to withdraw intruders upset the military so much that on October 12, he was ousted from power in a bloodless coup. When Musharraf, who is rumored to have been the architect of the Kargil war and who is called Mr. Kargil in India, heard on his return from Sri Lanka that he was being replaced by Sharif's confidant, Lt. General Khowaja Ziauddin, he had his generals remove Sharif on charges of hijacking and treason. Musharraf declared himself the Chief Executive, the Chief of Army, and later as President. Sharif, who was convicted and given a life sentence by a military court, was subsequently exiled to Saudi Arabia in December 1999.

The coup upset India and got Pakistan suspended from the Commonwealth Conference. Tensions between them escalated. Artillery fires across the LOC intensified and on December 24, a New Delhi-bound plane, carrying 178 passengers from Katmandu, Nepal, was hijacked to Kandahar, Afghanistan by the Pakistan-based Harakat ul-Mujahideen terrorists. They demanded a release from jails of 35 Kashmiri militants including the Pakistani cleric, Maulana Masood Azhar, in exchange with the passengers. When India's government refused to concede their demands, they killed a newlywed husband who was on his honeymoon with his wife. Pressured by the passengers' relatives, on December 31, India exchanged the passengers with three hardcore militants including Azhar. This was humiliating to India. India implicated Pakistan in this avail. Unlike his predecessors, Musharraf came out openly in support of terrorists by declaring that "Islam does not recognize political boundaries, and Jihad is a concept of God."

Emboldened by the successful results of their hijacking, the militants escalated their assaults and suicide bombings against innocent bystanders and the security forces. Realizing that negotiations with militants and the APHC leaders were essential to resolve this conflict, in November 2000, on the eve of the beginning of Ramadan (month of Muslim fasting) the Vajpayee government declared a unilateral cease-fire and invited them for talks. It also agreed to talk to Pakistan if the latter ceased supporting cross-border terrorism. The APHC leaders including its chairman Abdul Ghani Bhat at that time welcomed the initiative. They sought visas from the government to visit Pakistan to talk to the militant leaders living there. But they were denied visas because they wanted the Pro-Pakistani leader Syed Ali Shah Geelani of the Jamaat-I-Islami included in the team. The Musharraf government refused to cease supporting cross-border terrorism but agreed to abide by the cease-fire declaration along the LOC.

However, some of the Pakistani-based militant groups such as the Lashkar-e-Toiba, Hizbul-Mujahideen, Jash-e-Mohammed, founded later by cleric Azhas, and Al-Umar-Mujhideen rejected the cease-fire declaration as a sham and vowed to liberate Kashmir with a Jihad directed against pagan India. They escalated terrorism not only in Kashmir, but also in other locations like New Delhi. Their belief being that they will go to Paradise if they die as martyrs fighting pagan India.

Hoping to persuade the APHC leaders to talk to his government, Vajpayee appointed a noted politician and former Congress cabinet minister K. C. Pant as leaders, but also to other politicians from Kashmir who were committed to a peaceful resolution of the conflict. The APHC leaders rejected the invitation on the grounds that Pakistan was not included.

However, on April 30, one of its leaders, Shabir Ahmad Shah, the chairman of the Democratic Freedom Party (DFP), agreed to talk to Pant, even though he had earlier insisted on Pakistan's inclusion in the talks. When it became clear that India's unilateral declaration had only helped the militants to escalate their terrorism, and that the APHC leaders rejected negotiations the Vajpayee government ended the six month cease-fire on May 25, 2001, and invited Musharraf for talks without any pre-established conditions – which he accepted. The talks were held on July 14 – 16, 2001 in Agra, near New Delhi, but they failed because General Musharraf insisted that the Kashmir dispute be the core issue of the talks, which Vajpayee rejected. Although both leaders had agreed to meet again during the November UN General Assembly meetings, it did not take place as India was angered by the suicide bomb attack of the Jammu and Kashmir State Assembly building on October 1, in which forty innocent civilians and the three terrorists who had caused the blast were killed.

The Pakistani Cleric Maulana Masood Azher, leader of the Jaish-e-Mohammed, which is linked to Osama Bin Laden's Al Qaeda, took credit for the bombing. Vajpayee took a tough stance indicating that he would not talk to Musharraf unless he ceased supporting cross border terrorism. Moreover, India's foreign minister, Jaswant Singh, cancelled his scheduled trip to Pakistan to talk to his counterpart. Relations between the two countries again turned tense and resulted in an intense exchange of fire along the LOC. The Bush administration called on India to show restraint as it did not want to jeopardize its Al Qaeda that Pakistan had supported in the past. In January and June 2002 the tensions between India and Pakistan increased along with the threat of another war.

5

Cross-border Terrorist Challenges Facing India

THE BACKGROUND

India has been the victim of the use of cross-border terrorism by the State of Pakistan and its intelligence agencies since 1956 to achieve their strategic objectives, which are three in number. First, to create a religious divide between the Hindus, who are in a majority, and the Muslims, who are in a substantial minority. Second, to keep the Indian State destabilised and preoccupied with internal security tasks in order to hamper the economic development of the country. And third, to annex the State of Jammu & Kashmir (J&K), which is an integral part of India.

When India and Pakistan became independent in 1947, the Muslims constituted about 11 per cent of India's population. Today, they constitute about 14 per cent. In 1947, in the territory, which is now known as Pakistan, the Hindus constituted a little over 10 per cent of the population. Today, they constitute about two per cent. The rest of them were either massacred or driven out of the country or forcibly converted to Islam.

Today, India has the second largest Muslim community in the world with about 140 million plus, after Indonesia. India has more Sunnis and more Shias than Pakistan. They are guaranteed equal rights under the Constitution of India, which was inspired by the Constitution of the United States of America.

The Indian Muslims suffer from no discrimination from the State and are entitled to occupy any office of the Governments of India and the constituent States, however highly placed, however sensitive. Three distinguished Muslim sons of India have held office as the President of India. Mr.Abdul Kalam, the current President of India, was a distinguished space scientist and had served as the Scientific Adviser to the Ministry of Defence of the Government of India before he was elected as the President of India.

Illustrious Muslims of India have held office as Cabinet Ministers, as the Chief Justice of India, as Ambassadors to important countries, including the USA, as the Cabinet Secretary, which is the senior most post to which an Indian civil servant can aspire to rise in his career, as the Home Secretary, as the Chief of the Air Staff, as Lieutenants-General in the Army and as the heads of Police and Para-Military organisations. The Cabinet Secretary co-ordinates the functioning of the different Ministries of the Government of India and of its sensitive intelligence agencies. The Home Secretary exercises important internal security tasks and, in that capacity, monitors the working of India's Intelligence Bureau (IB), which is responsible for internal intelligence. No Hindu has ever been posted to such sensitive posts in Pakistan. Hindus have served as members of the Council of Ministers in Pakistan, but without any sensitive charge.

If one leaves aside the State of Jammu & Kashmir, which has been affected by Pakistan State-sponsored terrorism since 1989, no Indian Muslim from other parts of India went to Afghanistan in the1980s to join the jihadi mercenary force which fought against the Soviet troops. When the US-led international coalition launched its Operation Enduring Freedom in Afghanistan on October 7, 2001, no Indian Muslim, not even from J&K, responded to the call of the jihadi terrorist organisations of Afghanistan and Pakistan to go to Afghanistan to wage a jihad against the US troops. There were no major anti-US demonstrations by the Indian Muslims to protest against Operation Enduring Freedom.

Similarly, at a time when pro-Osama bin Laden jihadi terrorists are gravitating towards Iraq to wage a jihad against the US troops there, not a single Indian Muslim has responded to the call. Whereas the various fundamentalist and jihadi organisations in Pakistan have been collecting funds for the so-called jihad against the Americans in Iraq, there have been no such instances in India.

Hon'ble Chairmen, Hon'ble Members, if you happen to take a stroll in the streets of many Asian cities, you will find bin Laden T-shirts, bin Laden caps and other mementoes glorifying him. But not in India. Since 9/11, many books on bin Laden and his Al Qaeda have been published— some correctly projecting him as a contemptible terrorist and some glorifying him as a great Islamic leader. Many of these books figure in the best-sellers' lists of other countries. But not in India.

It is often not realised that as many young Muslim students from other countries come to India for their higher education as they go to Pakistan, if not more. There have been only two instances in the history of jihadi terrorism of foreign Muslims, who had studied in India, joining jihadi terrorist groups. In 1992, the Israeli security forces arrested a Palestinian terrorist, who was found to have been educated in India. The second instance is that of Abu Zubaidah, who used to be reportedly No.3 in Al Qaeda, and who was arrested in Pakistan in March,2002. He was a law-abiding student of computer technology in India, but when he crossed over into Pakistan, he joined Al Qaeda.

All other foreign Muslim students, who were educated in India, went back to their countries of origin as constructive, modern and law-abiding citizens of their country and are doing well as public servants, academics, media personalities etc. The most illustrious example of recent times is that of Mr.Hamid Karzai, the interim President of Afghanistan, who has rightly won the admiration of the international community and of the leaders and people of the USA as a proud, modern Muslim wedded to liberal ideas. Why? He did his higher education in India and spent some of his formative years in the two greatest democracies of the world—India and the USA.

Kindly do compare this with foreign Muslim students who go to Pakistan for their studies. Many of them returned to their countries of origin as destructive citizens—as jihadi terrorists, as narcotics smugglers, as counterfeiters of US dollar notes etc. It is said that the USA's counter-terrorism experts have been interrogating in the detention centres in Guantanamo Bay in Cuba and other places nearly 6,000 jihadi terrorists arrested during Operation Enduring Freedom. They are of many nationalities, but reports say that there is not a single Indian Muslim amongst them.

The USA has a large number of Muslims of Pakistani and Indian origin. In the 1990s, a Muslim extremist organisation called the Jamaat-ul-Fuqra was active in the US and Canada. Its activities figured in the annual reports of the Counter-Terrorism Division of the State Department on the Patterns of Global Terrorism. It had indulged in acts of violence against the Hindus and the Jewish people in the USA. It is said that Daniel Pearl, the young American journalist, who was kidnapped and brutally killed by the jihadi terrorists of Pakistan last year, had gone to Karachi to investigate reports of possible links between the so-called shoe bomber and the Jamaat-ul-Fuqra.

It was reported in the media that last year the FBI had arrested some Muslims of Yemeni origin at Lackawanna, near Buffalo, in the USA who were found to have been taken to Pakistan and Afghanistan by the Pakistani branch of an organisation called the Tablighi Jamaat (TJ) and brainwashed there. The TJ has its headquarters in India. Its Indian branch does the humanitarian work for which it was established during the British days, namely, to help the Muslims to become better Muslims. But, its Pakistani branch has degenerated into a front organisation for the recruitment of foreign Muslims to various jihadi terrorist groups.

Recently, the US law enforcement authorities were reported to have detected in US territory the activities of a secret cell of the Lashkar-e-Toiba (LET), a Pakistani jihadi terrorist organisation, which was designated by the US in 2001 as a Foreign Terrorist Organisation. It has been reported in sections of the media that some of its members were Muslims of Pakistani origin.

In February 1995, the "News", the prestigious daily newspaper of Pakistan, had carried a series of investigative reports on the activities of the Harkat-ul-Ansar (HUA), a Pakistani jihadi terrorist organisation, which re-named itself as the Harkat-ul-Mujahideen

(HUM) after it was designated by the US as a Foreign Terrorist Organisation in October,1997. The articles quoted an unidentified representative of the HUA as claiming that amongst the foreign Muslims trained by it were 16 Afro-American Muslims from various cities of the US.

The paper reported on March 27,1995, as follows: "Official investigation has revealed that dozens of Saudis committed to jihad all over the world have been visiting the military training camps inside Afghanistan. Sources estimated that at least 2,000 persons, mostly Pakistanis and Arabs of different nationalities, are currently engaged in military training in those camps for jihad in Kashmir and elsewhere in the world. These sources estimated that since the expulsion of the Soviet troops from Afghanistan, at least 10,000 Pakistanis belonging to the Islamic parties such as the Jamaat-e-Islami, the HUA, the Markaz Dawa Al Irshad and the Jamiat-ul-Ulema Islam have acquired training in making bombs, hurling grenades, firing from light and heavy weapons and in laying mines. The Harkat and all other militant organisations committed to Islamic jihad all over the world have acknowledged sending their guerillas to Tajikistan, Bosnia, Chechnya, the Philippines, Burma and Kashmir. The Jamaat-e-Islami, the Harkat and other organisations have never been challenged by the Government in their campaign to recruit committed Muslims to commit jihad anywhere in the world. These organisations are also permitted to collect jihad funds anywhere in the country."

One would be entitled to ask : How is it that the Muslim migrants from India conduct themselves as constructive and law-abiding citizens or residents of the USA and do not indulge in activities which could threaten US nationals or interests, but many Muslim migrants from Pakistan indulge in clandestine activities for carrying the jihad to the US homeland?

An objective examination of this question would show that one cannot blame Islam as such for the spread of jihadi bloodshed in the world. What one has to blame is a particular interpretation of Islam by some religious clerics and madrasas of Wahabi-Deobandi orientation in Saudi Arabia and Pakistan. This interpretation holds, firstly, that a Muslim's first loyalty is to his religion and only then to the country of which he is a citizen or a resident; secondly, that Muslims recognise only the religious frontiers of their Ummah and not the national frontiers; thirdly, that they have a sacred right and obligation to go to any country to wage jihad to protect the Muslims of that country; and, fourthly, that they have a religious right and obligation to acquire and use weapons of mass destruction (WMD), to protect their religion and the Ummah, if necessary. They project Pakistan's atomic bomb as the Islamic bomb to counter the Christian bomb, the Jewish bomb or the Hindu bomb.

This interpretation of Islam emanating from Saudi Arabia and Pakistan for some years now is as subversive of democracies and as threatening to international peace and security as international communism was before 1991 and has to be combated as resolutely by the liberal democracies of the world as they combated the evil of international communism. In fact, even more resolutely, because one did not find in international communism the kind of irrationality that one finds in pan-Islamic jihadi Islamism. International communism projected itself as forward looking and moving ahead. Pan-Islamic jihadi Islamism is backward looking and wants to take the Islamic world back to the medieval ages, with the Muslim communities of the world organised into a number of Caliphates.

The Indian Muslims have largely remained uninfluenced by the winds of medievalism blowing from Pakistan. The religious fundamentalists and the military-intelligence establishment of Pakistan cannot understand how a Hindu majority State like India can produce such good Muslims. What is called the two-nation theory is the basic philosophy of Pakistan. It holds that Muslims and non-Muslims cannot be part of the same nation. It is in pursuance of this theory that they campaigned for the partition of India.

This theory was falsified by the independence movement in the former East Pakistan and the consequent birth of Bangladesh. The remarkable spectacle of millions of moderate Muslims, not subscribing to the jihadi ideology, living and working peacefully and side by side with non-Muslims in the democratic State of

India further negates this theory. They are, therefore, determined to create a religious divide in India through the use of jihadi terrorism in order to re-establish the validity of their two-nation theory. It is this determination, which has been behind the use of State-sponsored terrorism by Pakistan against India. Its claim that the so-called dispute over J&K is the cause of the terrorist violence killing thousands of innocent civilians is a spin and a diversion. Kashmir is not the cause, but only a pretext for creating bloodshed in India. Just as Palestine is not the cause, but only a pretext used by Al Qaeda and others of the same persuasion for killing hundreds of Israelis and Americans. Unless and until this jihadi terrorism is crushed by the common understanding and joint efforts of India, the USA and Israel, the three greatest democracies and pluralistic societies of the world and the most bleeding victims of it, the international community will continue to bleed at the hands of the jihadi terrorists.

Since 1993, the international community has seen a prairie fire of jihadi terrorism spread across the world by Osama bin Laden, his Al Qaeda and the various constituents of his International Islamic Front (IIF) For Jihad Against the Crusaders and the Jewish People. Thousands of innocent civilians have been killed by the jihadi terrorists owing allegiance to bin Laden in New York, Washington DC, Nairobi, Dar-es-Salaam, Bali, Jakarta, southern Philippines, various cities of India, Karachi, Islamabad, Mombasa, Casablanca, Riyadh, Moscow, Chechnya, Xinjiang etc.

If one makes an objective analysis of these incidents, one would invariably find that practically all of them had a linkage to the jihadi terrorism triangle of Pakistan-Afghanistan-Saudi Arabia. Many of the terrorists were either the nationals or residents of these countries; or had studied there and had been brainwashed by the religious fundamentalists there; or were funded from there; or were trained, armed and motivated from there ; or provided sanctuary in those areas.

INDIA'S NORTHEAST: THE BEGINNING

It is against this background that one should examine Pakistan's use of terrorism as a weapon against India. Its initial use of the weapon in the tribal areas of India's North-East starting from 1956 had nothing to do with Islam. It exploited the grievances of the tribals of this region to instigate them to start a movement for independence from India on the ground that they were ethnically different from the people in the rest of India.

Its Inter-Services Intelligence (ISI) provided the tribal insurgents sanctuaries in the then East Pakistan, where they were imparted guerilla training and given money, arms and ammunition. The birth of Bangladesh in 1971 considerably reduced Pakistan's ability to sponsor insurgency and terrorism in India's North-East.

This led to a peaceful political solution being found to the problem of insurgency in Mizoram where normalcy has been prevailing since 1985. In Nagaland too, a large section of the Naga insurgents gave up violence and reached a political solution to their grievances through negotiations with the Government of India in 1975. Only a small section belonging to the National Socialist Council of Nagaland (Issac Swu-Muivah group) has not yet given up its insurgency, but it has been observing a cease-fire and is presently negotiating with the Government of India.

Insurgent groups in other parts of the North-East such as Assam, Manipur and Tirupura are still active. Some of them remain in touch with Pakistani intelligence agencies through clandestine contacts in Bangladesh and other third countries.

PUNJAB

After its ability to use insurgent and terrorist groups in the North-East was weakened because of its loss of East Pakistan in 1971, it instigated some sections of the Sikh diaspora in Western countries such as the UK, the USA, Canada and the then West Germany to start a movement for an independent State for the Sikhs to be called Khalistan in the State of Punjab in India bordering Pakistani Punjab.

Over half a dozen Sikh terrorist organisations came into existence. Their cadres were trained by the ISI in camps set up in Pakistani territory and provided with arms and ammunition and explosives. During their training in Pakistan, the ISI motivated them to emulate the Palestine Liberation Organisation (PLO) and other anti-Israel terrorist groups and indulge in attacks on civil aviation and large-scale use of improvised explosive devices (IEDs) in order to cause indiscriminate civilian casualties and weaken the confidence of the population in the ability of the State to protect them.

Religion was sought to be used as a weapon to drive a wedge between the Hindus and the Sikhs. Dozens of civilians were killed in explosions in Punjab and New Delhi, five aircraft of the Indian Airlines Corporation were hijacked to Lahore in Pakistan, an aircraft of the Air India called Kanishka was blown up in mid-air in 1985 off the Irish coast by an ISI-motivated and trained group of Sikh terrorists of Canadian origin, resulting in the death of about 200 passengers, an unsuccessful attempt was made to blow up another Air India plane in the Narita airport in Tokyo the same year, an abortive attempt was made to kill the Indian Ambassador to Rumania in 1991 and, the same year, a Rumanian diplomat posted in New Delhi was kidnapped in order to secure the release of some Sikh terrorists who were then in detention.

The Sikh terrorist movement in Punjab petered out after 1995 due to a lack of support from the local people and the close co-operation between the intelligence agencies of India and the West in countering the activities of the terrorists following their action in organising acts of terrorism in foreign territory. However, some of the Sikh terrorist leaders, including a hijacker of Indian aircraft, continue to enjoy sanctuary in Pakistan, which has consistently refused to arrest and hand them over to India for trial.

It was during the Sikh terrorist movement that the ISI tried unsuccessfully to inject suicide terrorism into Northern and Western India. During the training of some terrorists of the Babbar Khalsa, a Sikh terrorist organisation, the ISI asked them to join the Mumbai (Bombay) Flying Club, take a trainer aircraft up and crash it on the off-shore oil platform off Mumbai. They did not carry out the instructions since they did not believe in suicide terrorism.

It was also during the Sikh terrorist movement that the ISI started teaching the terrorists the importance of attacking economic targets such as the irrigation canal systems, oil production facilities, stock exchanges etc in order to disrupt the Indian economy. They did not carry out these instructions either as they were afraid that the resulting economic hardships for the population might turn public opinion against them.

Jammu & Kashmir and Other Parts Of India

In 1989, the Pakistani military-intelligence establishment turned its attention to Jammu & Kashmir and to the Muslim community in other parts of India in order to spread terrorism to the Muslim-inhabited areas and exploit the anger caused by the State's counter-terrorism operations for driving a wedge between the Muslims and the Hindus and between the Muslims and the State.

Even before 1989, there had been sporadic incidents of terrorism in J&K, but these were few and far between. For example, in 1971 two members of the Jammu & Kashmir Liberation Front (JKLF) hijacked a plane of the Indian Airlines Corporation to Lahore and blew it up with explosives given at Lahore by the Pakistani authorities after asking the passengers and the crew to leave the aircraft. In 1983, some members of the JKLF in the UK kidnapped an Indian diplomat posted in Birmingham and killed him when the Government of India refused to concede their demand for the release of their leader from jail.

In the late 1980s, the ISI set up a number of training camps in Pakistan-Occupied Kashmir (POK) and the North-West Frontier Province (NWFP) of Pakistan where recruits brought from J&K were trained and armed. They were then sent to Afghanistan to get jihad experience from the Afghan Mujahideen and thereafter infiltrated into J&K to indulge in acts of terrorism.

Since then, the Pakistan Army and its ISI have been waging a proxy war against the Indian Security Forces through these surrogates without themselves getting involved in any direct confrontation with the Indian Army. This proxy war has passed through the following phases:

1989-93: The terrorists involved were mostly Kashmiris from India and Pakistan. Very few foreign mercenaries were involved. They initially operated mostly with hand-held weapons, but subsequently started using explosive devices, land mines and hand-grenades to indiscriminately kill civilians. The average number of local terrorists killed by the Security Forces came to 848 per annum. As against this, the average number of foreigners, mostly Pakistanis, killed came to 32 per annum only. The average recoveries of military material other than AK-47 rifles, light-machine guns, rocket launchers etc by the Security Forces came to 100 KGs of explosives, 426 mines and 2760 hand-grenades per annum.

1994 to 1998:Finding that the indigenous terrorists were not making any headway in their operations against the Indian Security Forces, the Pakistan Army and the ISI started infiltrating foreign merceneries, who had fought against the Soviet troops in Afghanistan, most of them Pakistani nationals, in increasing numbers. There was an increase in the use of explosives, landmines and hand-grenades. The average number of local terrorists killed came to 1069 per annum and the average number of foreign jihadi terrorists killed came to 172 per annum. The average recoveries per annum came to 405 KGs of explosives,628 mines and 4085 hand-grenades.

1999 to 2003: This period saw two important developments. The Pakistan Army headed by Gen.Pervez Musharraf staged a coup and seized power in October,1999. Four Pakistani jihadi organisations operating in J&K joined Osama bin Laden's International Islamic Front (IIF) for Jihad Against the Crusaders and the Jewish People, which had been formed in 1998. These were the HUM, the HUJI, the LET and the JEM. Under the influence of bin Laden, they introduced suicide terrorism for the first time in J&K. Before 1999, there was no suicide terrorism in the State. Since, 1999, there have been 46 acts of suicide terrorism or fedayeen attacks, of which 44 were carried out by the LET and the JEM. The remaining two were by unidentified (possibly local) terrorists. The infiltration of foreign mercenaries, mostly Pakistani nationals, increased and they started operating under the guise of Kashmiris and took over the leadership of the militant movement. The average number of local terrorists killed came down to 726 per annum and the average number of foreign mercenaries killed went up steeply to 951 per annum. The average recoveries per annum were 866

KGs of explosives and 5336 hand-grenades. Figures in respect of mines are not available.

The killing of a large number of foreign mercenaries has not yet affected the capability of the Pakistani terrorist organisations to maintain a high level of violence since those killed are immediately replaced through fresh infiltration of trained mercenaries. The Pakistan Army and the ISI have managed to maintain a total of about 1,600 foreign mercenaries always active in J&K—more in the Jammu Division where the Hindus are in a majority and less in the Kashmir Division, where the Muslims are in a majority.

In addition to the foreign mercenaries, about 1,700 Kashmiris recruited from J&K as well as the Pakistan-Occupied Kashmir (POK) have also been got trained by the ISI in camps located in the POK and elsewhere and infiltrated into J&K. They largely belong to the Hizbul Mujahideen (HM), the militant wing of the Jamaat-e-Islami, which calls for the merger of J&K with Pakistan. The JEI of J&K is an appendage of the JEI of Pakistan, which is a strongly anti-US, anti-India and anti-Israel organisation. Khalid Sheikh Mohammad, of Al Qaeda, believed to be the master-mind of the 9/11 terrorist strikes in the US which brought down the World Trade Centre in New York killing over 3,000 innocent civilians and damaged the Pentagon building in Washington DC killing many more, was caught in the house of a women's wing leader of the JEI in Rawalpindi in Pakistan in March last. Some other Al Qaeda members were also found to have been sheltered by the JEI of Pakistan.

An idea of the extent of the Pakistani assistance to the terrorists in J&K could be had from the fact that the total recoveries since 1989 of hand-held weapons, rocket-launchers etc supplied by the ISI to the terrorists would be sufficient to equip one Division of a conventional army. One does not know how many weapons are still left with the terrorists. None of the countries which have been designated by the US as a State-sponsor of International Terrorism is known to have issued hundreds of mines of different kinds to terrorists as Pakistan has been doing.

Economic Terrorism & Use Of Dawood Ibrahim

There have been three other significant developments since 1993. Having failed in its efforts to motivate the Sikh terrorists to take to economic terrorism, the ISI started making use of trans-national crime groups for organising terrorist strikes against economic targets. Before March 1993, the Dawood Ibrahim group, which indulges in large-scale smuggling, money-laundering and other criminal activities, was operating from Dubai. In March 1993, this group organised at the instance of the ISI a series of explosions directed at important economic targets in Mumbai—such as the local stock exchange, which is the biggest in India, a local hotel for tourists run by the Air India etc.

Subsequent investigation brought out that the perpetrators of these acts of terrorism, all Indian nationals, had been got recruited, at the instance of the ISI, by Dawood Ibrahim in Mumbai, taken to Pakistan via Dubai for training in the use of arms and ammunition and explosives and then sent back to Mumbai via Dubai. The Pakistani Consulate in Dubai issued them plain paper visas so that their passports did not carry any entries of their visit to Pakistan for training. However, Indian investigators managed to get xerox copies of the passenger manifests of the flights by which they went to Pakistan via Dubai for training. After they returned to Mumbai from Pakistan after the training, the explosives and other arms and ammunition required by them for organising the terrorist attacks were sent by the ISI by boat with the help of Dawood Ibrahim and clandestinely landed on the Western coast of India.

After carrying out the explosions, the perpetrators escaped to Pakistan, some via Dubai and some via Kathmandu, and were given sanctuary in Karachi by the ISI. When the Govt. of India took up with the Dubai authorities the question of the involvement of Dawood Ibrahim, the Dubai authorities pressured him to leave their territory. He took shelter in Karachi and has been living there since then along with some of the perpetrators, who have been given Pakistani passports under different names. Repeated requests by the Govt. of India to Islamabad for arresting and extraditing/ deporting them to India have been turned down by Pakistan, which denies their presence in Pakistani territory. Red-cornered notices of the INTERPOL for their arrest have not been honoured by Pakistan.

This matter was again taken up by the Govt. of India with President Pervez Musharraf of Pakistan when he visited India in July,2001. He denied their presence in Pakistani territory. Subsequently, "Newsline", a prestigious Pakistani monthly, in its issue for September, 2001, carried a detailed article on their presence and activities in Karachi. The Pakistani media reported that the journalist who wrote this chapter (Ghulam Hasnain) was detained and harassed by the Pakistani authorities. The "Herald", the prestigious monthly journal of the "Dawn" group of Karachi, has also (August 2003) carried a detailed report on their presence and activities in Pakistani territory.

On October 16, 2003, the US Department of Treasury announced that it was designating Dawood as a Specially Designated Global Terrorist under Executive Order 13224 and that it would be requesting the UN to so list him as well. The designation would freeze any assets belonging to Dawood within the U.S. and prohibit transactions with U.S. nationals. The UN listing will require that all UN Member-States take similar action.

"This designation signals our commitment to identifying and attacking the financial ties between the criminal underworld and terrorism,"" stated Juan Zarate, Deputy Assistant Secretary for Terrorist Financing and Financial Crimes. ""We are calling on the international community to stop the flow of dirty money that kills. For the Ibrahim syndicate, the business of terrorism forms part of their larger criminal enterprise, which must be dismantled."

A press release of the US Department said: "Dawood Ibrahim, an Indian crime lord, has found common cause with Al Qaida, sharing his smuggling routes with the terror syndicate and funding attacks by Islamic extremists aimed at destabilizing the Indian government. He is wanted in India for the 1993 Bombay Exchange bombings and is known to have financed the activities of Lashkar-e-Tayyiba (Army of the Righteous), a group designated by the United States in October 2001 and banned by the Pakistani Government — who also froze their assets — in January 2002. "

A fact sheet attached to the press release said: "Ibrahim's syndicate is involved in large-scale shipments of narcotics in the UK and Western Europe. The syndicate's smuggling routes from South Asia, the Middle East and Africa are shared with Usama Bin Laden and his terrorist network. Successful routes established over recent years by Ibrahim's syndicate have been subsequently utilised by bin Laden. A financial arrangement was reportedly brokered to facilitate the latter's usage of these routes. In the late 1990s, Ibrahim travelled in Afghanistan under the protection of the Taliban."

It added: "Ibrahim's syndicate has consistently aimed to destabilise the Indian Government through inciting riots, acts of terrorism and civil disobedience. He is currently wanted by India for the March 12, 1993, Bombay Exchange bombings, which killed hundreds of Indians and injured over a thousand more."

It also said: "Information from as recent as Fall 2002, indicates that Ibrahim has financially supported Islamic militant groups working against India, such as Lashkar-e-Tayyiba (LET). For example, this information indicates that Ibrahim has been helping finance increasing attacks in Gujarat by LET. "

The US authorities also indicated that Dawood Ibrahim was living in Karachi and held a Pakistani passport, whose number was also given by them. The Government of Pakistan has denied the US contention that he was living in Pakistan and claimed that the passport No. given by the US authorities belonged to another individual and not to Dawood.

Spread To Other Parts Of India

The second significant development after 1993 relates to the spread of jihadi terrorism to other parts of India outside J&K. The Kashmiri terrorist organisations describe their objective as confined to J&K and claim that they do not have any agenda outside the State. But, the four Pakistani jihadi organisations, which are members of bin Laden's IIF, follow his pan-Islamic ideology and call for the re-organisation of the Islamic Ummah into a number of Caliphates, including one in the South Asian region.

In pursuance of this, they describe J&K as the "gateway to India" and say that after having "liberated" J & K, they would "liberate" the Muslims living in other parts of India, as a prelude to the formation of an Islamic Caliphate consisting of Pakistan, the "liberated Muslim homelands" of India, Bangladesh, the Muslim majority areas in the Eastern Province of Sri Lanka and the Maldive Islands in the Indian Ocean.

To achieve this objective, the LET has already set up secret cells in other parts of India such as New Delhi, Mumbai, Hyderabad in Andhra Pradesh, Chennai in Tamil Nadu etc. While the LET headquarters at Muridke, near Lahore, in Pakistan co-ordinate the activities of its cadres in J&K and other parts of North India, a branch of it located in Saudi Arabia has been co-ordinating the activities of its cadres in Mumbai and South India. The LET has been using a banned Muslim extremist organisation of India called the Students Islamic Movement of India (SIMI) for this purpose and has been making recruitment amongst Indian Muslims working in the Gulf region.

The JEM and the HUM have also been setting up secret cells in New Delhi and other parts of India. Since 1999, the LET has carried out a number of terrorist strikes in New Delhi (attack inside the Red Fort and on the Parliament House), Ahmedabad (attack on Hindu worshippers in a temple in Gandhi Nagar) and Mumbai, where a number of explosions has been organised, the latest being the twin blasts on August 25, 2003, which killed 53 innocent civilians.

Hijacking As A Weapon

The third significant development relates to the ISI's resumption of the use of hijacking as a weapon to force the Government of India to release Pakistani terrorists arrested and detained by the Indian Police. The ISI had instigated the Sikh terrorists to carry out five hijackings in the 1980s, but it gave up the use of hijacking as a weapon in its proxy war against India after the death of Gen.Zia-ul-Haq in 1988 which led to the restoration of democracy in Pakistan.

Between 1988 and 1999, when democratically elected civilian Governments were in power in Islamabad, there was no hijacking by Pakistan-trained terrorist groups. In December,1999, hardly two months after the army, under the leadership of Musharraf, seized power again, an aircraft of the Indian Airlines flying from Kathmandu to New Delhi was hijacked by terrorists belonging to the HUM and forcibly taken to Kandahar in Afghanistan, which was then controlled by the Taliban. On the way to Kandahar, they killed one of the Hindu passengers. Because of the non-helpful attitude of the Taliban in terminating the hijacking, the Government of India had to concede the demands of the hijackers for the release of three Pakistani terrorists, who returned to Pakistan via Kandahar. One of them subsequently played a role in the kidnapping and murder of Daniel Pearl.

In the 1980s,the Pakistani military-intelligence establishment refused to extend mutual legal assistance to India for bringing the Sikh hijackers to trial and gave them sanctuary in Pakistan. Similarly, the Musharraf Government too has refused to extend legal assistance to India for bringing the December, 1999, hijackers to trial and given them shelter in Pakistan.

Continued Support To Terrorism After 9/11

During his visit to India in 2001 for the summit talks at Agra with the Indian Prime Minister, Atal Behari Vajpayee, Musharraf refuted Indian charges of jihadi terrorism in J&K and described the terrorists as "freedom-fighters similar to the Palestinian freedom-fighters". While he did not deny that innocent civilians had died, he contended that such deaths could not be helped during a "freedom struggle."

However, after 9/11, apparently under US pressure, he started condemning attacks on innocent civilians as terrorism, but denied that these attacks were carried out by Pakistan-based organisations. In his telecast of January 11, 2002, he said that resort to terrorism could not be justified whatever be the cause. Subsequently, on January 15, 2002, he banned the LET and the JEM and ordered the arrest of their leaders and many of their cadres. All of them have since been released on the ground that there was no evidence of their involvement in acts of terrorism in Pakistani territory. Pakistan does not accept evidence of their involvement in acts of terrorism in Indian territory.

During 2002, following a visit by Mr.Richard Armitage, US Deputy Secretary of State, to Islamabad for talks with Musharraf, the latter gave an assurance that no more infiltration of trained terrorists into J&K would be allowed. Despite this, infiltrations continue to take place as would be evident from the following figures of detected infiltrations of armed terrorists into J&K from Pakistan-Occupied Kashmir (POK):

- 2000 —— 2284
- 2001—— 2417
- 2002——— 1400
- 2003——— 1410 upto September 30.

The number of armed terrorists infiltrated came down in 2002, but has gone up this year. 1410 new terrorists were infiltrated till September 30, 2003, as against 1028 during the corresponding period of 2002.

While co-operating with the USA in its operations against terrorists of Al Qaeda and other organisations such as the HUM, the JEM and the Lashkar-e-Jhangvi (LEJ), who pose a threat to American lives and interests in Pakistani territory, the Pakistani Government has refused to act against terrorist organisations and their members indulging in acts of terrorism in Indian territory. It has avoided implementing the provisions of the UN Security Council Resolution No. 1373 as would be evident from the following:

Mutual Legal Assistance In Bringing Terrorists To Trial

It continues to refuse to arrest and hand over to India for trial 20 terrorists involved in major acts of terrorism in Indian territory. Of these, one (a Sikh terrorist, who is an Indian national) is wanted for trial in the 1981 hijacking of an Indian Airlines aircraft to Lahore; five Pakistani terrorists, all members of the HUM, which is a founding member of bin Laden's IIF, are wanted for trial in the 1999 hijacking of an Indian aircraft to Kandahar; five terrorists (all Indian nationals) of the Dawood Ibrahim gang, which has links with Al Qaeda and the LET according to the notification dated October 16, 2003, of the US Treasury Department, are wanted for trial in the Mumbai (Bombay) explosions of March 1993, in which 250 innocent civilians were killed; four Sikh terrorist leaders, all Indian nationals, are wanted for trial in connection with acts of terrorism in Punjab before 1995; one Pakistani national is wanted for trial in the case relating to the attack on the Indian Parliament in December, 2001; two terrorists are wanted for trial in connection with a conspiracy to assassinate the Deputy Prime Minister of India; and two other terrorists, both Indian nationals, are wanted for trial in connection with some other terrorist incidents. Pakistan continues to ignore the red-corner notices issued by the INTERPOL for their arrest and handing over to India for trial. In the case of the Indian nationals, it has been taking up the stand that they are not in Pakistani territory despite the fact that the Pakistani media has been reporting about their presence and activities in Pakistan. In the case of the Pakistani nationals, it has been contending that there is no evidence of their involvement in terrorism.

Sanctuaries To Terrorist Leaders

Five Sikh terrorist leaders, the Amir of the Hizbul Mujahideen, and Dawood Ibrahim, the leader of a trans-national crime group supporting Al Qaeda and the LET, continue to enjoy sanctuary in Pakistan. All of them were Indian nationals, when they sought sanctuary in Pakistan, but Dawood Ibrahim, who was declared by the US on October 16, 2003, as a specially designated global terrorist, has been given a Pakistani passport under a different name.

Continued Use Of Pakistani Organisations For Sponsoring Acts Of Terrorism In Indian Territory

The ISI continues to use the HUM, the LET, the JEM, the HUJI and Al Badr, all Pakistani organisations, for sponsoring acts of terrorism in Indian territory. Of these, the HUM is a founding member of bin Laden's IIF. The HUJI, the LET and the JEM joined it subsequently. The US State Department designated the HUM as a Foreign Terrorist Organisation in 1997 under its then name of HUA. It designated the LET and the JEM as Foreign Terrorist

Organisations after 9/11. The HUM has not so far been banned in Pakistan despite its involvement in acts of terrorism not only against Indian nationals, but also against American and other Western nationals. There has been no ban on the HUJI either. Musharraf banned the LET and the JEM on January 15, 2002, but the ban order applied to only their activities in Pakistani Punjab, Sindh, Balochistan and the North-West Frontier Province (NWFP). It did not apply to their activities in Pakistan-Occupied Kashmir (POK), the Northern Areas (Gilgit and Baltistan) and the Federally-Administered Tribal Areas (FATA). Their leaders and many of their cadres were arrested and kept in jail or under house arrest for some weeks. They were subsequently released on the ground that there was no evidence of their involvement in acts of terrorism in Pakistani territory. Both these organisations continue to be active under different names. Their leaders travel all over Pakistan to collect funds and recruit volunteers for jihadi training. The Pakistani media has reported that even after the so-called ban the LET has acquired immovable property of considerable value in Pakistani Punjab and Sindh. On October 14, 2003, the US Treasury Department moved for the freezing of the accounts of a Pakistani charity organisatioin called Al Akhtar Trust on the ground that it was funding jihadi terrorist activities not only in Afghanistan and Pakistan, but also in Iraq. This Trust was founded by the JEM after Musharraf had ostensibly banned it. In September, 2003, the Pakistani authorities claimed to have rounded up Gungun, the brother of Hambali, who is reported to be the operational chief of the Jemaah Islamiya (JI) of South-East Asia and some other Indonesian and Malaysian students studying in two madrasas of Karachi. The JI is stated to have masterminded the Bali bombing of October last year. According to the Pakistani media, one of these madrasas is run by the LET and Hafiz Mohammad Sayeed, the chief of the LET, was taking a class in the madrasa when the police went there for the arrests. Even though he is the head of a banned organisation, he was not arrested.

Continued Terrorist Infrastructure In Pakistani Territory

No action has been taken by Pakistan against the training camps in Pakistani territory run by the Pakistani and Kashmiri terrorist organisations. These training camps are located not only in the POK and the Northern Areas, but also at Muridke, near Lahore, in Pakistani Punjab and at different places and madrasas in Sindh and the NWFP.

Continued Supply Of Arms And Ammunition, Explosives, Detonators, Timers, Landmines And Hand Grenades

There has been no decrease in their supply.

Avoidance Of Action Against Terrorist Funding

The action taken by the Pakistani authorities against all suspected bank accounts in Pakistan under the UN Resolution continues to be an eye-wash. The "News" of Islamabad reported as follows on January 1, 2002: " Experts said the policy to freeze the accounts in "pieces" gave ample time to most of these account-holders to withdraw their money." On June 14,2003, Shaukat Aziz, Pakistan's Finance Minister, placed on the table of the National Assembly a statement giving details of the accounts frozen by the authorities. In the statement figured three accounts in Peshawar banks held in the name of bin Laden and one in the name of his No.2 Ayman Al-Zawahiri (name of the branch not given). Of the three accounts of bin Laden, two were joint accounts held by him along with others and one was an account only in his name. The three bin Laden accounts, according to the statement, had balances of only US $ 306, US $ 342 and US $ 1585 and the account of Al-Zawahiri had a balance of US $ five only. The statement contained a remark that the account of Al-Zawahiri had remained dormant since 1993. There were no such remarks in respect of the accounts of bin Laden. Hence, they are presumed to have been active. The statement remained silent as to what were the various deposits made in the accounts and withdrawn or transferred from them before they were frozen, who were the beneficiaries etc. According to the same statement, the HUM had three accounts with balances of US $ 62, US $ 48 and US $ 35. The JEM had one account with US $ 14. The seizure of only such paltry amounts speaks eloquently of the insincerity of the Pakistani authorities in circumventing the directives of the UNSC to act effectively against terrorist funding. When the State of Pakistan itself, through its Inter-Services

Intelligence, has been distributing an estimated US $ 40 million per annum to different terrorist groups, where is the question of its acting against terrorist funding? More than a half of this goes to the four Pakistani terrorist organisations, which are members of bin Laden's IIF.

Implications For The Us Counter-terrorism Policy

The USA's continued reluctance to act against Pakistan and make it pay a prohibitive price for helping the jihadi terrorists is coming in the way of an effective counter-terrorism strategy. Encouraged by this US reluctance, the Pervez Musharraf regime continues to keep the jihadi terrorists alive and active in the hope of using them to retrieve the lost Pakistani influence in Afghanistan and achieve its strategic objective of forcing a change in the status quo in India's Jammu & Kashmir.

One is already seeing the result of this not only in the continuing acts of terrorism in Indian territory by terrorists sponsored, trained, armed and infiltrated by Pakistan, but also in the similar cross-border infiltration of re-grouped, re-trained and re-armed cadres of the Taliban from the sanctuaries in Pakistan into Afghanistan. According to Ahmed Rashid, the internationally renowned Pakistani expert on the Taliban, about 2,500 well-trained and well-equipped Taliban cadres are presently in the Pakistani territory waiting to be infiltrated into Afghanistan. About 1,400 plus trained and armed terrorists are infiltrated into India every year by the ISI. The continued availability of the terrorist infrastructure in Pakistani territory poses a serious threat not only to peace and stability in India and Afghanistan, but also to the US and other allied troops and the personnel of international organisations in Iraq, which are trying to restore normalcy in Iraq and lay the foundation for its emergence as a modern, liberal democracy. Osama bin Laden and his Al Qaeda and the Pakistani jihadi organisations subscribing to his ideology look upon India, the US and Israel as the main obstacles in their efforts to spread jihadi terrorism across the world and achieve their pan-Islamic objectives.

Any counter-terrorism policy followed by the US, in its capacity as the head of the international coalition in the war against terrorism, cannot be effective unless it acts firmly not only against terrorist organisations and their leaders, but also against States using terrorism as a weapon to achieve their strategic objectives.

Even if the US has difficulties in taking punitive action against Pakistan, it should at least ensure that Pakistan sincerely implements the provisions of the UNSCR 1373 against all terrorist organisations whether their terrorist activities are directed against the USA, India, Israel or any other country. Any further US economic and military assistance should be linked to this condition. As a first step, the US should insist on Pakistan arresting and handing over to India the 20 terrorists wanted for trial in India, effectively enforcing a ban on the HUM, the LET, the HUJI and the JEM and removing all training and other terrorist infrastructure in its territory, whether of Pakistani or Kashmiri organisations. Pakistan's claims of freezing terrorist accounts need to be closely scrutinised. If they are found to be false, Pakistan should be held accountable before the UN Security Council.

CHALLENGES OF CROSS BORDER TERRORISM FOR INDIA

The terrorism means all kinds of violent acts, undertaken by a person, group or a state with an aim to create fear/terror for a religious, political or ideological goal. This is aimed towards government and civilians equally. It can be broadly classified into Political terrorism for political purposes (This could be domestic or cross border and for ideology or control of state) and Non-Political terrorism – Terrorism that is not aimed at political purposes but which exhibits "conscious design to create and maintain a high degree of fear for coercive purposes, but the end is individual or collective gain rather than the achievement of a political objective."

India has been facing threat of cross border terrorism since independence, when Pakistan sponsored Azad Kashmir forces comprising of local militia of POK and FATA attacked J&K in 1947. The very fact that India shares its border with many nations, it makes its task of internal and external security more difficult. The ethnic mix of population also adds fuel to the fire, when ideology and aspiration of all religion in India are not met concurrently by the govt. This has been seen in Punjab terrorism in 1980s, followed by Assam and J&K problem in 1990s and now as Maoism in state of Chhattisgarh, Bihar and Andhra Pradesh, west Bengal and Orissa.

India shares ethnic, religious and cultural affinities with its neighbours and in times of conflict, certain portion of tension flows inward in form of state sponsored terrorism. Since these states can unleash the terrorist activities in different capacity, they may use their own directly recruited and controlled terror squads, or may choose to work through proxies and client movements across the border. The terrorist menace from across the border is supported financially and materially by the government and institutions of these countries. Therefore there are number of problems which poses a serious challenges to the national security of India, unless neighbors, India can hardly play its legitimate role in global affairs. Reasons for Cross Border Terrorism India is emerging as economically and military strong nation in both continental Asia as well as the Indian Ocean region. In the present scenario, India faces a great threat from all the countries with which it has borders, in one or the other form. The form of threat varies from pure military to a combination of military and non-military. Today India faces more security threat from Pakistan than any of its neighbours, because of multiple conflicts since 1947 partition on issues like J&K, water sharing, Sir Creek etc. Pakistan has not accepted regional supremacy of India and undertaken many military and terrorist actions to destabilise India since independence.

The dynamic nature of the problems concerning management of borders is brought out by manner in which the sensitivity of the India- Pakistan, Indo-Bhutan and India- Bangladesh borders have changed over a period of time. These borders, which have been open, were once peaceful and trouble-free. However, with the increasing activities of the Inter Services Intelligence (ISI) in Pakistan and frequent movement of militants in other States, the nature of the borders has changed completely. The Pakistan is resorting to Cross border terrorism, to covertly bringing pressure to bear on India across the border through violence, so as keep it engaged in proxy wars, divert its resources from other development and garner support of Muslim community in India for creating separate Muslim state and finally to degrade India's conventional superiority through a process of strategic fatigue.

SECURITY CHALLENGES FOR INDIA

India is very sure that terrorist activities of Pakistan will extend far beyond the confines of J&K and will cover all parts of the country. There is credible information of ongoing plans of terrorist groups in Pakistan to carry out fresh attacks. Hence India needs to be prepared for encountering more sophisticated technologies and enhanced capabilities of all terrorist groups operating out of Pakistan. India has been emphasizing at international level the need for combating terrorism and called for global action to counter terrorism and enactment of various political and economical sanctions against state responsible for sponsoring terrorism across international borders. However due to political and military interest of super powers like USA and China in and around Pakistan nothing much has been done to control rogue activities of Pakistan. India has to fight this war alone by strengthening its military, police and paramilitary forces and at the same time garner international support for combating terrorism. There is also a need to keep Pakistan politically engaged on bilateral conflict issues, so that Pakistan is motivated to reduce/stop their support for terrorist groups operating out of Pakistan. This three prong strategy will ultimately reduce cross border terrorism in India.

If India wants to assert itself globally in international politics and power game, it must control such misadventures from Pakistan. India is a growing nation and in few years from now it will be an international power to reckon with, for which it must concentrate in economic, trade, infrastructure and agriculture development, but at same time keep Pakistan under check and well humoured.

India's Counter-Terrorism Set-Up

- The state police and its intelligence set-up: Under India's federal Constitution, the responsibility for policing and maintenance of law and order is that of the individual states. The central government in New Delhi can only give them advice, financial help, training and other assistance to strengthen their professional capabilities and share with them the intelligence collected by it. The responsibility for follow-up action lies with the state police.

- The national intelligence community: This consists of the internal intelligence agency (Intelligence Bureau), the external intelligence agency (Research and Analysis Wing), the Defence Intelligence Agency that was set up a year ago, and the intelligence directorates general of the armed forces. The IB collects terrorism-related intelligence inside the country and RAW does it outside. The DIA and the intelligence directorates general of the armed forces essentially collect tactical intelligence during their counter-terrorism operations in areas such as Jammu and Kashmir, Nagaland, etc, where they are deployed.
- Physical security agencies: These include the Central Industrial Security Force, responsible for physical security at airports and sensitive establishments; the National Security Guards, a specially trained intervention force to terminate terrorist situations such as hijacking, hostage-taking, etc.; and the Special Protection Group, responsible for the security of the prime minister and former prime ministers.
- Paramilitary forces: These include the Central Reserve Police Force and the Border Security Force, which assist the police in counter- terrorism operations when called upon to do so.
- The Army: Their assistance is sought as a last resort when the police and paramilitary forces are not able to cope with a terrorist situation. But in view of Pakistan's large-scale infiltration in Jammu and Kashmir and the presence and activities of a large number of Pakistani mercenaries, many of them ex-servicemen, the army has a more active, permanent and leadership role in counter-terrorism operations here.

In recent months, there have been two additions to the counter-terrorism set-up:

(a) A multi-disciplinary centre on counter-terrorism, headed by a senior IB officer, within the IB, expected to be patterned on the CIA's counter- collection and counter-terrorism operations will work under a common umbrella and be responsible for joint analysis of the intelligence flowing in from different agencies and co-ordinate follow-up action.

(b) A counter-terrorism division in the ministry of external affairs, expected to be patterned after the counter-terrorism division of the US state department. It will be responsible for co-coordinating the diplomatic aspects of counter-terrorism, such as briefing other countries on Pakistan's sponsorship of terrorism against India, processing requests for extradition and mutual legal assistance, servicing the work of various joint working groups on counter-terrorism which India has set up with a number of countries, etc.

Options for India

India has to understand that there is a need to collectively address this problem through military means, bilateral diplomacy and international political support. At the same time India has to ensure that internal stability especially religious one is maintained and support of all religious groups is strengthened to fight the cross border terrorism.

Military Option- India needs to consider the military option seriously. This would not only enhance the deterrence in place against such attacks, but would ensure that the state-jihadi nexus is constricted. The state element would likely be more sensitive to the likely hurt that India could inflict militarily and therefore exercise restraint over jihadi impulses. Any such consideration would enable execution of the military operation better and integrate it with the political and diplomatic prongs of the strategy that would likely unfold in real time. India must invest more in strengthening its security forces including army by procuring state of the art weapon and equipment, surveillance devices, mobility vehicles including helicopter and aircrafts and logistic support. There should be more cooperation and inter- operability amongst all security elements for synergy of operation. All sensitive areas along the border must be guarded and infiltration routes covered by deploying adequate forces. The intelligence must be shared by all to detect and counter any form of terrorist activity in time.

Diplomatic Dialogue- India must diplomatically engage not only Pakistan, but also Nepal, Bhutan, Bangladesh and Myanmar, so as to formulate policies for cooperation in economic, military, cultural and terrorism fields and ensure mutual quest for regional peace, prosperity and stability. As far as Pakistan is concerned India need to adopt test and trust policy in all future relations and engage them actively by giving more economic facilities and trade concessions. India must also ensure that Pakistan remains politically viable nation so that it is not taken over by non state forces.

International Support- India has initiated many dialogues in international forum for formulation of combined policy and guidelines for combating terrorism, some of which are in force and being implemented. India need to especially motivate and convince USA and China to keep Pakistan under control, so that ISI can be checked for sponsoring and supporting various terrorist groups operating out of Pakistan. In wake of recent attack by Taliban on naval base of Pakistan, the security of their nuclear arsenal is threatened. If Taliban and al Qaeda are successful in securing nuclear weapon from Pakistan, then India will be the nation to face the brunt of their hatred.

Internal Stability- India need to understand the importance of maintaining peace and harmony amongst all religion and community in India, with special reference to Muslim and people belonging to NE states and RED CORRIDOR(Maoism). Over last decades ISI has targeted these people and fuelled insurgency in these regions. The importance of good grievances detection, monitoring and redressal machinery so that the build-up of grievances in any community is detected in time and the political leadership alerted and advised to take prompt action to redress them. The intelligence agencies have an important role to play as the eyes and ears of the government in different communities to detect feelings of anger and alienation which need immediate attention.

Conclusion

The fight against terrorism is very difficult and challenging task, for which concerted efforts by various responsible agencies, both national and international, is required. For fighting a successful war against cross border terrorism, an international political support and cooperation and coordination among the neighboring States is required. It is unfortunate that various states are pursuing cross border terrorism in spite of its prohibition, as International Law regarding the implementation and enforcement of its rules is not as strong as it should be.

India- Pakistan relations have deteriorated over period of time even though continuous processes by both nations are being initiated for peace, harmony and cooperation. However, due to ideological and historical differences not much has been gained by either side. Pakistan policy to degrade India's conventional superiority through a process of strategic fatigue is the main stumbling block in all peace process. ISI of Pakistan has taken up one point agenda of spreading terrorism in India by all means, and unless India takes all necessary actions to check its activities now, the threat of nuclear terrorism looms ahead.

6

Terrorism and its Impact on Pakistan-India Relations

Let me start with the proposition that terrorism has had an adverse impact on relations between India and Pakistan – and for two reasons. First is the cross border movement of terrorists (who say they are motivated by oppression of fellow Muslims) from Pakistan to India. Second is the proxy war that is emerging between India and Pakistan in Afghanistan as the former seeks to limit the power of militant groups with an anti-Indian agenda (such as the Taliban) and the latter has reacted to this by supporting the anti-Indian activities of the Taliban in order to limit Indian influence.

A second basic proposition is that the international anti-terrorist agenda has always had much greater popular support in India than in Pakistan. Besides the lack of popular support for anti-terrorist activities, which is widely characterized in Pakistan as anti-Islamic, the Pakistani government has always had a somewhat Janus-faced policy toward terrorism since the Musharraf dictatorship decided to back the global war on terrorism in the wake of 9/11.

A recent PEW public opinion study in 25 countries, for example, shows that a large majority of the Indian population has a favorable view of US foreign policy and the US. Only two countries had a higher ranking. This favorable Indian perception of the US is in marked contrast to the unfavorable view of the US in Pakistan, a fact that has forced the new democratically elected government in Islamabad to adopt a very cautious policy toward militant Islam and the activities of the US and NATO forces in Afghanistan. Of course, a basic reason for this stark difference between the two neighbouring South Asia states is that Indians consider themselves a victim of terrorist attacks over the past two decade, and the level of violence have surged over the past few years. This may explain why India was the first country to come out openly in favor of the US in the wake of 9/11. It took some American arm-twisting to get Musharraf to make a similar commitment and it was more a tactical move than a real commitment. In fact, Pakistan has become the victim of terrorist activities as well, as the bombing of the Marriott Hotel in Islamabad demonstrates, but there is a more conflicted popular response to such activities than in India.

Besides the lack of popular backing for the war on terrorism, Pakistan had several tactical reasons to be wary of backing it. Taliban control of Afghanistan suited Pakistan's foreign policy interest in denying India influence in Afghanistan, recalling that the royal governments of Afghanistan had historically had good relations with India. Moreover, the Taliban might be able to provide Pakistan strategic depth against the historic enemy, a country several times larger, more populous, and more prosperous. Pakistan is a relatively long country that could be cut in two by Indian military action. Afghanistan would offer convenient strategic depth to meet this challenge. Finally, Taliban control might result in Afghan recognition of the Durand Line that separates Afghanistan from Pakistan. It was a boundary drawn by the British over a century ago as part of a larger effort to separate Czarist Russian and Imperial British spheres of influence. Every Afghan government, including the present one, has denied the legitimacy of this colonial era boundary. The dispute is a standing invitation for Pakistan Pashtuns to separate themselves from Pakistan. In fact, there was historically a strong separatist movement among Pakistan's Pashtun population, though it is much less vibrant now than before. However, there is a contest for shaping the identity of the Pashtun on both sides of the border. President Karzai (a Pashtun himself) and the Awami Party in Pakistan's Northwest Frontier Province, which won the most recent assembly elections there, are pushing for a secular definition. The Taliban area seeking to give Pashtun nationalism a religious definition and Pakistan has historically supported an enhanced Islamic identity in part to undermine the separatist movement there.

Pakistan was one of three states (Saudi Arabia and the UAE were the other two) which offered official recognition to the Taliban in the 1990s, and was reluctant to abandon it. The Taliban's increasingly close ties to Osama bin-Laden's efforts was to force Pakistan to abandon the Taliban, at least officially. It tried unsuccessfully soon after 9/11 to get the Taliban leadership to separate itself from al-Qaeda and then to get the West to accept the notion of moderate Taliban in the new government. Both were clearly aimed at preserving as much Pashtu influence as possible. The Taliban supreme leader, Mullah Omar, effectively blocked both Pakistani moves. Mullah Omar, the poorly educated but charismatic leader of the Taliban, had increasingly come under bin-Laden's influence and came to accept his notion of a pan-Islamic world order, along with his views on the enforcement of a proper understanding of the Shariah, and an aggressive international effort against various designated enemies of Islam. Present evidence suggests the symbiotic relationship between the two organizations still exist. At the top of that list of enemies are the US and Israel, but other nearby non-Islamic states like India and Russia are also targeted. The Shia' dominated government of Iran has been a subject of its animosity, presumably because Shia' Islam in interpreted as apostate by the militants. Denmark has apparently also become a target in this post-cartoon era. This is demonstrated by the bombing of the Danish Embassy in Islamabad, and perhaps other incidents where Danish interests have been targeted.

The world is again now focused on Afghanistan because of the renewed Taliban activities in the southern Pashtun areas of Afghanistan and the increased danger that Taliban bases will serve as centers for international terrorist activity. Taliban activities are supported by sympathizers in Pakistan. What is particularly worrying is the porous nature of the Afghan-Pakistan border and the movement of militants to safe havens across the Durand Line in the mountainous regions of northwestern Pakistan. A 2007 US National Intelligence Estimate (NIE) representing the view of 16 agencies of the US government, concurred that al-Qaeda has re-established a safe haven along the Pakistan-Afghanistan border. The growing number of US and NATO troop deaths as a result of Taliban attacks is nudging the US to take a more unilateral approach to the issue of cross border activities, moving beyond "hot pursuit" to unilateral targeting Taliban/al-Qaeda centers in the border region of Pakistan when there is actionable intelligence. The danger of this policy, of course, is that it risks further alienating the Pashtun population and complicates the secular democratic government in Islamabad as it seeks to restore law and order in the troubled border regions. The better policy might be to build up Pakistani counter-terrorism capacity along with a regional approach to terrorism (more on that below).

The Karzai Government for its part has blamed Pakistan for doing little to crack down on the Taliban and al-Qaeda that now control a considerable part of the border region. Karzai's complaints go beyond this, however, to include Pakistani backing of terrorist

activities to advance Pakistan's foreign policy interests. Senior Indian figures, including the External Affairs Minister, have echoed these charges of Pakistani involvement against Karzai and Indian targets in Afghanistan, most prominently attacks on Indian highway construction workers and most dramatically the bombing of the Indian Embassy in Kabul, in which senior Indian officials, including the defense attaché, were killed. The situation is further complicated by the widespread belief in Afghanistan that Islamabad was involved in some way in efforts to assassinate President Karzai.

A third basic proposition of this chapter is that a transformation of Pakistan-Afghanistan ties can only take place in the overall context of improved Pakistan-Indian relations (more on that below). That diplomatic path may require considerable American – and perhaps Chinese — effort. In recent decades, Indo-Pakistan hostility has mainly revolved around the Kashmir dispute. Pakistan's support to militant groups fighting in Kashmir in the 1990s and into this century was aimed at forcing India to the conference table to negotiate the status of this disputed state. The situation in this Muslim majority state of India has recently deteriorated in the wake of a controversial land deal providing accommodations for the significantly larger number of Hindu pilgrims to a religious shrine located at the core Vale of Kashmir. Along with this there has been a surge of firing incidents along the Line of Control that threatens the cease first that went into effect in November 2003. India charges that Pakistan border troops engage in firing to serve as cover for the infiltration of militants in Kashmir.

It is Afghanistan, however, that constitutes the new battleground on which Indo-Pakistani hostility is playing out. Credible American media leaks indicate that US officials in mid-July confronted Pakistani officials with information linking Pakistani military intelligence to the July 7 2008 car bombing of the Indian embassy in Kabul. A meeting in July 2008 between Pakistani Prime Minister Gilani and Indian Prime Minister Manmohan Singh resulted in Gilani pledging to investigate the claims of Pakistani intelligence involvement in the bombing. Perhaps the long run solution of this issue is to separate Pakistan's military intelligence from military control, a proposal that was seriously considered by the new civilian government, but abandoned, presumably because the new army chief of staff opposed the idea. Continued Pakistani ambivalence toward the Taliban stems in part from its concern that India is trying to encircle it by gaining influence in Afghanistan. Pakistani security officials may calculate that the Taliban offers the best chance of countering India's growing regional influence. Pakistan believes that ethnic Tajiks and other ethnic constituents of the former "Northern Alliance" in Afghanistan that opposed the largely Pashtun Taliban prior to 9/11 continues to receive support from India and that India foments separatism in Pakistan's restive Baluchistan province from its multiple consulates in Afghanistan.

India in fact has increased its presence in Afghanistan significantly since the fall of the Taliban structure in late 2001. It is one of the major donors for the reconstruction of the country, with over a billion dollars pledged for a wide variety of projects all over the country. Many of these projects are in the Pashtun south, a clear effort to revive links to the Pashtuns that were once so close in the last days of the British Empire in South Asia. India is also paying for the construction of a splendid new parliament building in Kabul as part of its support for the democratic process in Afghanistan. It is building a major highway project in the west bordering on Iran. An estimated 4,000 Indians are in Afghanistan working on development projects, including highways and bridges, cold storage facilities, health centers, and electrical generating facilities. This does not count the return of thousands of Indian families, mainly Sikh and Hindu, who traditionally had been a key part of Afghanistan's urban mercantile middle class and who had fled to India in the wake of the Taliban takeover. An increasingly globalizing India is concerned about the well-being of its diaspora here and elsewhere. India has dispatched some 500 paramilitary Indo-Tibetan border police to guard its workers following attacks on them such as an April 12, 2008 suicide bombing that killed two Indian highway engineers in Nimruz Province. There are also news reports of Indian offers to train senior personnel of the Afghan armed forces in India. India is the largest donor for educational training and provides scholarships for hundreds of Afghan students and officials to study in India each year.

India has a soft diplomacy advantage in the popularity of its film and music industry. None of its neighbors has anything comparable to compete, and the Afghan film and music industries were virtually eliminated during the austere Taliban period. Within days of the defeat of the Taliban in late 2001, for example, billboards advertizing Indian films sprang up all over Kabul. CDs of Indian film music appeared on the shelves of shops as if by magic all over the city. The craze for things India has spilled over into clothing, food and art.

India in addition is investing significant sums in the Iranian port at Charbahar to gain entry to trade with Afghanistan and the Central Asian republics. It is also assisting in the construction of road and rail links from Charbahar to the Iranian border with Afghanistan and the Central Asian republics. These Indian links to Afghanistan also have the advantage of avoiding the unstable Pashtun areas of Afghanistan south of the Hindu Kush mountain chain that runs through the middle of the country. This investment is necessitated because of Pakistan's refusal to permit India cross-shipment rights across Pakistan to Afghanistan and beyond. The purpose of this Pakistani policy of exclusion is almost certainly for use as a lever on issues of dispute, like Kashmir. However, it has had limited success so far and undermines a basic US policy. I think it would suit US interests in the region to pressure Pakistan to lift this prohibition against India trade.

The strategic implications of this Indian-financed port/road/rail system to Afghanistan are significant. For the first time, Pakistan would be deprived of a veto power over Indian trading with Afghanistan. This could have implications for US efforts in Afghanistan if Pakistan would follow through on threats to block US resupply of its troops in Afghanistan.

Terrorism in South Asia is a regional problem, as is becoming increasingly clear by the demonstrated links among Islamic terrorist groups whose tentacles reach across state boundaries. Transforming regional security perceptions among the Afghans, Pakistanis and Indians will be a monumental challenge, but constitutes the only way to stabilize and secure Afghanistan so that it does not again become a terrorist sanctuary. The US in particular will have to focus on promoting regional cooperation among all three countries and defusing conflict between New Delhi and Islamabad, on the one hand, and Kabul and Islamabad on the other. More specifically, the US will have to consider other initiatives that reduce Pakistani fears of Indian hegemony and how the US can improve its own ties to New Delhi without setting off alarm bells in Islamabad. China, which is also trying to improve its relations with India and also faces the growing menace of terrorism that has roots in South Asia, confronts a similar dilemma as it reformulates its South Asia policy. The task of calming Pakistani fears of a dominant India is complicated by India's economic prosperity and Pakistan's recent virtual economic collapse. India as the larger and stronger party will need to take the initiative.

Indian policy toward Pakistan, while complicated by Kashmir and the cross border terrorist menace, has shifted somewhat over the past decade as the country has become a more self-confident player on the world scene. More specifically, India's preferred strategy seems aimed at reconciliation and stability, thus allowing it to play its "predestined" role as a global power. This policy is favored by the major national political actor (e.g. the Congress and the Bharatiya Janata Party). However, given the reality of instability in Pakistan and to guard against its future irresponsible behaviour, India is also working on a parallel strategy of containing, or even bypassing Pakistan, a policy that some of India's most important strategic thinks have supported for years. The other dilemma with Indian policy on this regard is its historic policy of keeping "outside" powers "outside" South Asia, though, at least with the US, this policy seems to have softened somewhat, given the American support for the Indian position during the 1999 Kargil crisis and the American push to make India an exception to its own nuclear non-proliferation laws and international protocols on the subject, an exception required because India is not a signatory to the 1970 Nuclear Non-proliferation accord – and it possesses nuclear weapons and the means to deliver them (as does Pakistan). It may thus be willing to permit the US as a good faith interlocutor on Indo-Pakistani relations. It would not provide a similar opening to the Chinese.

If a major effort is not launched to achieve regional stability, the danger of course is a revival of Indian Pakistani tensions, always dangerous for two countries possessing nuclear weapons and the means to deliver them. There is fortunately an institutional basis for negotiations, the Composite Dialogue that was initiated in early 2004 (and was to address the big outstanding issues), which followed a cease fire along the Line of Control in Kashmir that has by and large held since then. This Dialogue, however, has so far had limited achievements, in part because of political fragility in each country. The replacement of General Musharraf, who Indians largely distrusted, by a civilian government may help in the Dialogue. The departure of the communists from the Manmohan Singh coalition may similarly give his government greater room for manoeuvre in handling its own foreign policy. A major area for building links would be trade, which is presently at a very low level. Enhanced trade would build a constituency in each country for a stable relationship. The projected Iran/ Pakistan/India pipeline would be another economic factor binding the two energy short countries. That pipeline is now more notional than real largely because of the high prices that Iran is demanding and the difficulty in finding international financers, in part because of American and Western objection to any large scale project that could enhance Iran's economic situation.

Kashmir does remain a major stumbling block. It generates terrorist cross border activity from Pakistan, often with government backing. Terrorism makes any Indian move towards an innovative solution impossible politically, and it will take innovative thinking to get over the present impasse. General Musharraf had made a radical departure from Pakistan's stated position on Kashmir by suggesting that it would give up its territorial claim over Kashmir (and by extension the traditional demand for a plebiscite) in exchange for demilitarization and some forms of all Kashmir managerial functions. India never responded meaningfully to these out-of-the-box proposals. If the present Pakistani government were to raise them again, the chances are better for a positive Indian response. The problem is that a democratic government in Pakistan must be alert to any move that suggests that it is giving up Pakistan's historic demand for Kashmir. It must of course do so to get traction with India, but the challenge is to put this effort in a larger bilateral context that makes Kashmir more of a joint undertaking without transfer of sovereignty, a difficult proposition to sell.

I would like to close with six basic points on the issue of terrorism and its impact on Indo-Pakistani relations:

1. Terrorist violence attracts only a small part of the Muslim communities of South Asia. Islam is not a single unified religion, but is characterized by major cultural and theological differences. It would be both wrong and dangerous to tar the whole community with the violence of a small minority. What is dangerous about this is that a backlash against the whole community could in fact generate popular support for the militants.
2. Terrorist violence in the name of Islam probably has more to do with the voicing of dissidence than religious reformation. In Pakistan, for example, the widespread poverty and lack of opportunity in the rapidly growing urban sprawls is an attractive source of militant recruitment.

The militant leadership may be from the urban middle class, but the foot soldiers are not. One could say the same for India and Bangladesh.

3. Terrorist violence has both an official and an informal face and there is often a linkage between them. There are dozens of militant groups in Pakistan, for example, that function, and several are popular because of the charity they carry out in a country virtually devoid of social security benefits. However, some of them, particularly those that focus on Afghanistan or on India, have been supported officially because they advance the country's foreign policy goal of weakening India. It is these officially supported groups that have brought India and Pakistan to the brink of war a few times over the past decade and this kind of linkage must cease if there is to be lasting peace.
4. Terrorist violence in India increasingly is carried out by home grown groups and thus in some ways represents a greater danger than the expatriate groups that operate from Pakistan. They can blend in the local population more easily and they are in a better position to mobilize discontent. Surveys show that Indian Muslims are near the bottom of that country's socio-economic system and perhaps some kind of equal opportunity effort is needed to improve their situation.
5. Terrorist violence is more regional in nature than ever before and will not be contained without a regional solution, which requires the good faith participation of India, Pakistan and Afghanistan (and possibly other South Asian states, especially Bangladesh). The US, as by far the most important regional player, will probably have to get directly involved to make this happen given the high degree of distrust among regional states and likely bureaucratic resistance to innovative proposals. The foreign ministries of at least India and Afghanistan are very conservative institutions.
6. Democracy and economic growth are probably the best long term cures for terrorism, and may be the best hope

of preventing Pakistan from becoming a failed state. Closer economic ties between India and Pakistan would go a long way to achieve a better economic situation in Pakistan.

PAKISTAN'S SECURITY - TODAY AND TOMORROW

A conference of the Canadian Security Intelligence Service jointly sponsored by Canada's departments of Foreign Affairs and International Trade, National Defence and Public Safety.

In light of the volatile security situation which has developed in Pakistan in the aftermath of the terrorist attacks on the United States on 11 September 2001 and the subsequent invasion of Afghanistan, the Canadian Security Intelligence Service (CSIS), joined by Canada's departments of Foreign Affairs and International Trade, National Defence and Public Safety, hosted a two-day conference in Ottawa on the topic of *Pakistan's Security Today and Tomorrow*. Held at the CSIS headquarters in Ottawa, the conference featured presentations by leading Canadian, Pakistani, American and European experts drawn from academia, the media, think-tanks, as well as government. The objective of the conference, attended by upwards of ninety people, was to expose participants to a variety of expert views on Pakistan's security, enabling them to identify key drivers influencing the country's security, and to discuss alternative futures for Pakistan. It also supported the development of an informal community of interest on Pakistan's security within the government of Canada.

The conference was facilitated by Peter Jones, Associate Professor at the University of Ottawa's Graduate School of Public and International Affairs. The event was divided into five modules, each of which consisting of a series of expert presentations, followed by a panel discussion and a question period. The agenda also included discussions in small groups to encourage interaction amongst participants and generate new insights. The five modules focussed respectively on: salient issues in Pakistan today; the country's internal security; Pakistan and its neighbours; Pakistan in world politics; and three alternative future scenarios elaborated and presented by retired Lt.-Gen. Talat Masood, whose career was spent in the Pakistan army. Participants also benefited from remarks made by Canada's High Commissioner in Pakistan, Randolph Mank, as well as international affairs specialist Janice Stein, and CSIS Director Jim Judd.

Considerations for Canada

Pakistan faces several complex and interdependent challenges: the country's history has been marked by political instability, sectarian and tribal violence, as well as regional conflicts with lasting negative effect. Today, economic difficulties and, again, political instability present problems; Pakistanis do not appear united in tackling these issues, with sub-nationalism and ethno-linguistic regionalism dominating everyday life. These problems are exacerbated as the rule of law and democratic civilian institutions remain underdeveloped, while the central government's weakness in comparison to the military results in the latter dominating politics generally. Currently, large areas of the country are beyond the control of government, with different groups having taken advantage of a porous border with Afghanistan. Pakistan's frontier and tribal areas have been used by insurgent movements, including the Taliban and Lashkar-e-Taiba (LeT), to support their terrorist activity in both Pakistan and Afghanistan. Despite its wide-ranging powers, the military has been unable to counter rising insurgency and cross-border terrorism into Afghanistan and India.

A wide variety of regional issues further complicate the situation. Chief amongst these is Pakistan's complex and mostly antagonistic relationship with India. In the latest episode of this relationship, India alleged Pakistani involvement in a series of terrorist attacks on Indian targets, including the attacks in Mumbai in November 2008. Given the history of conflict as well as the nuclear capabilities of both South Asian states, rising tensions between the two are of serious concern.

For Canada, the deteriorating security situation in Pakistan has several critical implications, as described below:

1) Canada's involvement in Afghanistan. Canada has approximately 2500 troops stationed in Afghanistan. As long as Pakistan is not internally stable and secure, the

Taliban can utilise the lawless frontier regions of Pakistan to coordinate attacks on allied troops in Afghanistan.

2) Pakistan as a supply route for Canadian and NATO troops in Afghanistan. Because Afghanistan is a landlocked country, roughly 75% of supplies for NATO troops in Afghanistan pass through Pakistan.

   If the frontier and tribal regions that border Afghanistan are not secure and convoys come increasingly under attack, the ability to fight successfully against the resurgent Taliban in Afghanistan could be compromised.

3) Pakistan as a safe haven for international terrorists. Both Osama bin-Laden and Ayman al-Zawahiri are believed to be hiding in the frontier regions of Pakistan. They and likeminded individuals can plan attacks on international targets, including Canada.

4) Risk of India-Pakistan nuclear war with global repercussions. As long as tensions between India and Pakistan remain, the risk of a nuclear conflict will persist. Tensions between Pakistan and India are more likely to be diffused if Pakistan is internally stable.

5) Extremists' access to, and control of, nuclear weapons. Beyond conventional state-to-state warfare in South Asia, analysts must also consider the considerable security challenges associated with a nuclear state losing control of its nuclear capability to a fragmented set of extremists. The radicalisation of growing segments of Pakistan's army, noted by an expert at the conference, is therefore also of concern.

6) Pakistani diaspora in Canada. Canada has benefited from the presence of a large South Asian diaspora across the country. Solving the problems that are dear to Pakistanis, such as the Kashmir issue, sectarian violence, as well as inter-tribal and intra-tribal conflicts, will be instrumental in ensuring continued harmony amongst South Asian Canadians. In the eyes of many observers, the confluence of the factors and realities described above has made Pakistan "the most dangerous country in the world today".

To encapsulate the ideas of the conference, the results of the discussions have been used to highlight a list of drivers of change, which will influence Pakistan's future security.

These drivers were defined by the conference participants in plenary and during break-out group discussions. They can be grouped in the following four categories.

DRIVERS OF PAKISTAN'S SECURITY

Terrorism and State Integrity

Drivers of change

- The efficiency of the Afghanistan campaign and the possibility of controlling the porous Afghanistan-Pakistan border;
- The demobilisation of the jihadi sector and reintegration of jihadists into the mainstream;
- National unity, identity and nationalism;
- Ethno-linguistic diversity and Islamabad's ability to evoke a national politics that creates stakes for all groups, including differing tribes and classes.

The insurgency in Pakistan has taken a stranglehold of the country, as the Taliban have gradually taken control of the Federally Administered Tribal Areas (FATA) and are now slowly spreading east. The North-West Frontier Province (NWFP) may be lost to the Taliban, as terrorist attacks there are increasing and the Taliban are spreading their control of the area. The Swat Valley, in NWFP, once a paradise for tourists, is now controlled by the Taliban, who appear to have secured from Islamabad the freedom to enforce sharia law. Taliban violence as well as militancy by other groups demanding more autonomy are also spreading to Punjab and Baluchistan. Today, Mullah Omar, the reclusive leader of the Taliban, is widely believed to be living in Quetta, the capital of Baluchistan.

Whether and how the problem of rising insurgency will be contained is vital to how Pakistan will develop over the next years. If Islamabad does not succeed in securing the country from insurgents, the de facto integrity of Pakistan may be at play and international terrorism will continue to emanate from the country, while coalition troops deployed in Afghanistan continue to be the targets of terrorist attacks conceived in Pakistan. The country's economic situation will worsen significantly, as foreign investments disappear.

Several ideas were introduced during the conference to understand these issues. These emphasised that the insurgency can only be halted through a concerted effort by Pakistani security forces and the international community. Moreover, some participants stressed that Pakistan needs to understand that this is now "Pakistan's conflict", rather than an American problem being fought on Pakistan's territory. In addition to military engagement, experts offered that economic and political development should be a priority for all parties concerned with the country's stability. However, Pakistan needs to develop a national identity while balancing the interests of its regions. This would strengthen Pakistan's unity, moving away from tribal sub-nationalism and ethno-linguistic identities.

The Economy and Development

Drivers of change

- socio-economic development and poverty alleviation;
- education reforms, amongst others to equip citizens appropriately for economic life;
- approach to international development aid: focussed on the long term and reaching all parts of the state, not just the armed forces;
- foreign investment and international trade;
- the successful (re)integration of jihadists into the national economy.

In 2008, Pakistan's economic outlook took a dramatic turn for the worse given its political instability and security concerns, which have led foreign direct investment (FDI) to decline dramatically. The global financial downturn has exacerbated the problems, leading the country's stock market to dive while the

Pakistani rupee decreased significantly in value. In the light of massive trade and budget deficits, Pakistan and the International Monetary Fund (IMF) agreed on a US$7.6 billion loan in November 2008 to stabilise the country's finances and stave off a balance of payments crisis and possible default on its foreign debt.

Logically, persisting economic difficulties will have immense repercussions on Pakistan, as it attempts to solve its other problems. In support of this view, some indicated that the Taliban today appear to have a more vibrant economy than the state itself. While Pakistan may indeed benefit from foreign aid, several participants indicated that an increase in foreign aid money would no longer suffice. Instead, participants suggested that aid programs have to be tailored to meet Pakistan's needs. Those participants also argued that the international community needs to hold the Pakistani government accountable for the aid money it receives. This could be achieved by conditioning aid.

The completion of the 2700 km India-Pakistan-Iran pipeline (IPI) will also depend in large part on the security situation in Pakistan, especially in Baluchistan. It is unlikely that investors would invest the US$7 billion required for the project, given the uncertainty surrounding the security of workers and the pipeline itself. Nonetheless, the IPI is a project on which India and Pakistan are in principle dependent in order to fulfil their ever-growing need for energy. Similarly, the expected economic gains from the development of Gwadar, a deep-sea port on the Baloch coast of the Arabian Sea which was inaugurated by then-President Musharraf in 2007, depends on the security situation in Baluchistan. Gwadar sits at the mouth of the Strait of Hormuz, and thus by the Persian Gulf, through which 30% of the world's daily oil supply moves.

Governance and Civil-military Relations

Drivers of change

- institution-building and the stability of existing institutions;
- the role and power of the military in everyday life;
- whether the national interest will broaden and not be solely driven by security;

- the rule of law and accountability of the judiciary;
- the strength and authority of the police force.

The conference heard that the Pakistani state apparatus is marked by structural inefficiencies stemming from patronage politics, competing elite interests, corruption, as well as a lack of civilian institutions. Further, the Pakistani military wields a great deal of power, as the legal, political, and constitutional roles of the military remain virtually undefined and unchecked today. This has created a situation in which the national interest of Pakistan is defined almost exclusively in terms of security.

In this context, good governance has remained an elusive goal. Civilian institutions will have to be created or fostered to hold government accountable for its actions. However, institution-building is a long and arduous process that will require a significant commitment by many. On the other hand, Pakistanis overwhelmingly want democracy.

To establish an efficient system of governance, respect for the rule of law, a reliable judiciary and the existence of a professional police force are imperative. The conference heard that transparent and accountable governance would require a restructuring of the entire state apparatus, which would place the military under the control of the civilian government. Because the military have alienated parts of Pakistani society through its actions, and it is thus up to the people of Pakistan to take the initiative to effect change. However, since Pakistan's national identity is frayed, this will prove to be a monumental task, especially since the military is unlikely to surrender voluntarily to civilian authorities.

Geopolitics

Drivers of change

- the protracted tensions between Pakistan and India;
- the Kashmir conflict and its implications for regional security;
- nuclear weapons and issues of nuclear deterrence;
- the United States' involvement in the region;
- regional balance in Central and South Asia.

The rivalry between India and Pakistan, rooted in several factors, including disputed control of the Kashmir, has changed significantly over the past years, causing observers to be cautiously optimistic that a rapprochement between the two states could lead to lasting peace. After the 2002 crisis following the attacks on the Indian parliament, both states appeared actively to seek to normalise relations after more than half a century of conflict. In November 2003, a ceasefire was signed regarding the Line of Control (LoC) in Kashmir, ending years of fighting there. In January 2004, then-President Musharraf and then-Indian Prime Minister Vajpayee met in Islamabad, where the former stated that he would not permit any territory under Pakistan's control to be used to support terrorism. Based on this promise, the two countries agreed to start a composite dialogue in February 2004, tackling issues of bilateral concern.

Nonetheless, the situation remained volatile as real progress on the most pressing political issues – Kashmir and nuclear confidence-building – remained rudimentary. This was first illustrated when a series of train bombings shook Mumbai in July 2006, leading Indian police immediately to point the finger at Pakistani terrorists backed by Pakistan's Directorate for Inter-Services Intelligence (ISI), i.e. the Pakistani intelligence service. In May 2008, India then alleged that one of its soldiers had been killed by firings across the LoC, the first clear violation of the 2003 ceasefire. In July 2008, troops from both sides traded gunfire across the LoC, followed by the bombing of the Indian embassy in Kabul. This led India once again to accuse Pakistan of not doing enough to curb terrorist activity, while directly accusing the ISI of involvement. The Indian foreign secretary promptly asserted that relations had deteriorated to their "worst level in four years", illustrating the explosive nature of the situation despite the improvements in the relationship. From the Pakistani side, the reasons for this freeze in relations were India's nuclear deal with the U.S. and a perceived obsession with global power status on the part of New Delhi. The Mumbai attacks of November 2008 negated much of the progress that had been made over the past years. In parallel, the presence and actions of the U.S. in Central and South Asia may have also heightened already palpable anxieties in a region known for its frail geopolitical balance. Observers widely agree that the India-Pakistan relationship is now worse than it was at any point since 2002: as both sides have put diplomatic relations on hold in the aftermath of the attacks, while incendiary rhetoric increased, especially in India. Various sources have indicated that both sides had put their armies and air force on high alert, and that plans for Indian attacks on Pakistani targets had been made. Many analysts now agree that another major terrorist attack on Indian interests could well lead to a forceful retaliation by India.

While the possibility of war between India and Pakistan is deeply worrying, a deteriorating relationship will also mean that Pakistan's army will continue to focus on India, rather than concentrating on curbing the insurgencies previously referred to. An improvement in India-Pakistan relations would therefore have a direct impact on how Pakistan will deal with its many other problems.

How to Look at Pakistan Today

The Islamic Republic of Pakistan, along with India, became an independent country in 1947. At the time, Pakistan's territory was divided into two segments, namely West Pakistan, which is identical to today's Pakistan, and East Pakistan, which was separated from West Pakistan by approximately 1600 kilometres of land across India. In 1971, East Pakistan became independent, establishing the state of Bangladesh. With a population of around 170 million today, Pakistan is the sixth most populous country on the globe, home to the second largest Muslim population in the world after Indonesia.

The history of the country has been one marked by frequent if not constant turmoil: political instability and sectarian violence have been ongoing, conflicts in neighbouring countries such as Afghanistan have had frequent spill-over effects, and the military has had direct rule over the country on four occasions. As noted above, also, relations with India have been strained as the conflict over Kashmir, the root cause of armed conflict on at least two occasions, has evaded resolution for over 60 years. In addition, economic growth has been erratic, poverty is now widespread, and inflation high. Nonetheless, partly due to its rapidly growing population, Pakistan is projected by some to become one of the world's largest economies in the 21st century. However, the country is often seen as a failing state. In 2008, Foreign Policy's Failed States Index, which uses twelve social, economic, political and military indicators, ranked Pakistan ninth on the list of states most likely to fail. In 2007, Pakistan had been in twelfth position on the same index.

These statistics, as well as the historical anecdotes presented above, unfortunately reflect the current realities in Pakistan quite well. Over the last years, a faltering economy, growing levels of poverty, a weak government unable to assert control over its territory, as well as a nuclear arsenal shrouded in uncertainty, have made Pakistan a central concern to policy-makers around the world. These concerns have been exacerbated by a powerful Pakistani military that remains dominant in domestic affairs, yet is unable to contain growing insurgency and terrorist activity. Pakistani terrorists attacking targets at home and abroad have dominated headlines over the past years, in the process making the deteriorating situation in Pakistan a security crisis with effects far beyond its borders.

Examples of this are the assassination of Benazir Bhutto in December 2007, the attack on the Islamabad Marriott hotel in September 2008, as well as the attacks in Mumbai in November 2008, which analysts believe were conceived in Pakistan and carried out by Pakistani nationals. Moreover, as emphasised by the Norwegian Institute of International Affairs' Laila Bokhari, the United Kingdom, the Netherlands, Denmark, Germany, and Turkey all uncovered terrorism plots in the last few years with some connections to Pakistan. Former U.S. Secretary of State Madeleine Albright observed that Pakistan has everything that "gives you an international migraine". Equally pointed, Bruce Riedel, a former CIA official and a South Asia adviser to Barack Obama during his presidential campaign, recently stated that Pakistan is "the most dangerous country in today's world."

While many observers around the globe have tended to see Pakistan's deteriorating security situation through the prism of the war in Afghanistan alone, the country's situation has now become a flashpoint in its own right. To support this assertion, the Pakistan Institute of Peace Studies reported that, in 2008, an estimated 8000 lives were lost in the country to terrorist attacks, as well as in drone attacks and military operations against militants. This is only roughly 600 fewer than the number of lives lost in Afghanistan in the same period. An objective look at the situation reveals that the chief reason why Pakistan has been lifted to the top of the international community's agenda is not necessarily its precarious internal situation, but rather its critical geostrategic location next to Afghanistan, considered by many to be the central front in the fight against terrorism. In December 2008, then-President-elect Barack Obama asserted that "we cannot solve Afghanistan without solving Pakistan". This statement, echoed by many, is based on the fact that there are intricate linkages between a resurgent Taliban in Afghanistan and the volatile internal security situation in Pakistan, which has allowed the Taliban to establish bases in the frontier areas of Pakistan, from where it coordinates activity in Afghanistan. Approximately 75% of NATO supplies headed for Afghanistan have to transit through Pakistan, where such convoys have repeatedly come under attack from Taliban forces. It is in this regard that Pakistan has also become increasingly important for Canadian foreign policy.

UNDERSTANDING PARADIGMS

It is useful to discuss the consequences associated with the different frames, or paradigms, which we use to understand the country, as those may be constructive or misleading. In this regard, the frames describes below, put forth during the conference by the University of Toronto's Munk Centre for International Studies director, Janice Stein, are examined for their potential to help understand Pakistan's security. In sum, a qualified appreciation of those frames, together, depicts Pakistan as a deeply fearful state.

Pakistan as a failing state. Pakistan's alternating civilian and military governments have failed to provide effective governance and the state does not extend its authority throughout its full territory, specifically in the FATA and NWFP. However, because such control was effectively never secured since the birth of Pakistan, the country could be said to have been a failing state for more than 60 years already.

Pakistan as an unstable nuclear state and a proliferating state with poor nuclear safeguards. Prof. Stein indicated, however, that concerns about proliferation have also been raised about the former USSR when it collapsed, and that they are therefore not exclusive to Pakistan. Additionally, worries about the country's nuclear weapons being used accidentally or stolen, while they cannot be dismissed, are no more valid than in the case of other nuclear powers. Using that frame is hence perhaps "too facile", asserted Prof. Stein.

Pakistan as a fearful neighbour, obsessed with India's capabilities and intentions. Rooted in Pakistan's anxieties about being encircled by India, this frame may be useful to analysts and policy-makers in that it stresses the crisscrossing nature of regional politics and indicates that a stable Afghanistan is dependent on a secure Pakistan.

Pakistan as a society threatened by its own intelligence service and army, which have supported militants and are believed to have the necessary means to carry out their own strategy. However, it is easy to exaggerate evidence of "rogue intelligence" activity and very difficult to ascertain what is authorised and what is not.

Pakistan as a safe haven for global jihad. This is a useful frame, says Prof. Stein, which should be examined seriously. In what she qualified might be a controversial statement, she mentioned that the challenge of dealing with jihadism in this part of the world was one of "world-wide policing and intelligence", as opposed to a military one.

Pakistan threatened by Talibanisation, as militants already control large parts of the country (FATA, NWFP) and continue to spread their influence. This is a society that has been used to the reality of autonomous regions, and that frame is useful in emphasising the development and governance needs of the country.

Pakistan and Afghanistan as hostage to the Pashtun community, who sees the border as an inconvenient line separating artificially Pashtunistan, the homeland of Pashtuns extending across the Durand Line in Pakistan and Afghanistan. This frame is not persuasive because it ignores the sense of national identity that Pashtuns in both countries may feel, and the possibility of multiple loyalties.

Canadian Perspectives

Canada's High Commissioner to Pakistan, Randolph Mank, agreed that domestic security has been steadily deteriorating over the last year in the country, with the 20 September 2008 Marriott hotel bombing in Islamabad representing a watershed event in what appears to be an unstoppable downward spiral. The bombing, while not singularly the worst attack in recent history, carried with it a symbolism that made it a breaking point for Pakistanis and international workers in Pakistan alike. The attack not only killed several foreigners; the Islamabad Marriott is as much a favourite amongst Pakistanis and is located near government buildings and diplomatic missions. The deadly attack hit the psyche of the international community in Islamabad, serving as a stark notice that nobody is safe.

As mentioned before, Canada, as other Western countries, has tended to look at Pakistan through the prism of the theatre of conflict in Afghanistan. Canada currently has approximately 2500 troops deployed in Afghanistan as part of NATO's International Security Assistance Force (NATO-ISAF), making it the biggest Canadian military engagement since the Korean War. Since internal instability in Pakistan has been exploited by the Taliban to plan attacks in Afghanistan from Pakistan, targeting Afghan and NATO coalition troops and thus costing Canadian soldiers' lives, High Commissioner Mank highlighted the urgent need to understand concretely the situation in Pakistan, while working to strengthen the border between Pakistan and Afghanistan.

Other Canadian government officials joined HC Mank in reiterating the importance of the topic for Canada. As CSIS Director Jim Judd remarked, Canada's ties to Pakistan extend far beyond its current role in Afghanistan. Canada was involved in finding a resolution of the Kashmir issue as early as the 1950s, while Pakistan and Canada have cooperated on several UN peacekeeping missions. Trade and economic relations between the two nations is also important to both sides. Moreover, the Pakistani diaspora has played an important role in Canada, where it represents the fourth highest source of immigration. Pakistanis living in Canada, as well as Canadians of Pakistani origin, have made significant contributions to many aspects of Canadian society, many of them having succeeded in politics, finance, the public service and other fields.

Retired defence analyst Tony Kellett and Carleton University's distinguished senior fellow Elliot Tepper highlighted that Pakistan deserves attention from Canada because it combines dangerous elements: a potentially unstable government in Islamabad and an offensive nuclear capability. Because of the potential consequences of nuclear weapons theft or the inadvertent use of those weapons resulting from an unstable government having lost control over its nuclear stockpile, the experts contend it must be the objective of the international community as a whole to work together to stabilise the country.

The threat of terrorism emanating from Pakistan and affecting Canadians at home and abroad is another major concern that cannot be underestimated. Until recently, Canada's experience of jihadi terrorism has had a North African face (symbolised by Ahmed Ressam). However, of the two convictions to date under Canada's Anti-Terrorism Act of December 2001, one was a Pakistani-Canadian. Momin Khawaja was convicted in October 2008 for bomb-building, facilitating terrorism and receiving terrorism training. Like Khawaja, other Canadian residents have received terrorism training in Pakistan, and the ease with which extremists in the West can travel to that country greatly facilitates al-Qaida plots against Western countries. Mr. Kellett said that the training, organisational and networking support available through Pakistan greatly amplify the threat posed to Western countries by homegrown extremists in their midst (and was epitomised by Khawaja's links to a group of mostly Pakistani-Britons who were convicted on charges of plotting to bomb targets in the London area). Since 11 September 2001, some fifty Pakistan-origin residents of Western countries have been convicted on terrorism charges, with the incidence of conviction gaining pace. This demonstrates that the security problems associated with Pakistan are not confined to South Asia.

Dr. Tepper offered three suggestions regarding Canada and Pakistan.

- *Concentrating on the Pakistan-India nexus.* The Afghanistan-Pakistan relationship is now in policy focus and observers must bear in mind that Pakistan's relations with Afghanistan are closely linked to its relations to India. In Dr. Tepper's view, Canada would benefit from paying more attention to New Delhi: does India wish to be the "Elder Brother" or "Big Brother" on the subcontinent? Calls for a regional approach to Afghanistan are valid but can be too general. There is not one regional complex but
- several which affect Canada's interests.
- *Increasing strategic exchanges between Canada and Pakistan.* New entry points are necessary for working with Pakistan and, as stressed Dr. Tepper, an "architecture" has been lacking for us to do so. He pointed to the Parliamentary Democracy Project as a useful measure to address this gap. This and other measures, in his eyes, would strengthen elements of a stable democracy in Pakistan.
- *Wrapping initiatives into a comprehensive Pakistan strategy.* Canada would benefit from an all-of-government approach which is integrated and cohesive. This would draw on government and other capacities.

A participant contended that solving the issue of Kashmir, as well as other bilateral India-Pakistan subjects, would not solve all problems. Developmental indicators have been extremely low across Pakistan, and the challenges arising from the global economic crisis have been particularly acute. Democratic institutions are still at an embryonic stage, national unity is fragile, and the rule of law, which was never firmly rooted, is still generally absent since then-President Pervez Musharraf declared a state of emergency in

Pakistan in November 2007. This pessimistic account of realities leaves room for speculating whether the "India factor" is indeed still as relevant to Pakistan's internal security as many believe.

What is clear, however, is that a roadmap for Pakistan cannot treat Pakistan, India, or Afghanistan as isolated entities. Several speakers at the conference indicated that the provision to Pakistan of developmental aid, technical training, expert advice in several areas, and assistance with issues of federalism and institution-building would contribute to the stability of the country. At the same time, some analysts agreed that diplomatic initiatives would need to target India-Pakistan tensions, whether or not the issue is the key to stability in Pakistan. The appointment of Richard Holbrooke as U.S. President Obama's special representative for Pakistan and Afghanistan was welcomed, although it must be noted that the issue of Kashmir is not part of Mr. Holbrooke's mandate.

PAKISTAN TODAY: THE KEY ISSUES

The first module of the conference analysed the key issues facing Pakistan today. In a first presentation, an account of Pakistan's international identity was provided. The second key issue identified was the current freeze in relations between Pakistan and India, which has followed the recent terrorist attacks in Mumbai. A discussion on civil-military relations, followed by an exploration of Pakistan's civil society and public opinion completed the first morning of the conference.

Pakistan's International Identity

Speaking about Pakistan's international identity, the New York University's Centre on International Cooperation senior fellow, Barnett Rubin, indicated that the principal security threat emanating from Pakistan today is the confluence of Islamabad's poor record pertaining to nuclear proliferation, which is the worst of any nuclear weapons state in the world, as well as the issue of terrorism, since Pakistan, as a geographical entity, is the major source of global terrorism today. The expert blamed the security doctrine of the Pakistani military for the convergence of these factors and the resulting threat to global security, asserting that Pakistan's military still sees its primary mission as balancing and defending Pakistan against larger countries such as India or China, thus operating on the basis of a security doctrinewhich includes three ways of fighting. These are (a) conventional forces, (b) the use of deniable asymmetrical warfare, and (c) the possession of a credible nuclear deterrent.

The purpose of this doctrine may be to realise what some Pakistanis see as their country's destiny to become a "Muslim empire" (which may not necessarily be the army's point of view), while attaining certain specific military and security objectives, such as a favourable settlement of Kashmir. The doctrine is based on the fundamental belief that Pakistan's neighbours do not accept Pakistan's right to exist, a deeply entrenched paranoia that results from the often made assertion that Pakistan is an "artificial state". On this issue, Dr. Christine Fair (RAND Corp.) added that the idea of an Indian threat may have been inflated and in part nurtured by the Pakistani military to ensure that it does not lose power and influence, and that it can continue to secure a large percentage of the country's budget.

One may wish to note in that regard that President Asif Ali Zardari recently made several statements that are effectively antithetical to Pakistan's security doctrine. Most notably, he stated that India has never been a threat to Pakistan's security, further advocating that Pakistan ought to move away from current policies and embrace a no-first-use policy for its nuclear deterrent. The fact that these words have not resulted in any specific policy changes demonstrates the power that the military wields in Islamabad.

Pakistan's nuclear capabilities as well as its asymmetrical tactics, namely the statesponsored use of armed militants to pursue foreign-policy objectives, have at different points in history received the support of different states, such as China and the U.S. The conference heard that the U.S. has thus far considered the nuclear deterrent the bigger threat to global security, traditionally almost ignoring the issue of insurgency. Dr. Rubin stressed that there is a need for a policy reversal to cause Pakistan's military to stop using armed militant groups as tools of foreign and security policy.

Concurrently, the exact nature of the relationship between the jihadists and the military, which controls the nuclear assets, needs to be clarified. The Pakistani military and the ISI have so far relied on asymmetrical warfare to pursue foreign-policy goals. A demobilisation of the "jihadi sector", however, would hold the Pakistani state accountable for its actions, while adding transparency and eliminating any plausible denials. The eradication of the jihadi sector would carry with it an obligation to reintegrate the demobilised militants into the economy, as well as into society more generally, since jihadi activity has become an economy in itself. This economic complex, which according to Dr. Rubin is intrinsically linked to jihadi activity, would most likely prove a major hurdle in this effort.

The Fifth India-Pakistan Crisis and the Pakistani Army's Strategy

The India-Pakistan relationship remains one of the most potentially explosive bilateral relationships in the world. In addition to the three wars which the countries have fought, several minor conflicts have been contested, while skirmishes along the Line of Control (LoC), the de facto border in Kashmir, are the norm. Assessing the India-Pakistan relationship, the Brookings Institution's Stephen Cohen explained that the two states have been involved in four major crises over the last eighteen years. In each of these crises – the so-called "Brass Tacks" crisis of 1987, the 1990 Kashmir conflict, the 1999 Kargil conflict, as well as the "Twin Peaks" crisis of 2002 – there were significant policy and/or intelligence failures on the part of at least one of the players involved.

These four crises, all of which came close to full-fledged war, could be replicated today, said Dr. Cohen. The current chill in bilateral relations, after the Mumbai terrorist attacks, reminds observers dangerously of the other four scenarios, and a major conflict – or even war – could grow out of this crisis. While no military engagements have occurred since the Mumbai attacks, incendiary rhetoric has increased, and both states at least temporarily put their militaries on heightened alert. Dr. Cohen sees that this tension could lead to conflict in case of a renewed terrorist attack on Indian soil. The relatively weak government in New Delhi would be forced to retaliate, while the even weaker civilian government in Islamabad would be helpless as the military would monopolise decision-making and move towards war, seeing a perfect opportunity to justify its enormous budget, political power, as well as the abovementioned security doctrine.

Dr. Cohen sees three major obstacles to an improvement in bilateral relations. First, India's indecision towards Pakistan has persisted, ranging between wanting to annihilate its neighbour to developing a fruitful political and economic relationship. Second, Pakistan's incoherence also poses a major obstacle to improved relations. While Pakistan now once again has a civilian government, this government has its hands tied due to its fractious inter-party politics as well as its inability to rely on democratic institutions. At the same time, the military has maintained at least some of its grip on power, and terrorist activity has increased significantly since 2001; as many analysts would argue, this latter development has been a product of the close ties that exist between militants, Pakistan's military and the ISI. The third major obstacle to long-term rapprochement is the fragmented international approach to the issue. While most countries have expressed serious concern, a concerted effort to resolve or ameliorate the issue does not exist.

CIVIL-MILITARY RELATIONS AND CIVIL SOCIETY IN PAKISTAN

The Pakistani military remains the most powerful institution in Pakistan today and, according to Dr. Ayesha Siddiqa, hinders democratisation and institution-building. She envisages one of three possible scenarios for the future of civil-military relations in the country, ranging from the military's gradual loss of power to the Zardari administration, to the ousting of the current government by a political faction that nurtures closer ties to the military – if not the military itself.

In the first scenario, the military loses some of its power because President Zardari succeeds in implementing tactical change through a constitutional shift, taking power away from the military. In the second scenario, the military loses some of its power in the short-run as President Zardari succeeds in asserting himself as the legitimate leader of the country, and thus out-manoeuvres the armed forces to gain more power. In this case, the empowerment of political forces depends on the government's ability to strengthen civilian political institutions and fill the legitimacy gap between the public and politicians. In a third scenario, Zardari's Pakistan People's Party (PPP) government is replaced by Nawaz Sharif's Pakistani Muslim League (PML-N), a party that nurtures a closer relationship with the military and which has historically been suspicious of the PPP's intentions.

The factors at the root of the military's dominance of Pakistani politics are to be found in structural inefficiencies in the Pakistani political infrastructure.

These inefficiencies are the result of a system of patronage politics, elite interests inherently tied to this two-way patronage system, as well as a lack of civilian institutions. This leads to a military hegemony in the country, which has allowed the legal, political, and constitutional roles of the military to remain undefined, with no proper checks or control mechanisms. At the same time, the military is present at all levels of the formal and informal economy, thus enjoying a presence in the Pakistani national market which cannot be quantified due to what Dr. Siddiqa referred to as the "kleptocratic distribution practices" of the army.

Due to the immense power which it wields, societal perceptions are largely shaped by the military, which through its ideological influence defines social discourse and leads people to subscribe to its "right-wing point of view". Dr. Siddiqa said that this growingly conservative perspective – which has strengthened a "right-wing security state" – is detrimental to civil society and prevents the emergence of a human security perspective. It also benefits the military, the religious parties, the conservative political parties and the militants. Nonetheless, Pakistan's public opinion differs between different regions, social classes, and tribes, which means that a generalisation of the Pakistani "street", i.e. the general public opinion, is not possible. The Group Executive Director of a leading media group highlighted that there is no national unity in Pakistan, and that a Pakistani 'street' does not exist. Instead,

Pakistanis feel an allegiance to Allah, and fault-lines are drawn along sectarian and social divides.

A FRAMEWORK FOR UNDERSTANDING PAKISTAN'S SECURITY

The second module of the conference focussed specifically on Pakistan's immediate security situation. U.S. Army War College Prof. Larry Goodson provided a succinct framework for understanding Pakistan's security, remarking that five interacting and interlinked factors, described below, shape Pakistan.

Ethno-linguistic Regionalism

Pakistan does not have one single national interest. Rather, several sub-national groups hailing from four ethno-linguistically constructed provinces (Punjab, Sindh, Baluchistan, and NWFP), the FATA, and three other federal territories make up a federal republic. This republic is dominated by Punjab, which is home to about half of Pakistan's population and is by far the most prosperous region.

Demographic and Socio-economic Realities

Pakistan is one of the most populated countries in the world, home to approximately 170 million people, of which 61% are under 24 years of age. The country is subject at times to extreme economic hardship, and corruption is still widespread.

Pakistan's Human Development Index (HDI), an indicator combining measures of life expectancy, literacy, educational attainment, and GDP per capita, ranks the country 139th in the world, with up to 40% of Pakistan's people living below the poverty line.

These numbers, exacerbated by the current-account crisis and the economic crisis, prompted a US$7.6 billion IMF bailout in November 2008. In spite of these realities, the budget for education in Pakistan in 2007 was only US$400 million, while defence spending remained the single-largest budget item at US$4.5 billion. This, in Prof. Goodson's view, clearly reflects the state's priorities.

Political Pendulum

The Pakistani political pendulum swings between weak and underdeveloped civilian institutions on one hand, and a very strong army on the other. The federal system concentrates the majority of the power at the centre, making for a dominant executive and a legislative and judiciary that are generally feeble, at times even entirely superfluous. For its part, the military – the world's seventh largest standing army – has ruled the country on four separate occasions for a total of 35 years. It has an institutionalised position in politics, civil society, as well as in the economy and industry, and as previously mentioned often dictates foreign policy directions, especially with regards to India.

Geopolitical and Geostrategic Position

Pakistan finds itself in a critical geographic location: India has been the "resented big brother" ever since partition in 1947, while Afghanistan has proven to be a perennial source of trouble. China, despite the military assistance which it has provided to Pakistan for decades, is often regarded with scepticism. The United States, a traditional ally of Pakistan, is far away geographically and seen by many to be a "fair weather friend".

From Islam to Talibanisation

Pakistan was founded as an Islamic republic and the homeland to the Muslims of South Asia, as a country separate from its Hindu-dominated neighbour. Islamist militancy was not always a threat to Pakistan's security. Many regard the Afghanistan war of the 1980s as having created the conditions that opened Sunni-dominated Pakistan to deeper religious violence. Since then, militancy has gradually expanded in Pakistan. However, it was not until the U.S. invasion of Afghanistan, in December 2001, that the Taliban began to shift to the frontier regions of Pakistan, from where they have since coordinated their activities. Since 2001, these regions have become the epicentre of the global jihad, with the Taliban gradually taking control of the FATA, before slowly moving eastwards to NWFP, as well as Punjab and Baluchistan in the south. Since then, sectarian, anti-secular, and anti-Western violence emanating from these regions have become a serious issue in Pakistan and abroad. In 2008, a CIA official referred to a near-mathematical "incrementality" in fatalities when a terrorist attack originated in the FATA.

The Security of Pakistan's Nuclear Weapons

A presentation an official of the government of Canada assessed that Pakistan's nuclear assets are more vulnerable than any other nuclear country's atomic weapons have ever been. Nonetheless, Pakistan's nuclear program is expanding, thus increasing the chance that Islamabad will lose control over at least some of its nuclear weapons. The official, whose presentation was based on publicly available information, reported that Pakistan has approximately 60 to 80 nuclear weapons, as well as large amounts of highly enriched uranium (heu) and plutonium, which could be turned into weapons-grade material.

In light of the internal weaknesses of Pakistan's state apparatus, corruption and the military's close ties to Islamist militants, Pakistan's nuclear program has become a significant preoccupation in several capitals, most notably in Washington D.C., where the current and previous administrations have had serious fears about the security of Pakistan's weapons. While then-President Musharraf stated in 2007 that his country's nuclear safeguards are "already the best in the world", the U.S. has invested almost US$100 million since 2001 to protect Pakistani nuclear weapons from theft and subsequent use by terrorists. This aid, says the official, includes training and technical assistance, to enhance what is known in atomic energy circles as nuclear surety, i.e. the material, personnel, and procedures that contribute to the safety, security, reliability, and control of nuclear weapons, thus assuring no nuclear accidents, incidents, unauthorised use, or degradation.

While these and other measures have prompted officials such as Adm. Mike Mullen, Chairman of the Joint Chiefs of Staff of the U.S. Armed Forces, to assert that the security of the weapons is not in jeopardy at this point, many are not convinced. One of the reasons for this is that one of the principles of nuclear surety stipulates that weapons are to be concentrated in few places, rather than having them scattered across several locations and storage facilities, as was the case in the Soviet Union. However, Pakistan has practiced the opposite tactic, namely a dispersion of its weapons, in order to make it harder for India to destroy its nuclear stockpiles and thus increase its own second-strike capabilities against a possible Indian attack.

Untangling the Militants' Many Agendas

The intricacies and complexities of terrorism and militancy in Pakistan cannot be understated. Militancy is not the result of terrorist outfits pursuing the same or even similar objectives. The Norwegian Institute of International Affairs' Laila Bokhari aimed to untangle the militants' many agendas, before Sciences Po's Mariam Abou Zahab provided details about insurgency groups in FATA and NWFP. Pakistani insurgents may be grouped into four categories, according to Ms. Bokhari. However, individuals have been shown to move from one category to another for ideological and pragmatic reasons, creating diffuse mixes. The four categories are:

A) Cross-border terrorist groups, including those who attacked targets in India or in Afghanistan. A prominent example is Lashkar-e-Taiba (LeT), the group allegedly responsible for the Mumbai attacks;

B) Sectarian groups, both Shiite and Sunni, have traditionally been active on a more local basis;

C) Traditional jihadi groups, some linked to al-Qaida, have increasingly and predominantly attacked Western targets;

D) Groups targeting symbols of the Pakistani establishment, in the process attempting to challenge the legitimacy of the state itself. Such groups are protesting the "apostate" leadership as well as Pakistan's armed forces.

Grouping terrorist outfits into different categories may be useful to create an analytical framework, but it may also create a dangerous precedent by oversimplifying the matter. Ms. Bokhari argued that the fault-lines between these different groups must be analysed further in order to understand the ideological nuances and the differing agendas and purposes at play.

Extremist Networks in FATA and NWFP

The FATA, which includes North and South Waziristan, has been described as today's nucleus of the Pakistani Taliban movement (Tehrik-i-Taliban Pakistan, or TTP) as well as a critical safe haven for the Afghan Taliban. The area is home to an estimated six million people, and serves as a training ground and main sanctuary for the Taliban, which benefits from the lawlessness of the region to plan cross-border attacks on coalition and Afghan troops in Afghanistan. The FATA is so dissimilar to either Afghanistan or Pakistan that it is often referred to as Talibanistan, a lawless frontier region far beyond the control and influence of anyone.

The militancy in the region is not limited to Taliban activity and recruitment. Ms. Abou Zahab highlighted that while most of the tribal people conducting terrorist activity in this region overlap in at least some of their ideology – they oppose the Western-backed Afghan state as well as the Pakistani regime, thereby creating a "defensive jihad" against NATO forces and the Pakistani state – there is not one monolithically structured and disciplined organisation that coordinates all terrorist activity. Rather, on top of a clearly defined Taliban offensive against the above-mentioned targets, there exist widespread tribal differences and animosity which lead to several inter-tribal conflicts (e.g., the war between Mahsuds and Wazirs), intra-tribe conflicts between dominant and minor clans of a single tribe, wars over resources (e.g., water), as well as sectarian wars between Sunnis and Shiites. This mix of several civil wars in the area has created a large displaced population, creating in it vulnerabilities that makes it prone to recruitment by the Taliban.

Given the different ideologies and animosity described above, it is also unclear to observers what the relationship between the Pakistani Taliban and the al-Qaida network may be. While it is generally accepted that there are some links and that the Taliban continue – as prior to 11 September 2001 – to provide al-Qaida with invaluable protection and sanctuary, it is unclear just how concrete those links are. In fact, it remains difficult to determine whether there are structural links between the organisations that go beyond ideological likemindedness and criminal activities of elements linked to the Pakistani taliban to finance missions.

In NWFP, the smallest of Pakistan's four provinces with a population of just over 20 million people, problems related to militancy are similar to those described in FATA, although not quite as widespread yet. The trend in NWFP, according to Ms. Abou Zahab, is towards further deterioration, as religious extremists have expanded their activity from the FATA to NWFP over the past years. A widely held view in NWFP is that the Talibanisation of the province is a direct result of military operations in FATA, which has led the Taliban to move to other areas of the country. As this trend continues, analysts worry that the NWFP will soon spiral to the same levels as FATA.

In recent months, inter- and intra-tribal conflict and sectarianism have also increased tremendously in NWFP. Signs of class war within different Pashtu tribes have developed, as the majority Pashtu population has struggled with important socio-economic issues. Ms. Abou Zahab also stressed that an important and often overlooked aspect of Pakistan's security is sectarian violence between Shiite and Sunni Muslims. In the last year, militants have increasingly targeted Shiite Muslims, and there are several accounts of members of the armed forces being kidnapped, with the Sunnis later being released while Shiites are beheaded. Many argue that the phenomenon of sectarian violence directed at Shiites has increased especially since the Pakistani military's siege and subsequent storming of Lal Masjid (Red Mosque) in Islamabad in July 2007.

Today, eight of the NWFP's 24 districts have been declared high-security zones by the Pakistani government, demarcating these zones as areas in which Taliban activity is expanding and the chances of terrorist attacks have increased. The number of terrorist attacks in NWFP has increased steadily over the past year, and there is now a widely held view that the police are either helpless or unwilling to challenge the Taliban's expanding influence in the province. The Taliban are asserting themselves as the faction best equipped to perform in areas such as law enforcement, governance, and even the judicial process.

The movement has asserted itself as a strict enforcing agency of sharia law, punishing individuals for behaviour that is deemed anti-Islamic. Accounts from NWFP, which includes the Swat Valley, previously one of the most sought-after tourist destinations in South Asia, include such acts as men being punished for shaving their facial hair, or women for attending school. In several cases, the threat of using acid as a punishment for anti-Islamic crimes was reported in early 2009.

PAKISTAN AND ITS NEIGHBOURS

Afghanistan and Pakistan: One War in Two Countries

After hearing about internal issues in Pakistan on the first day of the conference, the second day focussed on Pakistan in the context of regional and global issues. Having noted that India continues to be the dominant issue for Pakistanis, the Centre for International Governance Innovation's Mark Sedra explored the relationship between Pakistan and its neighbour to the west: Afghanistan. This relationship has always been of great significance, having been marked by the anti-Soviet jihad in the 1980s and the corresponding birth of the Taliban, as well as Pashtun nationalism, a movement by both Pakistani and Afghan Pashtuns to unite and form a separate country of Pashtunistan in the border region.

In 2001, the relationship between Afghanistan and Pakistan entered a new era, as Taliban forces were expelled from Afghanistan by coalition forces and subsequently created new bases in Pakistan's border regions. Cross-border insurgency in both directions started to increase immediately after the invasion of Afghanistan, as the Pakistani government of then-President Musharraf was unable, or unwilling, to contain the insurgency especially in Waziristan. Mr. Sedra said the vast majority of supplies for coalition troops in Afghanistan had to pass through Pakistan via the Khyber Pass, a route that has been a target for Taliban militants on several occasions. Despite these issues and the challenges in curbing this activity, Islamabad continued to enjoy the support of the U.S., and the Bush administration was convinced that the Musharraf regime, backed by the Pakistani military, was the only faction capable of keeping the country's nuclear weapons away from militants, while at least maintaining control over the majority of the country's territory. At the same time, it became increasingly evident that ties between the militants and at least some elements of the Pakistani military, especially the ISI, persisted.

Today, as Afghanistan's president, Hamid Karzai, and the relatively new civilian government of Asif Ali Zardari in Islamabad appear intent on increasing cooperation, there is hope that the situation will become more stable. Moreover, President Obama promised a surge of troop numbers in Afghanistan on several occasions prior to taking office. This military commitment may be accompanied by several development initiatives led by USAID. Since 2001, there has also been a Tripartite Commission between Afghanistan, Pakistan and the U.S., to which NATO-ISAF is now also a member. The Ottawa conference heard that this Tripartite Commission has started to work very well in the recent past, allowing for optimism that progress on some of the bilateral issues of concern, such as border protection, will be made in the near future.

While there are thus several measures that leave room for optimism, Mr. Sedra also contended that Pakistan is currently following a dual-policy strategy in Afghanistan. If Pakistan has many reasons to stabilise Afghanistan, Islamabad is also concerned about the growing Indian influence in Afghanistan, and may wish to keep the country unstable. In fact, some suggest that Islamabad, and more specifically the ISI, sees Afghanistan as an extension of Pakistan's struggle with India. The reasons for this intriguing development are the increasingly strengthened ties between India and Afghanistan under the Karzai government, which have allowed Indian consulates to open in Jalalabad, Kandahar, Herat, and Mazar-e-Sharif. Another factor amongst a plethora of measures that have indicated a tightening in bilateral India-Afghanistan relations is that President Karzai also addressed the possibility of inviting India to help train the Afghan army. He also indicated he could ask India to help in the construction of a major dam project in northeastern Afghanistan. Last summer, India's prime minister, Manmohan Singh, also announced developmental assistance to Afghanistan totalling US$450 million, in addition to the US$750 million already committed by India to implement projects in various sectors (infrastructure development, education, health care and social development). Given these developments, some have argued that it was no coincidence that the Indian embassy in Kabul was the target of a terrorist attack in the summer of 2008; the ISI was the immediate suspect in the eyes of many observers.

Pakistan and India: Eternal Rivalry

In order to illustrate effectively the wide-ranging complexities of the India-Pakistan relationship, Balsillie School of International Affairs director Ramesh Thakur described the latter by situating it within three analytical frameworks: nationalism, nuclear weapons, and terrorism.

Viewing the two countries through the prism of nationalist ideology and the bilateral issue of Kashmir, Dr. Thakur posited that as a territorial dispute Kashmir would by now have been resolved, with reasonable people on both sides. What makes the dispute intractable, he said, is three competing views of nationalism that exist in the relationship: Indian secular nationalism, Pakistani religious nationalism, and Kashmiri ethnic nationalism. Pakistan, created as the national homeland for the subcontinent's Muslims, has had difficulty accepting that Kashmir, whose majority is Muslim, should not be part of Pakistan. India, as a secular country, has had difficulty accepting that the Union's only Muslim-majority state should join Pakistan. The perspective of India considering Pakistan as an artificial state and wanting to weaken it is shared amongst many Pakistanis but not amongst many Indians. Pakistanis' fear is supported by India's role in 1971, leading to the break-up of Pakistan and the subsequent creation of Bangladesh.

The India-Pakistan relationship can also be assessed through the prism of nuclear capabilities. Here, Dr. Thakur reported that India has always seen itself as having pursued nuclear power because of its ambition to become a global science and technology powerhouse, with the motivation to build nuclear weapons, and keep them under civilian control, coming later. In Pakistan, however, nuclear weapons as a deterrent against India were the prime motivation in the interest in nuclear technology. This is evidenced by the fact that the military alone controls the weapons in Pakistan and that Pakistan has still not adopted a no-first-use policy, and thus reserves the right to resort to nuclear weapons in retaliation to a conventional attack by India.

Lastly, viewing the relationship in the context of terrorism, Dr. Thakur contended that Pakistan's efforts in curbing cross-border terrorism by Pakistan-based terrorists have been half-hearted. However, given the severity of the Mumbai attacks and the effects they have had on the Indian psyche, he, too, predicted that India would feel compelled to respond in a significant and forceful way if another attack was to happen on Indian soil.

Pakistan, Central Asia, and the Web of Resource Politics

An analysis of Pakistan in the context of the wider region must also include an assessment of the relationship which the country nurtures with its Central Asian counterparts, with which Pakistan has traditionally had strong commercial and political relations due to its religious ties to these predominantly Muslim countries. However, as the RAND Corporation's Christine Fair presented it, starting in the 1990s, Pakistan was blamed by some Central Asian states for a wave of militancy in the neighbourhood, putting a strain on these relations.

With Iran, Pakistan enjoyed particularly good relations since partition, when Tehran was the first government to officially recognise Pakistan's statehood. In the 1960s and the 1970s, a strategic dimension was added to the bilateral relationship, as both became members to the Central Treaty Organization (CENTO), a U.S.-sponsored pact designed to contain the Soviet threat. The two states were also united in their battle against a widespread insurgency in Baluchistan, which runs through Pakistan, Afghanistan and Iran. In spite of this generally sound bilateral relationship, bilateral ties became increasingly strained in the 1980s, when Iran grew wary of Pakistan's sponsorship of the Taliban in Afghanistan. The events of 11 September 2001, says Dr. Fair, then provided Islamabad with an opportunity to shed the negative image which had followed it around for two decades; but it failed to do so amidst rising terrorist activity emanating from its territory, coupled with political instability, as well as uncertainty surrounding its nuclear weapons. Some observers maintain that Pakistan and Iran enjoy good relations, based on Pakistan's past sharing of nuclear know-how and assets with its Iranian neighbour. In reality, stresses Dr. Fair, Iran is now distrustful of Pakistan's ability to be a responsible steward of nuclear weapons precisely because of its poor record on issues of proliferation and its fear that weapons could end up in the hands of militants. Conversely, many Pakistanis also see Iran as being at the root of some of its problems, as the sectarian violence in Pakistan can be directly attributed to the Iran-Iraq war (1980-1988).

Pakistan and Saudi Arabia

Pakistan and Saudi Arabia have a strategic relationship that is deeply inter-dependent and highly discreet. In the words of former Saudi intelligence chief, Prince Turki al-Faisal, it is "one of the closest [bilateral] relationships in the world without any formal treaty". According to Michael Kalin from the Privy Council Office's International Assessment Staff, there are three main drivers for Saudi-Pakistani cooperation:

a) Islamic solidarity and a similar political crisis of legitimacy experienced by both states. Beyond Islam's status as the nominal raison d'être of both Pakistan and Saudi Arabia, the rulers of each state have promoted political Islam as a response to a problem of regime legitimacy at home. In Saudi Arabia, the royal family has cultivated the Kingdom's religious establishment to justify the unelected rule of a regime whose survival depends on an unpopular defensive alliance with the United States. In Pakistan, political Islam can be historically understood as an effort by Islamabad to strengthen the central government against the centrifugal forces of various regional and ethnic identities.

b) Saudi-Pakistani ties are actively driven by complementary military and economic profiles. The wealthy but vulnerable Saudi state and its poor but militarily powerful Pakistani counterpart have each employed their respective strengths to offset the other's weaknesses. Riyadh has lavished more financial aid on Pakistan than any country outside the Arab world while Pakistan has historically provided thousands of military personnel to Saudi Arabia to protect the Kingdom.

c) Saudi-Pakistani ties flourish within the context of the alliance that both states enjoy with Washington. Both Saudi Arabia and Pakistan were firmly anti-Communist during the Cold War and from 1982-1990, both countries worked with the United States to arm and train the Afghan mujahideen. Both states seek to pursue two major but often divergent foreign policy objectives: highlighting their respective value as an ally to Washington while also enhancing their status to be defenders of Islam.

In light of these realities, the Saudi-Pakistani relationship must be seen as part of a triangular axis with the United States, said Mr. Kalin and it is precisely for this reason that Saudi Arabia's recent foray into Afghan reconciliation talks cannot be understood without regard to Riyadh's broader and overriding interests in working closely with both Pakistan and the United States.

Strategy and World Politics

One module of the conference addressed Pakistan's role in current world politics. This included a debate on U.S.-Pakistan relations and counter-insurgency efforts, as well as an exploration of Pakistan's standing in the Muslim world.

The United States' unequivocal objective in Pakistan has been to transform the state into a stable entity that can help it achieve its chief objective in its fight against terrorism. In the pursuit of these goals, the U.S. has spent an estimated US$11 billion in Pakistan since the end of 2002, investing in such projects as nuclear weapons safety, strengthening the armed forces, and development initiatives through USAID. Nonetheless, Dr. Christine Fair was clear in conceding that the U.S. has failed in its objective to stabilise the country. This failure is the result of several factors, amongst them:

1) The vast majority of the expenditure has gone to the military, with the objective of strengthening the latter so

that it can successfully tackle rising militancy, as well as protect the Afghanistan border from the Pakistani side. However, despite these investments, the performance of the forces has not improved, while it continues to follow its own strategy. This favourable bias towards the military has bred resentment across Pakistan, as development aid to the Pakistani people is limited to approximately US$100 million per annum.

2) The U.S. has thus far refrained from attaching conditions to the distribution of aid to Pakistan. This is, in Dr. Fair's eyes, because Washington believes that if it continues to provide supply-side assistance, the U.S. will win the hearts and minds of Pakistanis. However, she stresses, there is no empirical evidence to support this hypothesis.

3) The U.S. has been very indecisive in its policy towards Pakistan, which has been the result of not comprehending the realities on the ground. While al-Qaida was from the beginning the defined adversary, Kashmiri terrorist outfits were largely ignored, as were the links between these groups and al-Qaida, and the Taliban were not recognised.

As a measure to address these failures, the expert indicates that the U.S. may first need to mitigate the trust deficit which exists between Pakistan and the U.S. Dr. Fair says that this trust deficit is built on several half-truths which have led Pakistan not only to question America's real intentions, but also to assume that the U.S. is only working for its own benefit.

If this trust deficit is overcome, she sees an opportunity for other issues of bilateral concern to be tackled more fruitfully. These bilateral issues would include reforming the judiciary and civilianising the military state through institution-building. As a media executive noted, however, it will be difficult to overcome the trust deficit if U.S. drone attacks into Pakistani territory continue.

Lastly, Dr. Fair also believes that Washington should rethink its cost-benefit analysis of what it does for Pakistan. This would involve conditioning U.S. aid in the country, and demanding real results from Pakistan in return for continued assistance. This may after all alleviate the problems related to Pakistan's inability to deal with the threats of al-Qaida and the Taliban. Another approach would be to bring traditional American allies into the fold. In following this objective, she indicated that the U.S. could make use of the political capital it has gained through the election of Barack Obama.

Regarding Pakistan and its place in the Muslim world, a former head of a state-run television network stated that Pakistan is now experiencing the tribal divide between Sunnis and Shiites which other Muslim countries have long experienced, as the tribal system continues to be very strong across the Muslim world. However, in Pakistan these problems have surfaced mostly as a result of Pakistan being used as a battleground for proxies. Noting that neither the Taliban nor al-Qaida existed in Pakistan at its birth, the media executive lamented that the U.S. supported the regime of General Musharraf for many years because of its belief that this regime was the best way of ensuring that Pakistan would remain stable.

Conclusion: One Country, Many Futures

The conference featured a multiplicity of views on different aspects of Pakistan's security today and in the future. Discussions allowed to identify several drivers which will influence the future of the country's security. Those addressed internal, regional and global issues.

The conclusions that can be drawn from the presentations and discussion are far from positive: as the centre of jihadist terrorism today, Pakistan has a monumental task to handle, and it will be a long road to overcome this scourge if the country does not act in a resolute and united manner.

The country must also face a faltering economy, widespread socioeconomic problems, ongoing tensions with its Indian neighbour, as well as developments in Afghanistan. While Pakistan now once again has a civilian government, a lack of democratic institutions and the limited prevalence of the rule of law make for a precarious situation.

In light of these problems, the concluding module of the conference offered three alternative scenarios for Pakistan's future. In developing these three scenarios, Lt.-Gen. Talat Masood (ret'd) considered the drivers of change which were discussed throughout the conference. These scenarios, described below, are meant as tools to stimulate further discussion.

The Best Case

In the hypothetical best case scenario, Pakistan's government succeeds in creating a strategic environment that can overcome the major challenges confronting the country today. The civilian and military leadership embrace the need for change and discard their outdated policies.

Reflecting the resilience of Pakistan's people, the leadership realises that the people are hungry for change, and Islamabad moves to build democratic institutions and a judicial system on which the people can rely. The military surrenders some of its political power and subordinates itself to the civilian government, redefining its role to match the realities of the 21st century.

This means that asymmetrical warfare is completely abandoned, Pakistan becomes a responsible steward of nuclear weapons, the military abandons its role in everyday politics, and the army's budget decreases so that emphasis can be put on other areas of the economy.

The major changes illustrated here are then applied to re-establish power and the rule of law in the tribal areas and the frontier areas in general. The Taliban and other militant movements are progressively brought under control as the people of the region realise that the violence and ideology these movements champion have not resulted in prosperity.

The insurgency in Baluchistan, which was intricately linked to the militancy in the other regions, also subsides, and former insurgent groups are integrated into the mainstream political process. As a result of these internal developments, the insurgency in Afghanistan also begins to subside, as the Taliban have lost their logistical base and sanctuary. The warlords are on the retreat, and the Afghan government in Kabul, whether under a new leadership or a re-invented Hamid Karzai, asserts itself with the support of the international community.

In the meantime, Pakistan's relationship with India also improves, because no further terrorist attacks take place on Indian soil. The re-invented civilian leadership in Islamabad has realised that the military can no longer sponsor, or even tolerate, terrorist activity.

This leads to a rapid decline of terrorist incidents in Pakistan, and cross-border terrorism into India is also finally curbed. The thaw in bilateral relations, which was witnessed prior to the events of late 2008, gains momentum again, and India and Pakistan finally make concrete steps towards a settlement of the Kashmir issue. India appreciates that peace in the region is the only scenario under which it will be able to attain great power status, and thus steps up its efforts in trying to find a viable solution on issues of mutual concern.

As a result, militancy in Kashmir also loses momentum as Kashmiris demand a lasting political solution to the Kashmir question and thus rise up against terrorism. Organisations like the LeT and the Jamaat-ud-Dawa (JuD) slowly disintegrate, suffering under the loss of public support while also no longer receiving the support of the military.

The economy also takes a significant turn for the better. The global economic downturn ends, and the Pakistani economy feels the ripple effects of this development. The IMF package agreed in late 2008 leads to significant improvements in economic policy. Because the leadership in Islamabad has adopted new measures to create civilian institutions and the rule of law, security improves and the economy once again has room to grow. Eager to meet the needs of a young population, foreign investors are more inclined to invest in Pakistan again, and trade goes up as international attitudes towards Pakistan improve and investors no longer have to fear for their ventures in Pakistan.

In general, Pakistan is again respected on the international scene, and relations improve with China, Iran, the greater Muslim-majority world, as well as with the United States. Tourism becomes the norm, as people from the world over visit resorts in Kashmir and Swat, and all regions of Pakistan attract tourists just like its neighbour, India, has done for a decade. As the economy grows steadily at an annual rate of 7% to 8%, the demobilised jihadi segment of society is reintegrated into the mainstream economy, reducing the likelihood of a retreat to extremist activities. Poverty in general subsides greatly, people have access to drinking water and food, and the budget for education is increased.

The Worst Case

The second scenario is diametrically opposed to the previous one. In it, the insurgencies currently affecting Pakistan's security continue to fester. The security forces are unable, or unwilling, to contain the Taliban and other groups in the FATA and NWFP, and these groups succeed in gradually spreading further east and south, in the process taking full control of FATA and NWFP, while dominating large parts of Baluchistan and even Punjab. Terrorism increases in scope, costing many lives on a consistent basis. The government has now widely lost control over huge areas of its territory, and the Taliban have asserted themselves as the main power in these parts.

A similar development transpires in Pakistan-administered Kashmir (Azad Kashmir). The LeT and JuD continue to play a significant role in the daily lives of Kashmiris, taking political initiatives while also using the territory to plan terrorist attacks across the border in India. These attacks target Indian security forces in Indian-administered Kashmir (Jammu and Kashmir) and other Indian cities, causing relations with India to deteriorate significantly. India now sees no other alternative than to begin operations in Pakistan in order to eliminate training camps as well as logistical centres of LeT and JuD in Azad Kashmir. Tensions increase, and a military stand-off ensues in a repeat of the 2001-02 crisis. As a result, Pakistan once again concentrates its entire military forces on the border with India, leaving the rest of the country to be an easy target for the Taliban and other forces moving in from the west.

At a national level, the strategies and policies adopted by the government are oblivious to the problems and realities in the country. The rule of law and constitutionalism has found no place, and functional democratic institutions continue to be rare or absent. At the same time, the army continues to wield incredible power, dominating national politics and the economy. The social sector is neglected, poverty and socio-economic hardship are on the rise, and the service sector stagnates.

The combination of a degenerating economy, a rising militancy and poor leadership in Islamabad lead to a total collapse of the country. As people realise that they can no longer rely on the government, more regional crises unfold, militants gain ever more power, and ethnic and sectarian violence spread as the country effectively atomises into a free-for-all".

As a result of these developments, foreign investment has completely vanished from Pakistan, as investors worry about the lack of rule of law, a non-reliable financial system, and a militancy that poses threats to foreigners anywhere in the country. The international community is forced to deal with competing centres of power, which in turn further erodes the authority of the central government. This leads the army once again to stage a military coup d'État, dismissing bureaucrats, politicians, and judges. In essence, Pakistan is no longer a cohesive state and has ceased to exist politically.

A Nuanced Case

Lt.-Gen. Masood described a Pakistan whose economic performance remains volatile and extremely uncertain in the foreseeable future. Growth picks up in 2011, only to slide again to a relatively low annual 4% thereafter, shaking the confidence of investors already unimpressed by the government's inability to launch serious economic reforms. Law and order improve slightly, but militancy and terrorism persist, especially in Baluchistan, FATA, and NWFP. Criminality and trafficking of all kinds make for a permanent economic "backbone" in FATA and NWFP. As the government proves unable to undertake social reforms, poverty worsens and unemployment increases. Moreover, the military is unwilling to surrender some power in the political and economic realm.

Some of these negative trends come to be neutralised by increased remittances from the diaspora and international assistance, when the economy improves globally. As the international community sees the urgency of the situation, international aid increases, and the November 2008 IMF package begins modestly to bear fruit. While the government is unable to quell the insurgency definitely, pressure on the military and the ISI increases, and cross-border terrorism into India starts to wane, leading to improving relations with India and progress in the peace process. In the West, terrorism also subsides, as international efforts are stepped up to help Pakistan secure the frontier areas with Afghanistan.

7

Fighting Terrorism: India and Central Asia

TERRORISM IN INDIA

India has been a victim of cross-border terrorism. Pakistan's role in spreading terrorist activities in Punjab and Jammu & Kashmir is well known. Proper coordination in interception and the commitment of the state and its police in countering such activity lay at the root of the control of terrorism in Punjab. But in the case of Kashmir, terrorism still persists because Pakistan has taken recourse to the concept of jehad to fulfil its long time policy of securing the independence of Kashmir from India. Actually Pakistan's inclination of using force to annex Kashmir has been apparent from the very beginning. The blueprint of aggression against Kashmir which was drawn in Pakistan in 1947-48 continues to be followed as policy even today. Attacks by infiltration in 1965, which led to the second Indo-Pakistan war, Pakistan's proxy war since 1988, and the Kargil offensive of 1999, confirm that Pakistan prefers to follow a policy of confrontation in Kashmir.

The separatist movement in Kashmir began to metamorphose into militancy in April 1988 due to the resurgence in the activities of the JKLF. Gradually, the movement was taken over by Pakistan-sponsored radical Islamist groups, making terrorism, insurgency and ethnic cleansing its main weapons. The involvement of Pakistan's intelligence agencies like ISI transformed the movement into a campaign of terror. By 1989, the situation underwent a sea-change with the use of sophisticated firearms and extensive use of explosives, which were smuggled in from Pakistan. Infiltration of Pakistan-trained Kashmiri youth also went up. Pakistan's role in sponsoring international terrorism and promoting insurgency in Jammu & Kashmir has been comprehensively unmasked in a report prepared by the Task Force on Terrorism and Unconventional Warfare, a Republican Research Committee of the US House of Representatives. It stated that Pakistan started playing this nefarious game as early as the 1970s, when Islamabad commenced training of Sikh militants and members of other separatist movements in India as part of Zulfiqar Ali Bhutto's strategy of "forward strategic depth", as also his effort to avenge the loss of Bangladesh. By mid-1980s, as brought out by the Task Force, "Islamabad began to broaden its horizons and set its sights on bigger goals", with growing experience in training, organising and running the mujahideen campaigns in Afghanistan and vast military supplies (through US, Saudi Arabia and other foreign assistance), Pakistan began "expanding its operation to sponsor and promote separatism and terrorism primarily in Kashmir, as a strategic long term programme."

It was estimated by the task force that a total of about 20,000 Kashmiris were trained and armed by/in Pakistan. "Logistical support, primarily weapons and ammunition, is brought from Pakistan. Training, organization, propaganda and indoctrination are carried out in the safety of Pakistani sanctuaries." It further stated that by 1990 there were well over 30 militant groups in Kashmir representing a wide array of ideologies. Of these, as many as 29 groups were receiving assistance and shelter in Pakistan. Yossef Bodansky, analyst with the Freeman Centre for Strategic Studies, aptly said: For Islamabad, the liberation of Kashmir is a sacred mission, the only task unfulfilled since Muhammad Ali Jinnah's days. Moreover, a crisis in Kashmir constitutes an excellent outlet for the frustration at home, an instrument for the mobilization of the masses, as well as gaining the support of the Islamist parties and primarily their loyalties in the military and the ISI.

These militant groups were used for terrorising the people of Kashmir, forcing them to accept rigid Wahabi codes of conduct, whip up anti-India feelings among them and to undertake various subversive missions to destabilise the state. They also acted as Pakistan's recruiting and motivating agents, whose job included sending disgruntled Kashmiri youth to Pakistan for undergoing arms training. During the most violent phase of terrorism in 1990-91, terrorist groups virtually ruled the congested urban areas of the major towns of the Valley. They ordered bandhs which brought life to a standstill and created fear. The police and other key elements of the government had now been penetrated by ISI agents, and a widening spiral of violence had engulfed the Valley. The Pakistani aim of isolating the people morally and physically from the state was largely achieved. This phase took a tremendous toll of Kashmiri lives and many popular Kashmiri leaders were gunned down for not cooperating with the terrorist groups.

Over the years, there was a considerable increase in Pakistani backed military organisations in the Valley. At one time there were about 120 militant groups in the Valley. With the passage of time some of the militant groups disintegrated due to security forces operations, while others merged with some of the major militant outfits. By September 30, 1999, there were about nine major militant outfits operating in the Valley. These are:

- Hizbul Mujahideen (HM)
- Jammu-Kashmir Liberation Front (JKLF)
- Lashkar-e-Taiba (LeT)
- Harkat-ul-Ansar (HuA)
- Harkat-ul-Mujahideen (HUM)
- Harkat-ul-Jehad-e-Islami (HUJI)
- Al Badar
- Tehriq-ul-Mujahideen (TUM)
- Dukh-Teran-e-Millat (DTM)

These militant outfits are carrying out their subversive activities in the Valley in pursuance of their jehad against India. And ISI of Pakistan is the main body facilitating movement of weapons across the borders to Kashmiri militants. It has set up training camps in Pak-occupied Kashmir and plays a crucial role in sustaining these camps. Everyone agrees that jehad cannot be carried on without the support of the ISI. Inded, the ISI's stranglehold over these groups is such that even an irresponsible press statement by a jehadi leader can put him in trouble. "Sometimes you find a junior level ISI clerk knocking at your door, carrying a clipping of your press statements asking for an explanation, recalls the once powerful chief of the Harkat-ul-Mujahideen, Maulana Fazlur Rehman. Adds another militant, "The moment the ISI feels that Jehad body is becoming powerful, it incites trouble in that party or tries to split it. Breaching the bigger groups by throwing money, arms and vehicles and putting new leaders in the driving seat is their style." Not only ISI, but the Pakistani Army and Pakistani terrorist groups also work in close coordination in their operations in the Indian State. There is hardly any difference between the attitude of the army and the militants towards the Kashmir issue and towards Pakistan's relations with India. This fact was highlighted in the recent past by the Kargil crisis which took the form of a major diplomatic brouhaha at regional level. The Kargil crisis reached a disturbing stage for India largely because of the inroads made by Pakistan-supported militants and soldiers into the Indian territory.

In the past few years, the form of militancy in Jammu and Kashmir has changed, showing greater evidence of the involvement of Afghan mercenaries in terrorist incidents in the Valley and the militants (who call themselves jehadis) have become more vocal in their militant calls against India. Maulana Masood Azhar, one of the three notorious militants released in exchange for the hostages on the Indian Airlines flight in December 1999, threatened to organise a 500,000 strong mujahideen force to wage jehad against India and declared that he would not rest until Kashmir is liberated. The casualties in encounters with security forces and identifying militants from Afghanistan and Pakistan has raised India's concern over the developments in Afghanistan too. As the Taliban captured nearly 90 per cent of Afghanistan by September-October 1998, the Afghan militants started pouring into the Valley. There are linkages between the Taliban and religious seminaries in Pakistan because the former claim to have been trained in these seminaries. It is a well known fact that the Pakistani Army has been actively involved in the internal affairs of Afghanistan. It has fought along with the

Taliban against the Rabbani regime in Kabul. Whenever the Taliban need reinforcement – many madrassas – the training centres for the Islamic militants and terrorists in Pakistan immediately send their students to Afghanistan, thus, the emergence of the Taliban on the political scene of Afghanistan in 1999 was the handiwork of Pakistan and the Taliban has become the main laboratory to prepare future Islamic mujahideen of Taliban variety. Lashkar-e-Taiba, which has been claiming close cooperation with the Taliban in Jammu and Kashmir, is one of the branches of this laboratory. In the three day conclave of Markaz-Dawa-Ul-Irshad. held in Muridke in Pakistan, it was claimed by the organisation that its militant wing Lakshkar-e-Taiba, is carrying out successful operations in Jammu and Kashmir. Pakistan has also released the list of persons belonging to Lashkar-e-Taiba from Pakistan and Afghanistan who were killed in encounters in Kashmir. Besides, the facts support the contention that these institutions work and thrive under the government patronage in Pakistan. The media has repeatedly highlighted the visits of the ministers in Pakistan to Markaz-Dawa-Ul-Irshad. Thus, India has equally large stakes in Afghanistan developments. The Taliban continues to threaten security in India; particularly after the Indian Airlines hijack and the drama in Kandahar, India has taken the Afghan problem quite seriously. As stated by Brahma Chellaney, "whatever the apparent and hidden costs of the Kandahar deal, the main lesson of the hijack crisis is obvious: India is under siege from fundamentalist terrorist forces fattened by the thriving heroin trade, plentiful supply of modern weapons, and aid from regimes lacking legitimacy". A leading national daily also deplored that, "the Indian Republic has been outmanoeuvered by terrorists and by a neighbour which supports them and unleashes them on this country" and that "the decision to free three notorious terrorists will be hailed as a great victory by Islamabad in its proxy war".

The US has also taken cognisance of these developments. US Under Secretary of State, Thomas Pickering, told the Voice of America, "Information about the military involvement of Pakistan with Afghanistan has come to our attention. We have talked to Pakistan about it. Pakistan is swift in its denial of that involvement, but we believe it continues to be true." Earlier, Clinton administration's top counter-terrorism official Michael A. Sheehan, while testifying before a Senate Sub-committee, accused Pakistan of becoming a base for terrorist attacks in India. "Within Pakistan, there are numerous Kashmiri separatist groups and sectarian groups involved in terrorism, which use Pakistan as a base … We have continued reports of Pakistani material support for some of these militants."

On the other hand, explaining the Pakistani stand, General Pervez Musharraf, Pakistan's military leader has asserted at various forums that the uprising in Kashmir is in no way terrorism, but jehad. He has drawn a clear distinction between acts of terrorism and the Islamic "freedom-struggle" in Kashmir. He argued that to call jehad in Kashmir as terrorism is not correct. According to him, "Islam does not preach terrorism – Islam believes in Jehad, a fight in the path of God. Wherever Muslims are being victimised or killed, Islam asks all Muslims to come to their aid."

It is expected that General Musharraf will speak in this manner to hide his support to the armed groups operating in Kashmir, who receive training, arms and financial aid on a permanent basis from Pakistan. Jehad, of course is not terrorism but what the so called jehadis are doing is terror in its most brutal form.

TERRORISM IN CENTRAL ASIA

Like it is doing in India, Pakistan is playing its game in the Central Asian region also. It is trying to involve these states in South Asian politics to bolster its own geo-strategic advantage. The fact that the newly accessible Central Asian region is experiencing an Islamic revival as a rallying point for cultural identity makes the region even more attractive for Pakistan. Pakistan wants to increase its political and economic role in Central Asia for three reasons:

- It views Central Asia as a territorial enticement to realise its quest for "strategic depth"
- It wants to encompass the 55 million Mulsim population of these states into a stream of "Islamisation"
- It has been taking economic steps to integrate them into one market in the form of ECO.

For attaining these three goals Pakistan is using the Islamic card and through strong support to the Taliban it is focussing on securing strategic and economic backing in Central Asia vis-a-vis India, winning friends in a region which had been totally shut away from Pakistani influence in the past. Central Asian Republics are more vulnerable to the Islamic card due to seventy years of religious oppression. Now there is a sudden resurgence of Islam in these republics. Islam as a religious tradition and as a form of cultural and national identity has acquired new meaning. In recent years, there has been a greater observance of Islamic rites, adoption of "Asslamwalaikum" as a form of greeting, religious marriages, performance of daily prayers and attendence at mosques. There has also been a phenomenal increase in the construction of religious places. The number of unaccredited mullahs has increased and there is proliferation of mosques particularly in rural areas. According to Soviet estimates the number of mosques has gone up to 5,000 from 160 during the past few years. A number of theological schools have been established in Azerbaijan and Tajikistan. Huge donations are voluntarily collected to be used for the construction of mosques and madrassas. Wherever there are no mosques, chaikhanas (teahouses) are used as prayer houses. Surveys conducted in Central Asia have shown that the level of religiosity among Muslims is higher than ten or twenty years ago, especially among the younger generation and intellectuals.

In fact, revival of Islam in the Central Asian Republics was a cultural, social and religious phenomenon as people publicly wanted to demonstrate their separateness from the communist system. Yet, popular knowledge of the religion of Islam was minimal and information on political activism, ideas and debates in the Islamic world beyond Central Asia was almost non existent. But the arrival of funds, Korans, literature and mullahs from Saudi Arabia, Iran and Pakistan spread their particular version of Islam in these countries. The vacuum created by the lack of leadership from the official Islamic hierarchy allowed fundamentalist groups to proliferate. The growing involvement of outside powers increased as Wahabi groups from Saudi Arabia, Iranian Revolutionary guards and some Sunni fundamentalist parties in Pakistan took advantage of the unprecedented political opportunities. The refusal of Central Asian Governments to allow Islamic education in government schools resulted in the spread of unofficial Islamic schools. People learned to bypass official Islam as they set up their own mosques and other structures.

At the beginning of 1992, M. Abdulla Islamailov (incharge of international relations at the Spiritual Administration of Religious Affairs of Central Asia) enthusiastically declared, "Three years ago Uzbekistan had eighty mosques. Today there are 1000 in the Namagan region alone (Namagan is one of the most religious regions). We had only two madrassas in the whole of the Soviet Union for the instruction of religious leaders. Today, there are twelve".

In March 1993, the Foreign Ministers of Uzbekistan and Tajikistan directly accused the fundamentalist Jamaat-e-Islami, that wanted an Islamic revolution in Central Asia, of arming and training Muslim radicals from their republics. During the Afghan war, the Jamaat had trained Muslim fundamentalists from Central Asia and encouraged them to fight alongside the mujahideen. By 1992 the Jamaat was helping these radicals in their own countries together with its main Afghan ally, Gulbuddin Hikmetyar. The Jamaat also helped Islamic Renaissance Party (IRP) leaders in Uzbekistan and Tajikistan to establish links with Arab Islamic groups.

It is worth mentioning that in the Ferghana Valley, which has always been the country's most religious region, radical Islamic elements are on the increase, and have transformed radical Islam into a stronghold for IRP. Today, it is the "educational centre" for Central Asia's fundamentalists. Most of Central Asia's religious figures are still in the 'proselytizing phase', more interested in training new clerics and increasing the level of religious learning among the population than in getting the laws of society to conform to those of Islam. A passive propaganda operation in underway in outlying villages in order to reconvert the population. "First Fergana, then Uzbekistan and then the whole Central Asia will become an Islamic state," said Imam Abdul Ahmad in Namagan. Imams said their aim is to overthrow the 'communist government of Karimov' and spearhead an Islamic revolution throughout

Central Asia. All this shows that Islam has regained its importance in Central Asia and provides a fertile ground to the Islamic fundamentalists for expansion. Pakistan's track record of support for religious fundamentalism, political extremism, international terrorism and armed subversion have become an important component of its regional strategy. Earlier it has used these tactics against India in Kashmir. The latest manifestation of this phenomenon is the Taliban, who were previously sent to fight in Afghanistan and presently in the Central Asian region. Apart from their destructive activities, Muslim extremists are carrying out a silent war of subversion and infiltration in the republics of Tajikistan and Uzbekistan. The long term aim is to arouse the religious and nationalist passions of the 30 million Muslims north of the Afghanistan border.

In fact, Tajikistan provides a special case since Islamic forces have played a very destructive role in that country's civil war. Fanatic Muslims of this republic were very actively supported by their mentors from Jamaat-i-Islami of Pakistan. In fact Pakistan had begun spreading the communal and ethnic virus much before the erstwhile Soviet state began showing cracks under the Gorbachev regime. Brutal violence against ethnic Russians of Dushanbe and other parts of the Tajik Republic had its roots in rapid Islamic fundamentalist orientation. After the declaration of independence by Tajikistan in September 1991, pro-fundamentalist elements hoped and tried to seize power. For the attainment of this objective, the Tajiks wedded to Islamic extremism crossed the Tajik border into Afghan territory. There Afghan mujahideen undertook to impart training in sophisticated weapons to these Tajik migrants and they conducted armed incursions into Tajik territory with the tacit support and connivance of Afghan warriors with the clear objective of bringing down the Tajik government and replacing it by a fundamentalist regime.

Now, despite a 1997 Peace Agreement that formally ended the civil war, the former Soviet Republic i.e. Tajikistan continues to be plagued by outbursts of violence involving groups that do not recognise the deal. On September 9, 2000, celebrating his country's Independence Day, Tajikistan's President Emomali Rakhmanov, expressed concern about the threat from across the border as represented by his opponents, called the United Tajik Opposition (UTO). Elements of the UTO have continued to battle his beleaguered regime despite the May 1997 agreement with this group and a sweeping parliamentary poll victory in early 2000. Rakhmanov appealed that the resolution of the long standing civil war across the border lay not in the use of force; but in the conducting of political negotiations by all concerned. But the fact remains that the Islamic rebels living in Tajikistan are keeping the security forces engaged in the region and there is a considerable increase in the number of rebel forces in Tajikistan, Kyrgyzstan and Uzbekistan. When the snow melts on the mountain passes between Uzbekistan, Tajikistan and Kyrgyzstan, the rebels typically migrate from Tajikistan to other countries, killing or taking hostage anyone who gets in their way. On August 9, 2000, about 100 armed men crossed into southern Kyrgyzstan from Tajikistan and clashed with Kyrgyz soldiers. Another group moved into Uzbekistan. The guards and invaders were reported to have suffered casualties.

The Taliban have stepped up help to disparate anti-government forces in Central Asian Republics that have all along been taking advantage of the volatile situation in the Pamirs and on both sides of the Hindu Kush mountains and the Karakorum range. The hilly terrain is difficult to guard. The border forces are ill-organised and ill paid. Besides, not used to border management some of the Central Asian Republics are still in the process of setting up check-posts and raising border-guards. While Russian forces guard the Tajik-Afghan border, the Uzbeks have sought American help. The US, besides training and kitting the border-guards while not supplying any lethal weapons—also provides transports like pick-ups, sniffer dogs and even handcuffs. The borders with CIS and alongwith Afghanistan, thanks to bad management and difficult terrain, remain highly porous. It is through this border, that anti-government forces, drug-traffickers and arms-peddlers operate.

Armed Islamist militants, using the Afghan sanctuaries, have been traversing the Tajik territory to join hands with United Islamic Movement of Uzbekistan, which wants to set up an Islamic state in the Ferghana Valley. Actually, after giving support to Tajik rebels, Pakistan's target has been Uzbekistan. The leadership of IMU—an extremist paramilitary group that the US Department of State ranks fourth in its list of international terrorist organisations—makes the backbone of bandit organisations. Judging by identity papers found on dead para-militaries, numerous Chechen, Arab, Afghan and European mercenaries are fighting side by side with Uzbeks under the command of warlord Jumabai Namangani – a Wahabi trained in Afghanistan and prominent among IMU chieftains. The IMU has its headquarters in Afghanistan. Several thousand Uzbek and Tajik religious extremists undergo training in Afghan-based camps for fighting and acts of terror and sabotage. It has announced that its primary aim was to focus world attention on the persecution of thousands of Muslims in Uzbekistan, and ultimately to overthrow the current Uzbek leadership and establish an Islamic state. Following this declaration, the IMU planned and conducted a series of terrorist attacks. Among attacks attributed to the IMU is an attack on an Uzbek policeman in Namagan in late 1997 and a series of bomb attacks in Tashkent in February 1997. The February bomb attacks were targeted against Uzbek President Islam Karimov. Though the President had a narrow escape, but in this attack 16 people were killed and 128 injured. The leader of the IMU, Tahir Yaldossev, then fled to Taliban controlled Afghanistan. In May 1999, the Taliban allowed Yaldossev to set up military camps in northern Afghanistan just a few miles from the Afghan-Uzbek border. Unconfirmed media reports say that he is training several hundred Islamic militants from Uzbekistan, Tajikistan and Kyrgyzstan, as well as Uighurs from Xinjiang Autonomous Region in China.

Initially, the Taliban denied having extended any help to the IMU. But in June 1999, when the Uzbek Government requested for the extradition of Tahir to Tashkent, it was rejected by the Taliban.

Besides Uzbekistan, IMU, led by Namangani, has recurited heavily in the Batken region of Kyrgystan, a swath of land on the border between southern Uzbekistan and northern Tajikistan. Batken has high unemployment and poverty, and the IMU has attempted to use this discontent for a political programme. Youth in Batken are quicker to join radicals than older traditional Muslims. According to social workers in southern Kyrgyzstan, the majority of homes have IMU leaflets advocating an Islamic state. High mercenary traffic in the region accounts for an increase of militants subordinate to IMU. Kyrgyz Security Council Chairman, Bolot Dzanuzakov reported in April, 2000 that Islamic militants from Afghanistan, Pakistan and Central Asian Republics collaborate in terrorist training and narco-trafficking. Kyrgyz officials are also wary that between 2,000 to 5,000 militants have received training in camps at Tavildara in Tajikistan.

IMU gets its funds by ransoming hostages, narco-trafficking and pooling resources from contacts at Kandahar, the headquarters of the Afghan-Taliban leadership. Ransoms have been lucrative over the year, specifically from the Kyrgyz government, which tendered $50,000 for the safe return of three district officials, and then $3 million for four Japanese geologists.

Thus, the Islamists are threatening the political leadership in all the three republics – Tajikistan, Uzbekistan and Kyrgyzstan. Although located at a distance from the Afghan border, Nursultan Nazarbayev of Kazakhstan is also threatened by the influx of these elements, which along with armed insurrection, also upset the social order with their fundamentalist Islam.

The Central Asian fears were heightened when the Taliban captured Taloqan, the key town that is also located on the main supply line of the Northern Alliance. The Taliban forces were within a few kilometers of the Tajik border. This prompted Tajikistan to put its forces on high alert. According to Voice of Russia, Nazarbayev demanded an emergency session of the UN Security Council to consider ways and means to combat the Taliban menace. Also, four of the CARs presidents made a joint appeal to various international organisations, pointing out that the Taliban were behind the extremist and terrorist outfits. A joint document was signed by the presidents of the four republics, after a two-day deliberation held recently under the aegis of the Council of Heads of States of Central Asian States. Urging the world bodies to intervene and resolve the Afghan conflict, the four Presidents accused the Taliban of diverting funds from narcotic deals for purchase of weaponry to continue its "fratricidal-war". Also, during the two day meet, Uzbekistan and Tajikistan signed a treaty of external friendship, which is expected to deepen relations between the two states.

However, there is little doubt that the Central Asian neighbours of Afghanistan are the worst sufferers. Free from the erstwhile Soviet Union, they are struggling to acquire their independent identities and walk the path of development. But the export of militancy that feeds off religion and earnings from drugs has bedeviled their political lives. Desperate armed groups have been operating from the sanctuaries in an unsettled Afghanistan. A UNI report from Moscow (April 3, 2000) said, "after burning their fingers in the Chechnya conflict, Afghanistan and Pakistan trained mercenaries are seeking fresh pastures to exploit their brand of fundamentalism, with Tajikistan, Kazakhstan and Kyrgyzstan emerging as their new hot-spots."

While the Taliban officially deny that they have any intentions of crossing the borders into Central Asia, their activities on the ground have caused massive, justifiable concern for the neighbours.

INDIA AND CENTRAL ASIAN REPUBLICS IN COMBATING TERRORISM

From the above discussion it is quite clear that the situation created by the Pakistan-Afghanistan combine has disturbed peace in India as well as in the Central Asian region. Both are victims of cross-border terrorism and consider it as a threat to regional peace and stability. The Central Asian Republics have been trying to combat terrorism by expanding cooperation among themselves and among like-minded countries. On the other hand, India has been seeking the help of the international community to contain terrorism from the very beginning. In this respect, convergence of their interests in combating terrorism is the next logical step.

In fact, India and the Central Asian Republics have had close historical, cultural and political ties since antiquity. In contemporary times, these have got further strengthened due to continued friendly and warm relations between India and the erstwhile Soviet Union. But with the demise of the Soviet Union, India faces the task of constructing a vibrant relationship under entirely new and challenging circumstances. Common perspective/approach on the issue of cross-border terrorism can provide a firm foundation for mutual cooperation between the two. A beginning has been made during the Uzbek President Islam Karimov's visit to India in May 2000.65 Most of the agreements signed during the visit were concerned with combating terrorism—common threat to security. In fact, this trip was aimed to underpin a common political understanding to counter common threats to their security.

India and Uzbekistan are aware that the spill-over of terrorism from the Afghan hub has larger geo-political ramifications. The spread of religious extremism towards Uzbekistan, for instance can destabilise resource rich Central Asia. For India, the security implications are also negative as the consolidation of radicalism in Afghanistan will harden extremist pressures on Kashmir.

For India, the problem of terrorism in Jammu & Kashmir has to be dealt with at the local, regional and international levels. By teaming up with like-minded countries, it may be easier to expose the elements behind the terrorist menace and evolve a framework of cooperation to contain the movement of terrorists as well as arms. This view was also expressed by the visiting Uzbek President Islam Karimov who stressed that there was need for both the countries to act together to counter the threats emanating from Afghanistan before it was too late. He gave a call for putting an end to external "interference" in Afghanistan and emphasised that New Delhi and Tashkent should coordinate efforts to control "threats". In this regard, India and Uzbekistan signed several key agreements to fine tune their political relationship to face the onslaught of cross – border terrorism from the Pakistan – Afghanistan mujahideen hub. Concerned about the serious challenge posed to regional and national security both the countries signed a joint declaration on principles, which will anchor their future relationship. The declaration has been signed against the backdrop of the urgency felt by both New Delhi and Tashkent for a joint front to counter the threat to Central and South Asia's security from Talibanised Afghanistan. In addition to other agreements, an extradition treaty and a legal assistance pact on criminal matters was also signed between the two countries. A 'mutual assistance' agreement between the two customs authorities was also finalised.

The visit of President Karimov has been seen as part of a new diplomatic effort in Central Asia to build a broad international coalition, including India, to isolate the radical forces being nurtured by Afghanistan and Pakistan. Led by Uzbekistan, Central Asian Republics are increasing security cooperation among themselves and reaching out to Russia, China, India and the US to combat the new threats of terrorism, emanating from their southern border with Afghanistan. Top specialists of the Institute of Strategic and Regional Studies of Uzbekistan, which functions directly under President Islam Karimov, said, "India is quite experienced in handling fundamentalism and religious extremism, and since we are faced with almost identical problems, we will be glad to have the benefit of this knowledge." Further, Muhammed M. Yukbov, head of the department of regional studies and his two colleagues, Abdullazia Abdullau, strategic expert and Isadjanov, secretary, scientific board, suggested that India, Uzbekistan and other countries of the region should cooperate and evolve a mechanism to fight fundamentalism and religious extremism.

India has so much more at stake and so much more in common with the region, since they were once part of the grand Indo-Soviet strategic alliance. Thus, it is in the strategic interest of India to cooperate and improve relations with the Central Asian Republics. The spate of bilateral agreements signed between India and Uzbekistan signify the growing importance of Central Asia on New Delhi's radar. For the new millennium, New Delhi is making a serious bid to forge new equations with chosen countries in Central Asia and the Islamic world. Uzbekistan fits ideally into both these realms and emerges as a key potential ally in that region, and she too looks upon India as a natural partner in combating terrorism, religious extremism and drug-trafficking. India cannot ignore the importance of Uzbekistan because the country shares a common boundary with the other Central Asian republics – Kazakhstan, Kyrgyzstan, Tajikistan and Turkmenistan – therefore it is Uzbekistan which is the fulcrum around which the security of resource rich Central Asia revolves. For India, the relationship with Uzbekistan is a matter of historical continuity, therefore, taking advantage of this fact India needs to further strengthen its ties with it. Now is the right time for India to further consolidate its bond of friendship. In this context, the visit of External Affairs Minister of India, Jaswant Singh, to Tashkent in May 2000 was a welcome development. It underscores the importance India attaches to its contacts with the Uzbeks. This visit laid a clear road map for future interactions between the two. Talks with his Uzbek counterpart, Abdulaziz Kamilov, covered the entire gamut of bilateral relations, regional security, environment and the general global scene. Both shared their concern over Islamic fundamentalism and over what was happening in Afghanistan i.e., adventurism of the Taliban, gun running and drug trafficking. Kamilov set the ball rolling by saying that Tashkent wanted to institutionalise a mechanism for "regular and substantive political contact," on the lines of the economic joint commission. Jaswant Singh welcomed the suggestion and assured that New Delhi would be "flexible about the level," at which these talks could take place. He also offered more training facilities under the ongoing technical exchange programme and also invited their military personnel to participate in the Indian Defence Colleges for advanced courses. These are right moves on the part of India which Jaswant Singh's interlocutors also welcomed without any reservation and these will bring the two countries closer, apart from giving them a strategic significance.

Earlier, similar views on terrorism were shared by Kyrgyzstan with India during Kyrgyz President Askar Akaev's visit to India in April 1999.[74] Kyrgyzstan is threatened by Islamic fundamentalism, especially in its Osh region, which opens into Central Asia's famous Ferghana Valley. Kyrgyzstan which has a cross border connection across Afghanistan and Tajikistan, wants to avoid being used as a bridge for the export of religious extremism in the region. India, on its part, fears that the spread of fundamentalism across the Afghan-Tajik bridgehead into Central Asia can be destabilising. New Delhi and Bishkek are also engaged in limited defence cooperation, but which is mainly confined to the training of senior level Kyrgyz personnel in some of India's top military establishments.

Further, while meeting new Indian envoy Y. Kumar in Dushanbe, Tajikistan's President Emomali Rakhmanov also called on India, "taking into account its prestige in the region, to intensify efforts for the early possible peaceful settlement of the Afghanistan conflict". "Regional security depends in many things on the peaceful settlement of the Afghan crisis", he said.

Thus, as borne out by these agreements and statements issued and signed by the visiting officials of CARS and India, it is clear that now CARS are looking towards India to help them combat this menace of terrorism. Therefore, India has to move fast and take the lead as cooperation in the field of containing cross border terrorism can provide a new direction in cementing a new partnership between the two. So far very little concrete initiative has been taken by India to build on their former relationship and to build a new and lasting relationship with CARs. The initiative should be more from the Indian side as the CARs are already facing economic problems since their independence and terrorism has added to their woes. The initiatives that can be taken up with respect to combating terrorism are:

- India can establish Joint Working Groups on Counter-Terrorism with CARs on the lines it has done with US and Russia. Regular meetings of the group can become an effective mechanism for the two to share information and intensify cooperation in combating terrorism.
- The experience of Indian para-military forces with counter-terrorist activities in Punjab and Kashmir can specially help the CARs. Raising/training a para – military force and providing it with arms and equipment would help the CARS have a first line of defence against infiltrators and terrorists.
- Intelligence regarding terrorist groups, their camps, their personnel; and their activities on a regular basis can forewarn and forearm the CARs and would greatly enhance their capability in this common fight against terrorism.

- India can provide training to their military personnel with the additional advantage of nearly the same equipment being used by both.
- By helping CARs develop their economy, India would help them strike at the root cause of terrorism i.e. poverty and unemployment.
- Like India, CARs are also plural societies surrounded by fundamentalist/authoritarian regimes. The best course for such societies is an open and liberal, secular and democratic political system. The Central Asian leadership, at present seems to be committed to establish such a political system. India can play a positive role in helping the CARs by offering training facilities to acquaint themselves with a functioning democracy in a developing society.

8

Comprehensive System to Fight Cross-border

TERRORISM

The twenty first century has welcomed many of new dimensions of human life, which includes both desired and undesired events. The most dangerous phenomenon in the form of terrorism has been questioning the peace, tranquility and progress of the world. The term 'terror' is not new but has been changing its form and impact from time to time. The word 'terror' was first used to describe Jacobin's 'Reign of Terror' that followed the French Revolution in 1789.

As much as more than hundred definitions are available in the current literature and even it may increase in the course of time. Of course, a definition of the terror may not be important in the present context but significantly important is its nature and impact. Quite interestingly after the 9/11 attack on the United States a new version of definition of 'terror' has come into existence. Generally the dictionary meaning of terror is extremely simple in its meaning. Genuinely, the lawyers, politicians, legislative bodies, public and private establishments, national and international organizations are also duly accepting the chronological transformation of the definition of terror according to the need of the situation. In the same style, the United States has also tried to give a new dimension to terrorism, not to change the meaning of the word, but to avoid the international criticism or to enjoy the freedom of attacking few countries according to their choice. In history, although different major terror events have taken place, the spectrum of time, intentions and the targets are not the same. Setting aside of the events in the 20th century, similar intensions and purposes have been exposed in the September 11 incident and terror attacks in Bali, Madrid, London and the recent attacks on September 26 (Mumbai). The attacks instigate us to evolve a new mechanism to contain the wide spreading terror attacks.

One more significant dimension of terrorism may be its origin and the responsible factors. Innumerable studies are available on different issues of terrorism. Tore Bjorgo, Professor of Police Science, and John Horgan, Director of the International Centre for the Study of Terrorism, have made an attempt to simplify the processes and factors involved in forming terrorist organizations, Religious 'cults', racist groups and criminal youth gangs which appear strikingly similar in spite of the great differences in ideological content, background and aspirations. They opine that a few measures like disengagement from youth gangs, desistence from criminal life styles, and disengagement from fundamentalist religious movements, racist and right-wing movements can contain the origin of the terror. In the present context, India is not allowing any terror group or groups for any sort of terror training within its soil but few religious fundamental groups are vulnerable attracted by well trained terrorists out side the country.

India's economy has been progressing mammothly and even sustaining far better in the current world economic crisis. Emerging as one of the economic superpowers of the world, India has also been identified as the most responsible state irrespective it's economic, political, military, strategic relations and it has won the admiration of all the countries across the world. On the other side, India has also been one of the countries targeted by the terrorist groups, resulting in irreparable damage in different forms. In the recent past, India has attained unimaginable solidarity from different corners of the globe. Such a situation can't be assured for ever, but capacity building is required in the areas of countering terror attacks, specifically with its own domestic strategy. The Indian history has evidently proved that India or Indians are known to be very strong enough in continuing their traditions and conventional style of life and they should also cultivate and continue a new spirit and culture in fighting the highly sophisticated terrorism. This is the time to awaken and strengthen our hands not to dominate or to be aggressive at international arena but to protect our own citizens and further strongly building confidence on our democratic life with peace and prosperity. The recent Mumbai attacks have exhibited not only the weaknesses of India's mechanism of internal security measures but also the seriousness and possible frequency of attacks by different non-state organizations. The terror attacks have not damaged the Taj Hotel, but have only challenged the public spirit, administrative strength, political consensus and eventually the preparedness to fight against terror.

This chapter attempts to propose a certain mechanism to curb terror attacks in the context of secular and multicultural India. For this purpose a few broader objectives have been articulated within the existing political and institutional system. These objectives are aimed at constitutional reforms in major areas – law and order, public participation, institutional strength, inter-departmental and international linkages, judiciary, confidence building activities, national identity of citizens and so on.

DIVERSIFIED ORIGIN AND RESPONSE AND UNIVERSAL IMPACT

Responses to terrorism are crucial to understand the context in which political and policy strategies are developed. A contextualized approach allows for an understanding of specific *capabilities* in a context where normative, procedural and institutional resources have developed over time and in relation to social practices. For instance, the United States' government position towards terrorist threats which appears to be squarely

grounded in the world of modern nation-states, the EU, displays an altogether different set of strategies and perceptions. Compare, for example, the either/or position displayed by US President George W. Bush when associating terrorist activities with 'state sponsorship', addressing the reaction to this activity as 'state' warfare and ultimately presenting a choice – from one head of state to others – as 'every nation, in every region, *now* has a decision to make. Either you are with us, or you are with the terrorists' quipped President Bush in his 2001 address to Congress. Due to the wide scope of international response to the global terror, in view of the limitations of this chapter the context of the terrorism is confined to India, for discussion.

Many believe that the terror attacks in general and the recent Mumbai attacks have been plotted by few individuals or non-state organizations with certain self imposed aims and objectives. At this juncture, a basic understanding of the ideology or philosophy of terrorists is very important to counter the terror acts, followed by identifying the vulnerability and the frequency of such attacks. Here, it is needed to have a brief discussion about the internal pull factors of terrorism. In the Indian context, a different scenario appears to be responsible for frequent terror attacks, reflecting the subsequent failure in preventing the attacks. Diversified domestic conditions may not be noticed in any of the other countries where terror attacks have been plotted.

The complexity of such a scenario in India, evidently exhibits its history. India has been appreciated by the world for its unity in diversity. But the same character is attributed for the vulnerability of terror attacks on India with a changed version of 'disunity from diversity'. The character of unity in diversity requires a careful scrutiny over a period of time. The Indian history speaks of how the entire subcontinent was attacked and ruled by others. Obviously, for the benefit of doubt, one may raise a reasonable question, is there any direct or indirect relationship between historical events and the on going terror attack? The answer should be 'Yes'. The diversified nature of Indian society has given an opportunity for different versions of rights and ambitions to grow. In the process of achieving their goals, certain individuals or groups have not been hesitating to define their own arguments based on certain loopholes in the governance. The establishment of the Moghul Empire in the 16th century and the reasons for such an expansion of their kingdom in the subcontinent and their continued ruling for more than two centuries is an example. This was followed by the British rule for another two centuries, thereby explicitly exhibiting the weaknesses of unity among the diversified sections of the Indian society.

Nothing can be done to avoid diversity but lot more needs to be done to achieve unity. Of course, it is more of a political game rather than constitutional treatment. In this context, the treatment for such a doubt may not be within the scope of this study, but proper emphasis has been given to have one angle of comprehensive understanding on why terror attacks are common phenomena for India and what mechanism can stop such attempts. A comprehensive national anti-terror strategy must address many issues – defence, law enforcement, intelligence, diplomacy, economic development, education, promotion of socio-political justice – within the context of policies promoting national security. *Tactically*, in the short term, how does one employ the wide portfolio of tools available to policymakers to reduce pressing and immediate threats? *Strategically*, in the long term, how does one win "hearts and minds"? In addition, a strategy ideally attracts allies. How does one both maximize international "buy-in" and national effectiveness?

Religion should be away from politics specifically in a country like India, accommodating more number of religions and ethnic groups. Moreover, the changing international scenario is also much attributed to religion. For other countries it may not be a big issue, but for India it matters a lot. Taking advantage of loopholes from the system, a few political parties are trying to corner a section of society which may directly or indirectly benefit their political mileage. For instance, muslims across the country are a worried lot post 26/11. Whenever there has been a terror strike in the country, Muslims are subject to suspicion and discrimination from the other communities and investigating agencies. Their loyalty to India is doubted. Unfortunately, some elements from both the communities (Hindus and Muslims), along with the dubious political class always ensure that there is continuous rift between the two communities so that they may take advantage of it. Terrorism in India has affected the Muslims of this country badly. It has provided a more conducive atmosphere for the political parties who survive on divisive ideology and destructive politics. Unfortunately, on the other side of the coin, a new nomenclature (Hindu Terror) for Malegao attacks has been attributed. At several platforms, the Bharatiya Janata Party (BJP) leadership is strongly blaming the Indian media for such a type of propaganda.

In general, the relationship or coordination between the police and political leadership has been failing in many instances in winning the appreciation of the public. Within the police department, cohesion is also lacking in different hierarchies. Many police officers are not happy in discharging their duties in difficult times. As Ashish Gupta (batchmate of Hemant Karkare) writes: "But why do we, educated people, not raise enough hue and cry so that the political parties are forced to change the policing system and hence improve your security? Friends, please become aware of the realities of policing and beware of rhetoric of political parties – the solutions they offer are superficial and will not improve security situation. You can't build an edifice of security organisation with a weak and hollow foundation."

Again it may be a difficult task to pinpoint exactly one or two people or groups in certain instances of such nature, but it is open secret. Unless, efforts on such lines are put in practice it may be, to some extent, a difficult task to establish safety through the existing political system. The recent Mumbai incident flares up the public anger, irrespective of political parties and the entire political system has been blamed across the country. Mr. Jaipandey, an Indian journalist, viewed that the political leadership wanted the best security for itself but what about public security? Senior police officers are totally corrupt and they just want to make money and are always ready to sell the country's interests.

Why is the entire spectrum of the mechanism of anti-terror attacks being debated? The following analysis develops a framework; elaborates and examines the Indian potential responses to terrorism within the socio-economic and political situation of India. The international literature has established different means of responses based on the need, capabilities and the local social order. No doubt, India requires a framework which suits its capabilities and neighbouring relations. It may be difficult to exercise any one of the well established anti-terror mechanism, as it is.

CROSS-BORDER INFILTRATION

Once the topic is on India and about terrorism, Kashmir and its international border will be the first issue to be propagated in the international arena. It is all history, currently the entire international borders of India have been proved as the most vulnerable for cross- border terrorism. Moreover, the 26/11 Mumbai attacks proved that the Indian maritime international borders also brought out the weaknesses in preventing terror plots. In recent times, India has declared war in Kargil to clear off its soil from the terrorists/militants. On the Eastern border of India it is a different scenario – at the early the infiltration has taken place in the form of refugees from Bangladesh. The former Assam Governor Lt Gen (Retd) Ajay Singh's assertion of around 6000 illegal Bangladeshis entering Assam daily is only partially correct, as the fate of India's North East is at stake.

The horrific demographic imbalance will see Bangla migrants outnumber the entire population of the region in the next two decades. Of course, currently, the scope and intention of infiltration has been changing even in the recent Mumbai attacks which evidenced some sort of linkages from Bangladesh. The abnormal increase in the number of madrasas in Assam numbering about 1466, of which 810 are registered, is a matter of concern.

Intelligence agencies have been warning for years that many of these madrasas could be safe havens for radical elements. Surprisingly, Islamic groups have been silent on the tumultuous issue of illegal migration from Bangladesh to Assam. Intelligence inputs have expressed trepidation about these groups being instigated to violence by external Islamic groups, on the pretext of safeguarding the interests of the minorities. For instance, they face harassment in the hands of outfits spearheading the oust-Bangladeshi campaign in the region. Strategists in the Home Ministry fear that the tug-of-war over migrants of suspected Bangla origin could become the trigger for groups such as Harkat-Ul-Jehadi-Islami (HUJI) to fish in the troubled waters of the North-

East. Therefore, the argument can't be ruled out that the infiltration is the basic source of terrorism (some authors quoting as mother of terrorism) and it should be considered as one of the major components to be given equal importance in the mechanism aimed at fighting terrorism.

India is naturally gifted with 3,600 km of coastline, which is exposed to international navigation. The recent Mumbai incident exposes the weakness of the coast guards. The proposed measures to be taken by the Indian Naval Force, may be very difficult to specify, but in general there is a dire need to improve the existing plans and strategies of coast guards. Comparatively, the more difficult task may be that of protecting India's continental boundaries with Pakistan, Nepal and Bangladesh. Naturally, much concentration has been attached to the Pakistan border and significantly the eastern border, exposing its weaknesses. In the north of India, Nepal can't be ignored from all possibilities of engaging terrorist activities.

Many reports appear at national and international platforms on India's emphasis on establishing good relations with its neighbours – apart from the US, China, East Asia and European Union – to win peace and prosperity. One of the government reports has quoted that the dialogue process of January 6, 2004 has shown the commitment of the Pakistani President Pervez Musharraf not to allow any territory under Pakistani control for supporting terrorism against India. Unfortunately, till today the Indian government is demanding the same and building international pressure on Pakistan. The foreign ministers of India and Pakistan met in Islamabad on May 21, 2008 for the fourth round of the so- called composite dialogue process. It is the first high level bilateral talks between the two countries since the civilian government took over in Pakistan in March 2008. Indian officials say they will raise the issue of alleged infiltration and "cross border terrorism" with Pakistan. The developments which are likely to dominate bilateral talks are the first since the civilian government in Pakistan took over in March 2008. Earlier, the two countries held three rounds of dialogue since initiating a peace process in 2003. Many a time, Pakistan has been daunting from its commitment towards stopping non-state terror groups from its own soil. India should realize from the earlier experiences with Pakistan and try to find a permanent solution to the issue of Pakistan border, instead of raising India's voice occasionally or on the need of the day at different international fora.

Once the process of bilateral talks began, a chain of loopholes have exposed our weak security system in protecting the security of the people and the country at large. Terrorism specifically through infiltration has reached its peak. India currently has been running out of the ways in containing infiltration from international borders including maritime and continental borders. The research community in large should also probe into the micro- level issues of infiltration and explore the possibilities of suggesting different kinds of solutions and helping the government to strengthen the security mechanism of the nation for its prosperity through peace.

Institutional Reforms

The immediate need is, a strong institutional mechanism which aims at curbing both national and international terrorism. It is imperative to have an exclusive treatment for every serious issue of expected anti-terror mechanism. It should be a multidimensional approach, using intelligence, armed forces, confidence building, international cooperation, modernization of communication technology, border security, public participation and concern, modernization of armed weapons and a strong inter-state cooperation. All such objectives should aim at prevention of attacks and post-terror attack mechanism. By all means, the prevention of terror attacks may be the best but it requires consistent efforts and updating every dimension of institutional efforts and may also be a test for internal/domestic strength.

In the Indian context, the important weakness may be institutional lacuna. Traditional form of institutions can't find a solution for the modern terrorism. For instance, terrorists are in advance in getting their plans implemented than the national and international institutions aimed at curtailing the terrorism. India needs a broadly defined strong institutional support to fight terrorism, which should also be autonomous like Election

Commission of India. Raj Kumar, an honorary consultant to the National Human Rights Commission, India, has been advocating the forms and modalities of anti-terrorism mechanism and even coined a name 'Central Anti-Terrorism Commission (CAT-COM)'. India has been creating many laws in tune with the need of the nation to fight against terror. In this process 'Prevention of Terror Attacks (POTA)' was enacted by the National Democratic Alliance (NDA) government and recently on 16 December 2008 the United Progressive Alliance (UPA) government has introduced a bill called 'National Investigation Agency (NIA).

While introducing the POTA bill in the parliament L.K. Advani, the then Deputy Prime Minister and Home Minister gave the rationale of the bill. With the intensification of cross-border terrorism and the continued offensive agenda of Pak ISI targeted at destabilizing India and the post-11 September developments, it became necessary to put in place a special law to deal with terrorist acts. Accordingly, the Prevention of Terrorism Act, 2002 (POTA, 2002) was enacted and notified on 28.03.2002. The POTA 2002 clearly defines the terrorist act and grants special powers to the investigating authorities under the Act. However, in order to ensure that these powers are not misused and the violation of human rights does not take place, specific safeguards have been built into the Act. Within the Parliament, many political observers and media viewed that NIA and POTA are similar in many respects. In fact, the existing laws are more than sufficient and what is required is a mechanism which can help in implementing the stringent available laws.

For instance, USA has also been updating its laws to fight against terrorism. On December 17, 2004, President Bush signed the Intelligence Reform and Prevention Act of 2004 (S. 2845, P.L. 108-458) establishing the position of National Intelligence Director (a position separate from that of the CIA Director) to serve as the President's principal intelligence advisor, overseeing and coordinating the foreign and domestic activities of the intelligence community. Established as well is a National Counterterrorism Centre designed to serve as a central knowledge bank for information about known and suspected terrorists and to coordinate and monitor counterterrorism plans and activities of all government agencies. The Centre will also be responsible for preparing the daily terrorism threat report for the President. Many developing countries are obviously, depending on the US in many respects including domestic intelligence alerts. In view of huge investment requirements, India may be exempted from this excuse, since India is in possession of all resources to compete with the US in combating terrorism. The entire process is being much influenced by socio-political issues rather than economic support.

Personal Identity

Identity of citizens is another important aspect to be seriously considered. Generally, everybody is serious about the police and their infrastructure to fight against the terror. In fact, there are many deeper issues to be solved to avoid the terror in the initial stages of attack so that there would be no need of post-terror attack mechanism. Out of such desired acts, issuing a citizenship card or national identity card to every citizen is an important mechanism to cross-verify the identity of any one in the country. This process facilitates an initial stage of scrutiny of suspects by any official or an ordinary citizen of the country.

Judiciary

One of the most sensitive and significant organs of democracy is undoubtedly the judiciary. Although the concept of justice is universal, the nature and definition of judiciary has been always undermined with the political ideology/system of a state. Therefore, there is a range of diversity in safeguarding 'human rights'. In a given point of time and situation, the controversy seems to be phenomenal, because of the gap between the specific/local situation and the general concept of human rights. With this simple background many a time states/countries are obviously customized to bring out certain reforms in the political system or amendments in the constitution. Modern society under the umbrella of globalization, requires globalized judiciary, which suits to maintain the security, peace and prosperity of the world at large. International evil acts and non-state actors are aiming to disturb the human life at global level. In the process of countering such acts International Criminal Court (ICC) was established in 2002.

The ICC is typically recognized as a product of the cosmopolitanization of international law. Much of the debate on the ICC has centred on whether or not international politics and law can or ought to be reformed according to cosmopolitan moral standards. Many have sought to understand the ways in which the ICC was brought into being as a result of successfully framed cosmopolitan arguments. The ICC is an interesting phenomenon because it consolidates earlier reforms to international law with seemingly more radical departures from the traditional, state-based order. Many miss this fusion of more "conservative" and "radical" politics that the ICC represents; there is a tendency to either exaggerate or underestimate the novelty and potential impact of the Court in world politics. The first treaty-based tribunal was designed to hold individuals accountable for the most egregious international offenses—war crimes, genocide, and crimes against humanity. In 2005, the nascent court became a genuinely global tribunal when the UN Security Council (UNSC) referred to it, the situation in Darfur, Sudan. Antonio Franceschet, a political analyst, submits four dimensions of international law of *control, order, governance,* and *citizenship* which should be interpreted in cosmopolitan terms. Moreover, these projects have been the basis of significant reforms to the practice of international law. All these arguments certainly do not have any relevance to the present study, but evidently support to say that any judiciary must be subjected to the order of the day and deemed to be reformed according to the demand to deliver justice, primarily at the state level, stronger to serve the purpose and aimed at coordinating international laws.

Promotion of unity and harmony among the citizens of India would send strong signals to the terrorists. An exclusive and fast track judiciary system can answer all the questions of confidence building and warnings to terrorists. It is quite unfortunate to see that there is a provision of filing a mercy petition before the President of India, by an individual who directly or indirectly participated in terrorist activities and sentenced to death. Such acts indirectly help dampen the confidence in judiciary and exhibit the lacunas of judiciary to the terrorists and further instigate them to multiply their attacks. On the other hand, some other groups are trying to carryout the parallel terror acts. This chain of actions and reactions may not help individuals, nation and the peace and progress of the world at large. Therefore, this is high time to bring out reforms in the judiciary at least targeting terror activities. Few of the expected reforms in the judiciary are as follows:

- the provision of filing the mercy petition by any terrorist or who is involved in terror act indirectly irrespective of their background must be removed;
- no terror criminal will be released against the demand of terrorists at the time of hijacking, irrespective of the damage at specific point of time;
- certain reforms are required to define the severity of punishment against the involvement of local civilians, political leaders and police personals who directly or indirectly helped and joined with the terror groups and the degree of punishment for such personals should be on the lines of terrorists and even some times more severe;
- fast track courts are exclusively required to deal with the terror criminal cases;
- immediate implementation of court judgments;
- controlling the freedom of press and media in specific situations.

MULTIDIMENSIONAL INTERNATIONAL STRATEGY

Indirectly, this triangular strategy has pushed toward, another dimension of terror's nature and impact. Terrorism can be called one type of natural calamity (cyclone) but it can't be interpreted completely a natural calamity. In general, in the origin of any cyclone, direction of its movement, quantum of damage, the target, duration of impact, severity of attack, possibilities of controlling mechanism etc., may be possible to define, to notify any of the components including the frequency. Terrorism, which has been targeting India, has not been originated from its own soil and knowingly from its neighbouring country. Naturally, a cyclone does not affect the place of its origin, but in the case of terrorism, the place of origin is no way exempted. To be honest, it is an open secret that Pakistan is the first country affected by terrorism. Of course, Pakistan is hit by its own bullet. Many people may not be satisfied with such a conclusion including many Indians. Fundamentally, the historical analysis of Pakistan's political belligerency, economic turmoil and religious attachment (jihad movement) or fundamentalism, certainly give the rationale for such a commendable conclusion. Shazadi Beg and Laila Bokhari viewed that military operations in Pakistan have demonstrated that traditional counter-terrorism measures such as the use of force and intelligence gathering alone can never defeat the ideological and political battles. One of the major challenges in the Pakistani context is to change an extremist mindset drawn on its history of domestic sectarian strife and the strong national strategies on the jihads in Kashmir.

Such a strong historical background emulates to have a multidimensional formula to stop terrorism. Any attempt of anti-terror should not forget to bear in mind, a few significant bilateral and multilateral issues. Firstly, in understanding Pakistan's element of Jihad and related issues, India should basically try to widen the gap between the government/public and the Jihad militants. Secondly, India should have a special package to establish good relations with its neighbours, which may promote peace and prosperity not only within India but also in the entire South Asia. Finally, international cohesion is highly required. All such acts must not be seasonal and need consistent efforts to promote regional and national security issues at large.

Conclusion

With the limited scope of this chapter, a few recommendations are forwarded: strong measures are required along the international mainland and maritime borders; though the curruption is general, it has to be immediately stopped within the concerned departments of national security. The process of issuing photo national identity cards should be started immediately which helps in identifying the terrorists. Of course, judiciary is an important component of our constitution. But it has been constrained to forward certain recommendations. However, in the best interest of the nation, serious reforms are required – the provision of filing the mercy petition by a terrorist, should be done away with. In dealing with the jijackers national interests should be given top priority. Strong message should be sent to civilians and political elite that the punishments against those involved in terror process will be more severe. Fast track courts are the need of the day. Other measures to counter terror attacks include immediate implementation of judgments and controlling the freedom of press and media in specific situations. Above all, certain programmes are required to change the mind set of the corrupt political leaders and officials who are playing a significant role in indirectly encouraging the cross-border terrorism.

9

Cross-Border Cooperation against Crime and Terrorism

Paradoxically, regionalism implies both an increased and lessened flow of crime within the region in question. Crime is in some respects lessened as tariff barriers are broken down and the profits of smuggling are consequently reduced. But regionalism also amplifies the potential flow of crime because it usually entails an opening up of the regional countries to trade, travel and cultural exchange. This permits criminals, terrorists, illicit firearms and other illicit products, along with illegal migrants and victims of trafficking, to move more freely throughout the region.

Implicit in the regional contract is not only an undertaking to break down barriers to trade and transit, but also develop cooperative means to address the results of that process in terms of increased criminality. Such agreements usually relate to sharing of information and intelligence, joint investigations and the tightening of the barrier around the regional collective. Thus the Schengen Agreements (1985, 1990) in the European Union (EU) ultimately necessitated the creation of the 'Frontex' border control agency and EUROPOL.

The problems arising from regionalism in relation to increased criminality are further exacerbated by the fact that 'crime regions'—that is, regions of intense cross-border criminality—often closely reflect the geography of the regions themselves. This is because the very lines of trade, proximity and familiarity that give rise to the idea of the region in the fist place also enhance the possibilities of cross-regional criminal cooperation. The globalization of crime is, however, increasingly challenging the apparent primacy of regional cross border crime. In particular, illicit commodities originating outside a region, such as cocaine and heroin, need to cross the regional barrier. Cybercrime—a truly global phenomenon—has also progressively broken down regional barriers. And finally, people smuggling and trafficking, by their very nature, often involve the illicit transfer of people from a poor to a wealthy region, such as from Africa to Europe.

This combination of regional with global crime leads to a symbiotic relationship between the two. On the one hand, growing globalization enables illicit products and people to be brought to specific regions and to cross the regional barrier. On the other, regional crime, often enabled by the breaking down of regional barriers, enables these products and people better to move around illicitly within the region once they have entered the regional barrier. Further, the regional defence against global crime is only as strong as the weakest link in the external chain.

This symbiotic relationship between global and regional crime in some respects complicates the processes of regional cooperation against crime. Failing adequate regional responses, a multiplicity of agencies become involved in the cooperative process. On the other hand, sound regional responses can simplify and render more effective the international response, in that a unified regional response can limit the number of entities involved and give leverage to the collective of countries that is the recipient of global crime problems.

Not all emerging regions, however, have been able to address the escalation in cross-border crime associated with more lax internal barriers through anti- crime measures adopted under the rubric of regionalism. Nor have they been able to stave off the vulnerability that comes with globalization of crime. European regionalism—as exemplified by the EU—has done better in this regard that Asian regionalism—represented in this chapter by the regions covered by the Association of South East Asian Nations (ASEAN) and the South Asian Association for Regional Cooperation (SAARC).

In this chapter, we examine in greater detail some of the impediments to cooperation against international crime and terrorism within emerging regional associations, as distinct from more mature associations such as the EU. We consider the role of politics, and in particular the spoiling role of paired antagonistic states, within regional associations in erecting barriers against much-needed regional cooperation against crime and terrorism. We examine issues surrounding 'securitisation' of crime and terrorism and how securitisation can result in negative outcomes in terms of exacerbating existing political problems. And we consider some ways in which these political and securitisation problems might be mitigated in emerging regional associations.

MODE OF COOPERATION AGAINST CRIME AND TERRORISM

As McFarlane points out, there are both problems with international cooperation against transnational crime and terrorism as well as successes.

The problems he enumerates are less in evidence in a mature regional association such as the EU than they are in less mature cases. According to Frost, "modern European integration sprang from the bones and ashes of centuries of war between France and Germany". Cooperation only commenced once the war-weary protagonists concluded that it was the only viable way forward. And even then, a community of like-mined opinion leaders had to be in existence for many years. Europe appears eventually to have reached a 'tipping point' in which regional cooperation emerged as a more valued way forward in dealing with problems (including cross-border crime and terrorism) than competition.

That is not to say, of course, that competition has disappeared, or that problems in cooperation are no longer in evidence. We have only to observe the EU's difficulties in dealing with the current global financial crisis to know that they are. But the essential difference between the situation now and that in the pre-cooperative era is that it is possible for competition and cooperation (or as Tow puts it 'realism' and 'liberalism') to coexist within the same framework and for competition to be constrained and contained by cooperation. In the two Asian regional associations that form the subject of this chapter, however, the situation is very different. Antagonisms in this part of the world are still raw and both associations still lack confidence in their cooperative mechanisms. While cooperation in ASEAN is far advanced of SAARC, both, we suggest, are well short of any 'tipping point'.

More to the point, there is no reason to suppose that neighbouring members of a regional association should be intrinsically more able to cooperate than more distant countries. Indeed, according to the Kautilyan dictum, neighbours are often enemies and such enemies often seek to balance their enemies with powerful friends in more distant places. This dictum has certainly proven true enough in two of the areas we cover—South and South East Asia.

For example, within the ranks of the ten ASEAN countries, Thailand and Myanmar are traditional competitors. They have engaged in conflict and competition for hundreds of years. At the time ASEAN was formed, tension lingered between Malaysia and Indonesia as a result of the policy of *Confrontasi* exercised by Indonesia under Sukarno. Singapore had recently broken away from Malaysia because of the city-state's Chinese majority and the two remained uneasy partners. And Malaysia and the Philippines had also been in competition over north Borneo. Indeed, given the diversity and tensions that existed at the time ASEAN was established in 1967, the fact that the association exists at all is something of a miracle.

In view of the initial difficulties in establishing ASEAN, it is not surprising that the model chosen for cooperation was a 'consensus' one in which the agreement of all was needed to make any decision. Such a model was also deemed to be consonant with the so-called 'Asian-way'. According to this model, non-interference and mutual respect would allow the flow of cooperation amongst hitherto difficult neighbours gradually to increase, including through informal mechanisms capable of dealing with difficult issues in non-threatening ways. Wesley also notes how the 'Asian way' arose out of the colonial past and represented to an extent an expression of pride and a warning to western nations "to keep their advice about economic planning, human rights and democracy to themselves". Some argue that the 'Asia way', with its reliance on family and respect for sovereignty rather than supra-legal structures, will lead to a quite different form of regionalism to Europe—one in which the idea of region supersedes any action that should be deemed to flow from such a concept.

For these reasons, among others, the cooperative mechanisms in ASEAN are still relatively weak. This is especially true in sensitive areas like crime and terrorism. For example, an original resolution to set up a shared criminal intelligence database in 1992 was not implemented until the Electronic ASEAN Data System (e-ADS) came into existence in 2007. And even in the case of e-ADS, Burma and the Lao People's Democratic Republic (Lao PDR) have not yet been included.

In South Asia, the reality is even more stark. India and Pakistan have had a long-standing rivalry since the partition imposed on India by the British in 1947. This rivalry has been far more damaging to SAARC than the rivalries within ASEAN. SAARC was established in 1985 and is generally agreed to have been very limited in its performance in solving regional issues.

According to Rajan,

Many reasons exist for the uneven progress of SAARC: most have to do with intra-regional political tensions, and most involve India. [Factors include] the chronic tension, occasional conflict, and perennial absence of trust between India and Pakistan; the periodic hiccups in relations between India and her other neighbours—Sri Lanka, Nepal and Bangladesh; and so on.

So the Kautilyan dictum of antipathy amongst neighbours seems to apply readily to the SAARC region and to a lesser extent to ASEAN. But as we shall see, such cross-border political tensions do not seem to be reflected in reduced cross-border criminal and terrorist activity. Crime, like business, is essentially neutral in international politics: it will go where demand takes it and enforcement allows it.

The kind of attenuated cooperative regimes witnessed in SAARC, and to a lesser extent ASEAN, provide little, if any, restraint on criminal and terrorist activity. Unfortunately, they exist both bilaterally between antagonists and also in terms of multilateral arrangements within the region. They are extended into the multilateral sphere because the pace of cooperation is usually kept to the lowest common denominator, which is in turn the regime dictated by the antagonists.

Crime, encouraged by lack of effective law enforcement cooperation, further exacerbates existing frictions between neighbours because of its capacity to do harm across borders and to attract blame thereby from victim countries, thus perpetuating the vicious circle. Terrorism in such antagonistic circumstances is even more problematic than crime. Cross-border terrorism is often actively supported as a 'cat's paw' to weaken the disliked neighbour, or at best treated with indifference by turning the proverbial 'blind eye'.

'SECURITISATION' FURTHER COMPLICATES THE PICTURE

Although securitisation has been very useful as a means of fighting cross- border crime and terrorism at the level of the nation state, it can also complicate the process of international cooperation against these phenomena.

'Securitisation' is said to occur when issues like cross-border crime, terrorism and environmental problems become manifest at such a level that they threaten the integrity and security of the state, or at least are perceived to do so. A key implication of securitisation is that all agencies of the state—not just civilian agencies such as police, health authorities and environmental agencies—need to be brought to bear to address non- conventional threats, since such threats are deemed to threaten the state existentially. This 'whole of government' approach also naturally involves the conventional security agencies, including the military.

According to Emmers, securitisation of crime in ASEAN has been a 'rhetorical device' rather than an actuality. That is, such crime has been identified as an existential threat, but ASEAN has not actually moved to treat it as such by adopting a "military-security response".

While that may be so at the level of ASEAN itself, it is certainly not the case at the level of individual countries. In many instances, the state security apparatus has been fully coopted to assist police to deal with crime and terrorism. Often, indeed, the security apparatus already operates in the domain of crime and terrorism suppression by virtue of its pervasive influence through society itself.

This latter point is certainly true of Burma. Until it was dismantled in 2004, the Directorate of Defence Service Intelligence (DDSI) not only had a central role in military intelligence and state security, but also in managing the state's relations with the various drug lords (and some say actively participating in the drug trade). Pakistan's infamous Directorate of Inter- Services Intelligence (ISI) is also widely involved in internal security as well as providing military intelligence support. In Thailand, the military is actively involved in the attempt to interdict drugs along the border with Burma, in terrorism suppression in the southern provinces and in turning away illegal immigrants and refugees. In Indonesia, the police and military were only separated as recently as 2000 and are still under a joint command in West Papua. The elite military response and intelligence group, KOPASSUS, is actively involved in counter-terrorism. In China, the all-powerful Ministry of Public Security (MPS) covers all aspects of non-military security, including internal security against political unrest and terrorism, separatism and insurgency, counter-espionage and more traditional aspects of criminal policing.

Even in regional countries that subscribe to a supposed 'separation of powers', such as Australia, the involvement of security agencies in traditional policing has increased markedly in recent years. Military services such as the Navy and the Army (especially the special forces), and agencies like the Defence Signals Directorate (DSD) and Defence Imagery and Geospatial Organisation (DIGO) have been closely involved in countering international drug and people smuggling and terrorism and working closely with police to do so. In the case of Australia, however, such involvement is enshrined in sets of legislation and encrusted in rules designed to prevent misuse either of the police or security services against Australian citizens. Ironically, as a corollary to securitisation, international cooperation against crime and terrorism tends to be severely compromised, thus effectively increasing the insecurity that the concept is intended to address. This problem occurs when there is no adequate separation between traditional community policing and military and security agencies. This lack of separation itself poses a dilemma, since it is deemed (and is likely to be) useful to eliminate the 'stove-piping' that traditionally characterised the security apparatus in many Western countries. 'Stove-piping' was considered to be a key factor in the intelligence failures that presaged the 9/11 attacks.

Although 'stove-piping' can be a negative, it also has a wider purpose and its absence can itself complicate the process of international cooperation. For example, any country cooperating with Burma prior to 2004, say on a drug matter, must have expected the information it conveyed as part of that cooperation—say police-to-police—to end up in the hands of the DDSI.

This could involve information about a criminal being used for political ends, say to coerce a member of an alleged criminal's family to do something political in order to keep the family member from being punished as a criminal.

Or to take another example, information obtained through special means in one country involving a specific technique of military and security value beyond its criminal interdiction purpose could leak across the permeable borders between police and the security apparatus in the receiving country, to the security detriment of the providing country. This kind of concern arises in the case of China, where there is no separation between police and security agencies—as least as far as their political control is concerned.

China also has a poor reputation in using such techniques for purposes of industrial and military espionage. Countries dealing with China on normal police matters therefore need to be conscious of possible leakage of intelligence methods into the state security apparatus. The converse of this principle is true also: by giving police access to state security secrets, we increase the vulnerability of those secrets and reduce the normal protective mechanisms placed around them.

It need hardly be stated that such concerns about the securitisation of non- conventional threats are 'turbocharged' in a situations like that between Burma and Thailand, or India and Pakistan, which are 'traditional' enemies or antagonists.

Human rights issues also often come to the fore in cases of securitisation. This occurred between Australia and Indonesia, which were otherwise cooperating strongly against terrorism in the post-Bali bombings environment. However, when KOPASSUS was invited to be involved in counter-terrorism cooperation, Australia balked because KOPASSUS nominated personnel who had allegedly been involved in serious human rights abuses. Similarly, Australia was for many years chary of cooperating with Burma against the flow of drugs from that country because of human rights concerns. Eventually, the benefits of such cooperation in terms of interdicting the then very large and damaging flow of heroin into Australia were deemed to outweigh the human rights considerations associated with cooperation. However, that decision, and a subsequent decision to provide intelligence training to the Burmese police through the Jakarta Centre for Law Enforcement Cooperation (JCLEC), raised questions amongst NGOs and in the parliament about possible leakage of intelligence methods from the police to the military.

In the case of counter-terrorism cooperation, such problems are manifold. By its very nature, terrorism is a political activity and therefore tends to feed into existing inter-state political difficulties. Moreover, it often also involves an intense crossover between criminal and political activity, which results in a further blurring of the lines in terms of the separation of powers. This, in turn, muddies the waters of cooperation and reduces transparency.

In short, what we have in some regional associations is the confluence of enhanced cross-border crime and terrorism as a result of greater regional exchange with the existence of paired sets of antagonists. The equation is then further complicated by the securitisation of transnational crime and terrorism, which in turn feeds into the existing sets of antagonisms in a vicious feedback loop.

In order further to explore these phenomena and develop some insights into how they might be addressed, we will now turn to an examination of cross- border crime and terrorism between antagonists in two crime regions—South Asia and South East Asia.

Antagonism and Cooperation in Two 'Crime Regions'

Although the 'crime regions' of ASEAN and SAARC do not always correspond exactly with the cooperative regions, such correspondence is broadly the case. For example, the SAARC region is characterised by smuggling networks that criss-cross the region and that originated from the extremely high sets of tariffs it had been subjected to, especially in the case of the popular precious metals, gold and silver. The region also has a flourishing cross-border illegal arms trade supporting various criminal and insurgency activities. *Hawala*, or the traditional money transfer business, is also in evidence for both licit and illicit purposes. These criminal smuggling routes, methodologies and modes of contact have strong traditional roots, sometimes stretching back hundreds of years. This is especially true of *hawala*, an age-old form of exchange now adapted to a globalized criminal setting.

In the case of ASEAN, the crime region not only covers ASEAN itself, but also extends into North Asia and Australasia. It originally focused mainly on the production and movement of the illicit drugs heroin and methamphetamine, but in recent years has evolved to include maritime piracy, intellectual property piracy, identity fraud and other kinds of fraud and white collar crime, people smuggling and trafficking, money laundering and terrorism.

South and South East Asia are also increasingly connected through terrorism and crime. South Asian criminals are active in Bangkok in providing false documents and also use the city as a safe-haven from both law enforcement and rivals. Precursor chemicals move from India into Burma and from China to Afghanistan. South East Asian terrorists have frequently received training and indoctrination in Pakistan and Afghanistan.

There is a flourishing illegal arms trade from South East Asia (mainly Cambodia and Thailand) into South Asia. Increasingly, the Mumbai, Karachi, Dubai 'triangle' has emerged as a major *hawala* based source of illegal money laundering for criminals in South East and East Asia and Australasia. And we have seen recently increasing numbers of refugees and illegal migrants departing South and South West Asia for destinations in South East Asia and Australasia.

In both regions, however, long-standing bilateral disputes and tensions have seriously undermined the overall progress of regional and inter-regional cooperation against these problems. Let us examine two of these disputes in greater detail to see what they have meant for regional cooperation against crime and terrorism.

INDIA, PAKISTAN AND SAARC

SAARC has progressed very little since its foundation and could even be described as a case of 'dysfunctional regionalism'. Although a number of measures are in place, they are often honoured more in the breach than implementation, particularly in the case of traditional competitors such as India and Pakistan.

SAARC nations have implemented a SAARC *Regional Convention on Suppression of Terrorism* and an *Additional Protocol to the SAARC Regional Convention on Terrorism*. These documents emphasise cooperation against organised crime and terrorism amongst relevant agencies, especially in information exchange, completion of all law harmonisations and the criminalisation of terrorism, as mandated by UN Resolution 1373 of 2001. SAARC also has a *Regional Convention on Narcotic Drugs and Psychotropic Substances* and has finalised a text of the SAARC *Convention on Mutual Legal Assistance in Criminal Matters.*

The actual state of cross-border cooperation against terrorism and crime within the SAARC region, however, is a far-cry from the declared policy. India and Pakistan have no extradition or MLAT arrangements and a SAARC policing arrangement ('SAARCPOL'), establishing the equivalent of EUROPOL or ASEANAPOL, has yet to be formally established. Although information exchange appears in the exhortatory policy, it does not occur to any significant degree. Again, Pakistan-India and to a lesser extent India- Bangladesh problems and suspicions lie behind these failures. One of the manifestations of SAARC's overall failure has been the region's low intra-regional trade. Rajan notes that intra-SAARC trade is only 5 percent of the region's total trade (in other words the aggregate value of trade of all SAARC countries), compared with 62 percent for the EU and 55 percent for the North American Free Trade Association (NAFTA). Despite the introduction of the first phase of the South Asian Free Trade Area (SAFTA) regime in 2007, South Asia has significantly higher sets of tariffs than other comparable regions and very much higher non-tariff barriers.

As mentioned, one result of these very high sets of tariffs was to produce a region with some of the most entrenched smuggling networks of any on the globe, especially in relation to areas of high demand, such as gold, silver and foreign consumer goods. These networks were often funded through the *hawala* indigenous systems of money exchange. Such smuggling and *hawala* networks in turn proved invaluable for terrorism purposes.

While falling tariffs have diminished the role of smugglers, they have not yet been lowered to the extent that the incentive to smuggle has been entirely removed. According to one estimate commissioned by the World Bank in 2004, 'informal' trade within South Asia is still between US$0.5 billion and US$3 billion *per annum*. The same report found that this massive illegal trade consisted of smuggling via Afghanistan through the UN facilitated Afghan Trade and Transit Agreement (ATTA) trade corridors and thence on to Pakistan, by means of direct shipment from India with false bills of lading (purchasable for as little as US$50) or via more minor routes across the India-Pakistan border. Another commentator puts the 'informal' trade between Afghanistan and Pakistan as high as US$10 billion, which compares with an official trade of only US$2 billion. According to a reporter from *Dawn*, this volume of smuggled goods outweighs demand in Peshawar (the principal initial destination in Pakistan) and is presumably intended for elsewhere in South Asia. Another favoured smuggling route is via Nepal, which, as a land-locked country, has a virtual open border with India. An arms smuggling route also extends out of South East Asia and thence via the Bangladeshi ports of

Cox's Bazaar and Chittagong into South Asia proper. These arms are either used for insurgencies in northeast and central India or are sold onto the illicit arms market throughout South Asia. An alternate route, having left Thailand, goes through the Ten Degree Channel and thence to fuel the civil war in Sri Lanka. Arms and explosives, including the military-type explosive RDX, are frequently smuggled across the India-Pakistan border for use of criminals and terrorists. There is also a flourishing trade throughout the region in illicit gelignite stolen from mines and factories.

Vicziany points out that some commentators believe that economic liberalisation forced the noted gangster, Dawood Ibrahim (of 'D Company'), to abandon smuggling, leave India and fall into the arms of the ISI, from whence he progressed to stage what is still the most destructive terrorist attack in India, the 1993 Mumbai serial bombings. According to others, however, Ibrahim is still in the business of smuggling, including heroin smuggling. A recent Rand Corporation publication also covers D Company and points out that the gang is now heavily into film piracy, including as a means of funding terrorism.

'D Company' provides an interesting example of the fact that criminals do not recognise political and religious differences. In a world increasingly bifurcated between Hindus and Muslims and shaped by the India-Pakistan competition, the gang remained syncretic. It contained Muslim, Christian, Hindu, Parsi, Pakistani and Indian members and facilitators, right up to the time of the 1993 bombings. These attacks, however, finally forced some of the non-Muslim members, such as 'Chhota' (or 'Little') Rajan, out of the gang. But prior to that, profit knew no religious or national boundaries.

The broader point is that the long-standing antagonism between India and Pakistan, based partly on the religious divide, does not mean that criminals within both countries are unable to cooperate to make a profit. They certainly can, and do. On the other hand, the antagonism between India and Pakistan has been notable in preventing concerted action against both terrorism and criminality, even in cases such as the massive cross-border smuggling between the two, where it would seemingly be to mutual advantage to cooperate. This failure has been manifest both in terms of the lack of bilateral arrangements such as MLATs and extradition treaties, and in terms of multilateral action through SAARC. Nowhere is this failure more obvious than in the field of counter- terrorism.

The problem is that Pakistan has little incentive to cooperate in this area with India. Pakistan uses the cross-border terrorism of groups like Lashkar-e- Taiba (L-e-T) and Jaish-e-Mohammed (J-e-M) as a cat's paw in its proxy war with India, especially over the Kashmir dispute. There is ample evidence that Pakistan has officially fostered, supplied and trained such groups.

As far as any involvement of the Pakistani state was concerned at the time these relationships with sub-state actors were forged, however, the intention was probably only to use such means in the disputed territory of Kashmir, not in those parts of India outside Kashmir. The fact that groups like L-e-T and J-e-M have increasingly become involved in terrorist attacks outside Kashmir has greatly complicated the picture.

The 2001 attack on the Indian parliament was not the first such attack outside Kashmir, but it was the most prominent and dangerous up till that time. Following the attack—attributed by India to L-e-T and J-e-M—India remained in a state of military mobilisation for almost a year and demanded that Pakistan extradite over twenty alleged terrorists and criminals, including Dawood Ibrahim. Pakistan refused and continues to refuse to this day. In the context of the investigation and trial of the sole surviving alleged perpetrator of the 26-29 November 2008 attacks in Mumbai, Indian prosecutors passed another list of twenty-two to Pakistan, requesting extradition. Again, Pakistan refused.

This use of the cat's paw of terrorism *vis à vis* Kashmir was for a long period seemingly acceptable internationally on account of the disputed nature of Kashmir and Pakistan's role as a front line state in the so-called 'war on terrorism'. Pakistan was taken off the US State Department's list of states in support of terrorism after it became an ally in the US 'war on terrorism' in 2001, and has not subsequently been re-included.

If wider international pressure was lacking in India's attempts to get redress, the mechanisms of SAARC were even less productive. According to Crispin, India tried extradition under the principle of *aut dedere aut judicare* (extradite or prosecute) using the *SAARC Convention on Suppression of Terrorism*, signed in 1987. But this approach did not work and in the 2007 SAARC meeting India angled to have included a proposal for a regional MLAT under the auspices of SAARC, to which Pakistan would automatically be forced to subscribe. Although the SAARC Convention on Mutual Legal Assistance has recently been agreed in a text form, Pakistan and a number of other countries are still to ratify the agreement.

In 2006, India and Pakistan established a bilateral panel at Additional Secretary-level for exchanging counter-terrorism information. The panel was established in the aftermath of the so-called 7/11 bombings in Mumbai, in which over 200 people died and which were initially blamed by India on the ISI and Pakistani-based L-e-T. Following the bombings, India froze the Kashmir peace process and the new thaw did not occur until the two heads of state met informally at the Cuba Non-Aligned Movement leaders' summit. Subsequent talks at Foreign Secretary level established the panel. At the time of writing, the panel has met five times—well short of the stipulated quarterly meetings.

To date the panel has failed to make any real progress. Although it proposed to set up a mechanism to exchange information, to the knowledge of the author, no such mechanism was ever established and no information of substance exchanged. The essential problem was that the process was politically constituted and had a security focus, consisting of members of foreign ministries, ministries of home affairs and intelligence services on both sides, rather than police services. This political orientation meant it became mired in political issues, such as whether India can provide details of terrorism in Kashmir, which Pakistan regards as disputed territory. As well, members of the intelligence services of antagonistic states are hardly likely to want to pass over sensitive information. A better beginning might have been made had the panel been confined to police, who at least do not have to deal with high level national security issues (or not as their core business) and can rely on the so-called 'international brotherhood of police'.

Indeed, discussions in criminal matters, which also commenced in 2006, are somewhat more promising. They even covered formation of 'SAARCPOL', also mooted by SAARC in 2006 but so far not yet in place. The dialogue is being conducted at police-to-police level, but with representation from Home Affairs and External Affairs ministries. As an illustration of just how bad the state of cooperation is, however, it is noteworthy that this dialogue has only recommenced after an interregnum of seventeen years. By 2008, the international community's myopia in relation to Pakistani sponsored terrorism in India was starting to be cured. The initial trigger of this change was the apparent involvement of the ISI in the bombing of the Indian embassy in Kabul in July 2008, in which 54 died. Afghanistan was, of course, integral to the 'war on terrorism' and an attack in Kabul was not equivalent to one in India. But to be fair, the United States appeared to have direct knowledge of the ISI's involvement on this occasion, since following the attack the US intelligence services apparently leaked intercept information suggesting ISI involvement. Information based on intercepts was also leaked, suggesting that the top brass of the Pakistani Army regarded a leading Taliban figure, Maulavi Jalaluddin Haqqani, as a 'strategic asset' to be tipped off when Pakistani attacks against the Taliban occurred.

In the case of the Mumbai attacks of 26-29 November 2008 (referred to as 26/11 in India), the international community could no longer tolerate Pakistan's indulgence of terrorist groups like L-e-T. Two problems caused this to happen. The attacks involved the deaths of 26 foreigners, including westerners. And the dangerous escalation in tension between India and Pakistan in the aftermath caused Pakistan to withdraw troops from the western frontier—crucial in the 'war on terrorism'—so they could confront a belligerent India to the east. Pakistan played this concern about a withdrawal of support for the 'war on terrorism' to the hilt in order to try to get the United States to restrain India.

Despite the sharp escalation in international pressure on Pakistan, Islamabad has had to be forced against its will to cooperate with India on the Mumbai bombings. Initially, the recently elected civilian government had undertaken to send the head of the ISI to New Delhi for consultations. This would have been an amazing move on Pakistan's part, even a major break- through in terms of possible cooperation. However, the military evidently soon intervened. It could not allow one of its senior members to be 'dressed down' by India. The government had to back down.

India also attempted to garner international support by allowing the FBI and British police to interrogate the lone survivor of the Mumbai attacks. (This in itself was a breakthrough, because police-to-police cooperation with India is notoriously difficult.) The foreign agencies assisted with analysis of telephone intercepts and GPS data. Subsequently, the FBI confirmed that the attacks had emanated from Pakistan under the auspices of the L-e-T. India then released a series of dossiers which it said it had passed to Pakistan, in which was laid out what New Delhi referred to as the 'proof' of Pakistani involvement. The dossiers included phone numbers allegedly contacted by the attackers in Pakistan, the GPS data detailing the maritime route by which the attacks came and photos of various items and weapons allegedly seized from the attackers with Pakistani markings.

Pakistan initially denied the attacks came from Pakistan. Instead, Islamabad claimed they were supported from within India (probably true but not strictly relevant). They also delayed their official responses. Eventually they admitted that the lone surviving attacker, Kasab, did come from Pakistan but claimed he and other involved Pakistanis were 'sub-state actors'. When Islamabad did issue a reply to the Indian dossiers, it initially did so through the press rather than directly to India. Through leaks to the press Pakistan 'asked' further questions and made demands that India supply DNA for all of the attackers, including the nine deceased.

This prompted an angry response from Indian Home Affairs Minister Chidambaram. He claimed that nothing had been communicated to India officially by Pakistan. Moreover, he said, India had evidence of official Pakistani involvement. Eventually, Islamabad formally issued 30 questions to India that it demanded be answered before the investigation could be progressed.

Pakistan's 30 questions were issued after Cabinet consideration rather than directly by the investigating authorities. The charade of 'cooperation' was played out at the political level and as public theatre by both sides rather than behind closed doors as is more normal for legal cooperation.

If terrorism is political drama, so too is 'cooperation' against it, when played out by antagonistic states. On its part, India continued to apply pressure on Pakistan by holding out the possibility of a limited use of armed force through a surgical strike. Some argue such a response was not available to India due to continuing failure of the process of military modernisation. However, it is likely that the Indian Cabinet decided not to attack on other grounds, believing that a limited strike could well have led to a 'hot war' with devastating consequences on both sides. Probably also it was subjected to considerable pressure from the United States not to attack Pakistan. But the possibility of a surgical strike is still very much alive should India consider that Pakistan's response is never going to be adequate.

India's dissatisfaction with Pakistan's response was further increased by the release by a Pakistani court of the head of the L-e-T, Hafiz Saeed, on grounds there was insufficient evidence associating him with the attack. The Indian Foreign Minister said Saeed's release made India question the sincerity of Pakistan's offer of further talks.

Thus, the attempt to cooperate following 26/11, such as it was, actually had the effect of inflaming the situation further. To India, Pakistan appeared to be obfuscating instead of sincerely cooperating, a manoeuvre the Indians found infuriating in the circumstances. The process was politically driven and played as public theatre by both sides. That does not mean that some kind of cooperation may not eventually occur, but if it does, it will be due to unremitting international pressure on Pakistan and will have nothing to do with regional mechanisms.

Indeed, in all of this, the mechanisms of SAARC were worse than useless. It appeared that the organisation is seen in New Delhi as little more than a vehicle for the lesser powers of the region to gang up on India. Regionalism showed itself to be a 'dead letter' when it came to solving cross border problems between enemies.

But that does not mean that regionalism has no role to play in difficult circumstances like those between India and Pakistan. SAARC could ultimately prove very useful should India and Pakistan reach a modicum of workable cooperation on terrorism and transnational crime as a result of bilateral efforts and other external pressures, for example from the wider international community. Should such as state of affairs eventuate, SAARC would be well placed to 'wrap that cooperation around' with more formal regional mechanisms in order to ensure that it becomes embedded in the regional norm. SAARC's MLAT document could even be used as a vehicle for future cooperation between India and Pakistan.

Nevertheless, SAARC clearly has difficulties as a result of the intense India- Pakistan antagonism. But are prospects any better for ASEAN? Has ASEAN at least started to progress down the path to a 'tipping point' when cooperation actually instils confidence? To explore this issue, let us examine another relationship tainted by cross border violence and criminality—that of Burma and Thailand.

BURMA, THAILAND AND ASEAN

One of the best-known examples of the vicious circle mentioned above is the series of short border exchanges fought between Burma and Thailand in 2001 and 2002 over the trafficking of illicit drugs and the on-going tensions between them over the flow of refugees and illegal migrants into Thailand.

Independently of any problems relating to cross-border criminality, there is no love lost between the two countries when viewed in the historical context. After hundreds of years of intermittent warfare, competition and invasion, they are what might be called 'traditional' competitors, albeit ones with a strong cultural and religious affinity. Ball reports that problems along the border between the two are 'perennial'.

In the latter part of the 20th century, these tensions were exacerbated by the massive flow of methamphetamines (so-called *ya ba* pills) over the border from Burma into Thailand, particularly under the agency of the United Wa State Army (UWSA—a hitherto separatist group now sponsored by the Burmese military regime). According to one estimate made early in 2001, as many as 700 million *ya ba* pills were to cross the border in that year. Such was the negative effect on Thai youth that the Thais were provoked to tighten their grip on sections of the ill-defined northern border, resulting in military clashes with Burma involving artillery and air attacks in early 2001 and 2002.

The history of the flow of *ya ba* across the border is complex. It involves the crack-down in Thailand itself on the production of *ya ba* in local labs in the 1980s and 1990s; the movement of heroin production from the border region to the UWSA region more to the north west after the drug lord, Khun Sa, was 'brought in from the cold' in 1996; possibly the deal struck by the Wa with the Burmese regime to cease heroin production by 2002; possibly UN and US sponsored heroin eradication efforts in the latter part of the 1990s; probably the sharp crackdown by China on cross-border trafficking of heroin from the Wa regions into China; and certainly the complex market shifts, economics and risk assessment of methamphetamine production in relation to heroin production. In any case, it is not the purpose of this chapter to assess the reason for the massive flow of *ya ba* across the Thai-Burmese border in these years, but rather to examine its consequences.

Ya ba dependency had begun as a lower-order problem in Thai society, one involving sex workers, truckers and shift workers who needed to stay awake to fuel Thailand's booming economy and tourism industry. By the late 1990s, however, the problem had started to filter into Thailand's school, college and university populations.

This meant it also became a middle- class problem. Moreover, at whatever level it struck society, vicious side effects were exposed involving a rapid rise in morbidity and crime. Thailand, having cracked down on the internal trade in the 1990s and closed down large numbers of manufacturing laboratories, now saw millions of *ya ba* pills crossing the northern border from Burma. Bangkok directed its attention to interdicting the flow, including by military means. It was these endeavours that caused the two militaries to become embroiled in conflict.

By 2003, the Thaksin Shinawatra government was engaged in its so-called 'war on drugs' against *ya ba*. In this 'war', hundreds, and possibly thousands, of alleged, but untried, traffickers were killed in execution-style killings, often left clutching a firearm and bag of *ya ba*. Reported use of *ya ba* fell sharply (although the data may well have been distorted due to fear of self-reporting) and the Burmese drug routes were re-directed from the northern Thai border to the Lao PDR, Cambodia and Vietnam, with deleterious consequences in terms of addiction in those countries.

Another set of tensions triggered by cross-border criminal activity related to illegal migration into Thailand from Burma. Thousands of Burmese women were smuggled and trafficked from Burma into Thailand to service the sex industry in the 1990s and early 2000s. Many were minors, and many more became infected with HIV/AIDS. Upon such infection, they were unceremoniously pushed back into Burma, where they received further ill-treatment at the hands of the Burmese authorities. Others arrested by the Thais were simply re-trafficked, which was indicative of the fact that border relations were corrupted and mutual data were not maintained.

In addition, many Burmese young men also came across the border to find paid labour in the more affluent parts of Asia. This irregular migration was at first ignored by Thailand, but with the Asian financial crisis of 1997-98, the Burmese were less welcome and many were sent back. As the economy quickly resumed its higher growth rate, however, the flow of migrants again increased and numbers reached perhaps a million by 2004.[71] At least some of these were Rohingyas, Muslims from the northern border region of Burma near Bangladesh. The Rohingyas were discriminated against by the Burmese regime and had initially been pushed into refugee camps in Bangladesh. But by the early 1990s, Burma was attempting to show its more benign side in order to obtain membership of ASEAN. For a period, it therefore accepted the Rohingyas back.

Political refugees from the draconian military regime also established themselves in semi-permanent camps along the Burma-Thai border and in Bangkok. The existence of these camps further exacerbated tensions between Thailand and Burma. These tensions came to a head in 1999. The Burmese regime was outraged when a group of Burmese political refugees in Bangkok seized the Burmese embassy. Instead of being arrested by the sympathetic Thais, they were subsequently flown out to a jungle camp.

If that was the bald history of the tensions generated between Burma and Thailand over *ya ba* and illegal migration, how was ASEAN involved, if at all, and what has happened in the relationship since?

As a founding member of ASEAN, Thailand had initially favoured a relatively soft position on Burma. This occurred despite the historical antipathy between Thailand and Burma and on-going cross-border problems. It was the Thai foreign minister who coined the term 'constructive engagement' for ASEAN's dealings with Burma in 1991.

This softer attitude to Burma was related to the growing interconnectivity between the two economies following the establishment of the State Law and Order Restoration Committee (SLORC) junta in 1998. In order to win much-needed friends, the junta gave the Thai military under General Chavalit Yongchaiyudh valuable concessions in Burma in the logging and fishing industries and in cross-border trade, causing the two economies to become increasingly enmeshed. The Singaporeans and Malaysians also had significant investments in Burma. And with the softer policy towards the Rohingyas, the religious qualms of Indonesia and Malaysia were put to one side. These—and perhaps a desire to make a point to the Europeans and Americans who were critics of South East Asia's illiberal regimes—were among the factors that contributed to Burma's admission to ASEAN in 1997.

But following Burma's admission, Thailand's problems over illicit drugs and illegal migration caused its attitude to Burma to change. Thailand's return to democracy also contributed to this change. Constructive engagement had given way to 'flexible engagement', implying the right of ASEAN member states to criticise the activities of others, where those activities impacted across the border. Thai Prime Minister Surin referred to the flow of Burmese refugees across the border as an example of such Burmese 'interference'.

ASEAN's role in mitigating these frictions was limited by its policy of non- interference. This was despite the desires of Thailand, and to a lesser extent the Philippines, to use ASEAN to settle troubling cross-border issues. Non-interference in turn meant that there was little basis for real (as opposed to exhortatory) cooperation in matters like transnational crime and terrorism. With the attacks on the United States of 11 September 2001 and subsequent Bali bombings of October 2002, however, much changed. In part these changes were induced by outside intervention and money, particularly from the United States and Australia. In part also they were progressed by extra- ASEAN mechanisms, such as the collection of activities surrounding the so- called 'Bali Process', the Asia-Pacific Group (on money laundering), JCLEC and APEC. That said, it is also true that the years of hard work in ASEAN, including through expansionary mechanisms such as the ASEAN Regional Forum (ARF) and 'ASEAN plus 3' and second track mechanisms like the Council for Security Cooperation in the Asia-Pacific (CSCAP), also oiled the wheels for this additional level of cooperation.

As to ASEAN itself, progress in law enforcement cooperation continues to be slow but should not be dismissed out of hand. ASEAN often works through informal mechanisms. For example, the Australian Department of Immigration and Citizenship (DIAC) commented to an Australian parliamentary inquiry into Australia's relationship with ASEAN that Australia's involvement in the annual ASEAN meeting of senior immigration and consular officials (known as the DGICM) provides an excellent network for on-going cooperation throughout ASEAN. Through this involvement, DIAC has been able to work with regional countries to strengthen training of immigration officials and move towards a collective database. Also, bilateral as distinct from multilateral cooperation amongst regional countries is often far stronger than the regional association's progress would suggest.

This is exemplified by the excellent cooperation at a police-to-police level between the Australian Federal Police (AFP) and a number of regional police services, such as Indonesia's POLRI. A visit to the ASEAN Secretariat web site, however, is mind-numbing in its focus on exhortatory and declaratory strategies. The site contains thirteen joint communiqués; seven press releases; six declarations; and eight other documents, only a few of them of a more practical bent, such as MLATs and MoUs. But beneath this rhetoric, some good work has been done, especially in the areas of illicit drugs training and people smuggling and trafficking.

The issue for the present inquiry is: what has this work achieved in terms of mitigating the negative effects of cross-border issues between the two competitors, Burma and Thailand? Both countries subscribe to the various multilateral mechanisms in play around the issues of drugs, trafficking in persons and illegal migration. Both are part of the Bali Process; both are signatories of the Bangkok Declaration on Irregular Migration of 1999; and both have acceded to the UN's Convention on Transnational Organised Crime (CTOC) and its associated convention on trafficking. ASEAN has also played a role, at least to an extent, with the two countries signing an MoU on the employment of migrant workers in the sidelines of the 36th ASEAN Ministerial Meeting held in Bangkok. (But as Than notes, there is no evidence that this MoU led to any further coordination between the two.) In 2006, however, they did agree to set up joint border documentation centres and some progress has been made in establishing them.

Perhaps some of the best progress has been made against trafficking under the auspices of the Australian aid-funded Asia Regional Project to Prevent People Trafficking (ARCPPT), involving Myanmar, Thailand, Laos and Cambodia. This project involves NGOs, the establishment of specialised anti-trafficking police units, legal reform, protection of victims and exchange of information. It has led to an MoU on trafficking between the six members of the Mekong sub-region and a ministerial level coordination mechanism between them. It is noteworthy that the ARCPPT project works closely with the ASEAN Secretariat, which assists in spreading the mechanisms developed amongst the four original participants more widely. It remains to be seen whether this broad range of cooperative mechanisms, including under ASEAN, has provided a means of addressing the latest Thai- Burmese crisis—that over the Rohingyas.

By late 2008 and early 2009, the Thais were picking up growing numbers of Rohingya boat people. Normally, Rohingyas had drifted into Thailand to find work in the fishing and other low-paid industries and the Thais had not worried too much about them. But on this occasion the Thai authorities took a different attitude. According to some estimates, 1000 were put back to sea by the Thai military, some after being beaten. The Thai authorities were also accused of setting them adrift with little food and water and in some cases in boats without engines. Thailand's Foreign Ministry vigorously denied these charges of inhumane treatment, but in an interview on CNN the Thai Prime Minister, Abhisit Vejjajiva, eventually admitted that Rohingyas were put back to sea. The problem was exacerbated by the fact that the Burmese junta denied that the Rohingyas were even originally from Burma. The decline in the Thai economy caused by the global financial crisis was one factor in the changed attitude on the part of the Thais to the Rohingyas.

The Thai military and security agencies were also concerned that an additional population of discontented Muslims might feed into the discontent already manifest in the Muslim majority southern provinces. Indeed, from the outset, the matter had been given a strong security focus. For example, the coordinating authority between the different agencies involved with countering drug and people smuggling is the Internal Security Operations Command (ISOC). ISOC was established in 1965 with a heavy military bias in order to deal with the communist insurgency. With the insurgency defeated, and under civilian control, it still retains strong military links and the Army Chief-of-Staff is Chief-of-Staff of ISOC. In 2001, following the 9/11 attacks, General Chavalit said it should become "the Thai equivalent of the US homeland defence command" and placed in charge of "all border threats". Another aspect of this securitisation policy is the involvement of the major Thai paramilitary organisation, the *Or Sor*, in policing borders, combating drug running and dealing with refugee and illegal immigration flows.

In the face of mounting criticism from the international community and predominantly Muslim ASEAN neighbours such as Malaysia and Indonesia, Thailand turned not to ASEAN, but demanded an international conference of concerned countries, which would include India (which had picked up Rohingyas adrift on the high seas), Bangladesh, Burma, Malaysia and Indonesia (both of which had been destinations for Rohingya refugees).

The Thais, however, were facing severe international censure and disquiet from their Muslim ASEAN neighbours. In a significant shift from Thailand's initial approach to the issue, the Thai foreign minister agreed with the Indonesian foreign minister to "put the whole thing back under the Bali process". This decision both had the effect of bringing more familiar cooperative mechanisms to bear and implying a mutual agreement that the Rohingyas were *not* refugees but part of the regional people smuggling and trafficking problem. The subsequent 14th ASEAN Summit confirmed this position, finding that the Rohingyas were part of a wider Indian Ocean illegal migration problem "best addressed by other fora [than ASEAN]".

As far as Thailand was concerned, it appeared that initially ASEAN had little to offer in resolving this complex issue. The issue of the Rohingyas cut across the ASEAN region and into South Asia, so ASEAN itself was not an ideal vehicle. And ASEAN was replete with sensitivities and tensions, including those between Thailand and Burma and between Thailand and its Muslim majority brethren. Thailand was perhaps nervous that the Muslim ASEAN countries would argue that the Rohingyas were genuine refugees and therefore to be looked after by Thailand as the country of first refuge. (Thailand had refused to refer the matter to the United Nations High Commissioner for Refugees for the same reason). The fact Burma disowned the Rohingyas, and that ASEAN apparently accepted Burma's position, enabled ASEAN to shove the issue to one side by claiming it was extra-mural. Ultimately, however, it was at least an ASEAN-related process—the Bali Process—that offered Thailand a way out. Apparently the Thai and Indonesian foreign ministers were able to reach this position in accordance with the 'Asian way' of non-interference, in which human rights issues are, essentially, subservient to perceived security issues and in which the behaviour of other member states in support of their own security is not criticised.

THE IDEOLOGICAL FOUNDATION OF TERRORISM

Before the war against terrorism can come to any definitive conclusion, its underlying philosophy must first be identified, along with the means to be employed. This book, therefore, deals with terrorism's basic starting point, as well as the disasters to which it leads. Its starting point is the assumption that violence is a virtue in itself and a powerful means to solve social or political problems. While killing the innocents, damaging public order, and disrupting peace, any terrorist acts under the influence of ideas that have been imposed on him, coaxing him to believe that he's engaged in a justified struggle.

Terrorism can be healed only when such people understand the mistaken illogic of any ideology that inspires terrorism and incites to violence—and when they realize that going along with it can never get them anywhere. Until those ideologies' errors and contradictions are revealed, all measures taken against terrorism can be short-term only. Soon terrorism will emerge again, in different places and under different circumstances, behind a different mask.

We can put an end to terrorism only by destroying its ideological infrastructure. The modern terrorism's ideological foundations in fact go back to Social Darwinism and the materialist tendencies derived from it. People exposed to this indoctrination believe that life is a field of struggle, and that only the strong survive. The weak are condemned to be eliminated. Man and, in fact, the entire universe, are both products of chance. Therefore, no one is responsible for his actions to anyone else. These and similar ideas inevitably coax people into leading an animalistic form of life, where ruthlessness, aggression and violence are regarded as acceptable or even virtuous.

Anyone who resorts to terrorism, maintaining that violence is the only way to achieve his aims, is actually under the influence of Social Darwinism and materialist thought, no matter what his religion or race, or what group he belongs to. Modern terrorist groups that claim to act in the name of religion are also under Darwinism's influence and materialism, even though they claim to carry out their terroristic acts in the name of religion.

This is because for anyone who lives by the morality of religion revealed by God, it's impossible to approve of violence of any kind, much less achieve a "higher" aim by murdering others. Those who resort to such methods are therefore pursuing the exact opposite of the moral values upheld by religion, carrying out their actions under the influence of materialist ideologies.

In *Islam Denounces Terrorism*, it was made clear that Islam fiercely rejects all forms of terrorism, no matter whom it may be directed against.

In the light of verses from the Qur'an, it was explained how religion's morality calls people to peace, tolerance, and convenience. Also stressed was the dishonesty of condemning only those acts of terrorism directed against one's own side: Such an attitude only weakens the fight against terrorism; and anyone living according to Islamic morality needs to fight terror in all its all forms. The foundation of that intellectual struggle is based on revealing the true morality of religion.

Today's politicians, political commentators and academics agree that by itself, military force isn't enough to root out terrorism. This book concentrates on the only way it can be eradicated: by means of peace, tolerance, and love.

All the divinely-inspired religions that God sent down by means of His messengers are helpful guides. This book offers examples from the Qur'an as well as from the Bible (even though the latter has been partially distorted) to show how each of the three divine religions forbids the use of unjust violence. It also gives examples to show that the only way to fight terrorism is to heal the root causes through the love, affection, compassion, humility, forgiveness, tolerance and concepts of justice that religion's morality instils in people—whom, following the verse from the Qur'an (10:25): "God calls to the Abode of Peace... " Such fortunates will do their utmost to build a world full of peace and love.

ATHEIST IDEOLOGIES AND THE RISE OF TERRORISM

If a sick person is to be treated properly, an accurate diagnosis is essential. Whatever treatment follows that diagnosis must be followed meticulously and decisively, until the sickness is finally expelled from the body. If not, the illness will inevitably recur. The same applies to one of the most serious ills affecting society. One of the chief reasons why we can't find effective solutions to this century's social problems is that their causes aren't properly identified. When dealing with any social problem, the first thing to do is establish what causes give rise to it. Otherwise, whatever measures are taken can only be temporary.

The roots of terrorism are often sought in concrete matters; and thus the fight against it, aimed at these superficial targets, cannot provide lasting results. In order to free the world from terrorism, the principal factors behind it must be identified and eliminated.

TERRORISM IS CLOSE TO HOME!

There are an estimated 500 terrorist groups in the world. These include international cartels controlling trade in drugs, arms and prostitution, as well as underground organizations, marginal movements, various radical ideological groups, and deviant cults that stage actions allegedly in the name of religion. Many terrorist organizations do operate within their own countries' borders, but a number target what they have decided as "enemy" countries, through attacks on prominent sites and individuals that, they calculate, will elicit a huge public reaction. From the reaction, they seek to achieve fame, in fact notoriety, which they hope that will add to their power.

Though terrorism has existed since the earliest times, through esoteric organizations like the Sicarii or Assassins, and flourished in the modern times through revolutionary cadres like the sans-cullottes of the French Revolution or the Russian Nihilism of the 19th century, its threat really came to the fore in the 20th century, which saw an explosion in acts of terror and in the number of terrorists who committed them. Weapons of mass destruction and the rapid advance of technology made terrorist attacks much easier and vastly increased their destructiveness.

By the 1960s, people began to wonder seriously what might happen, if a terrorist group managed to acquire some kind of nuclear weapon that could result in the deaths of tens of thousands. A biological or chemical attack could wipe entire populations off the map. No such attack happened, fortunately. But by the 1990s, the chances of such attacks increased. These concerns only heightened with the collapse of the Soviet Union and the weakening of control over its nuclear arsenal. The spread of the Internet and the facilitation of all forms of information increased worries still further. Fear of terrorism became the subject of hundreds of films and books. Reports were written about the possible consequences; research was carried out. Now, all too obviously, terrorists could go beyond familiar, limited actions like bombings, armed robberies, skyjackings and kidnappings, to attack entire communities. Such attacks could be carried out by remote control or computer, with no direct human intervention.

A number of recent fears in the US involving biological weapons like of the anthrax bacteria revealed the scale of the threat posed by bio-terrorism and biological weapons. With the help of an experienced chemist in a simple laboratory, terrorists can now threaten the lives of thousands. One of the first examples of this occurred in 1984, when 750 people were poisoned in four restaurants in a small town in Oregon. Later, it was revealed that a Hindu-inspired New Age cult under the leadership of Baghwan Shree Rajneesh was responsible. Disciples had grown salmonella bacteria on their farms and placed them in salad bars in area restaurants. In 1995, the Aum Shinrikyo ("Higher Truth") cult released the poison gas sarin in the Tokyo underground subway system, leading to the deaths of 12 people and another 5,500 injured. Subsequent inquiries revealed that the cult had tried to construct biological weapons in its own laboratories—revealing just how large a threat terrorism poses to the public.

In the 21st century, computer technology is expected to play an important role in terrorist attacks. Meanwhile, more "conventional" ways of terrorism, like bombings, arson attacks, skyjackings and kidnappings are still going on all over the world, from Europe to America, from Asia to Africa. Since 1962, for example, members of the ETA (Euskadi Ta Askatasuna) terrorist organization, fighting for the Basque region's independence, has carried out many terrorist attacks in Spain, resulting in the deaths of more than 800.4 For years, the Irish Republican Army has seized world headlines with its bloody attacks to gain independence for Northern Ireland. The central aim of the IRA is to end British control of Northern Ireland and to achieve the reunification of the island of Ireland. Generally it has operated in Northern Ireland and London, but has also been involved in bombings in various European countries such as Germany. Since 1969, the IRA's terrorist attacks, and Britain's methods of "counter-terrorism", have caused the deaths of more than 3,200 on both sides of the conflict. Millions of dollars' worth of damage has been caused by IRA bombings of airports and underground stations, again aimed at civilians. During a European Football Championship match on June 15, 1996, an IRA car bombing in a Manchester shopping centre resulted in some 200 injuries.

Currently, no country can feel safe from this kind of threat. The few examples just cited show just how deeply terrorism has come to influence peoples' lives. No longer the problem of just a few specific nations, it's a threat that faces all mankind. Because no one can tell when, where or how terrorists will strike, the fight against them can no longer be considered the duty of a handful of countries or organizations. Terrorism, threatening the entire world, can be resolved only if well-intentioned people support each other in search of peace, friendship and brotherhood.

GLOBAL RESPONSE TO TERRORISM

Since terrorism is not restricted to any one jurisdiction, it mandates a global response. Repercussions are felt everywhere, and at some point, counterterrorism must require more than the ability of one state to combat terrorism. Extradition and deportation schemes have been the traditional global counterterrorism tools. Extradition is the surrender by one state to another of an individual accused or convicted of an offence outside its own territory and within the territorial jurisdiction of the other, which, being competent to try and punish him, demands the surrender.

Political offenses, however, are normally exempt from extradition, and death penalty concerns are an additional complication. Deportation procedures, likewise, rely upon cooperation, and usually create problems for whatever country the terrorist is deported to. Deportation is often used in the United States whenever a defendant is not allowed to view classified material against them. Aliens convicted of serious crimes are regularly deported.

The G-8 countries (which include Canada, the United States, Britain, Germany, France, Italy, Japan, and Russia) have long made counterterrorism an agenda item at their summits. Most of their proposals rest on using Interpol as a formal association of police agencies everywhere, or more recently Europol, the embryonic Europe-wide police agency. Other recommendations involve military installations, municipal operations, defence contractors, and the private sector. Most well-known, however, is the call for a permanent International Criminal Court (ICC), an idea spawned in 1993 by a U.N. committee and ratified by the Rome Statute in 1998 and taking effect in 2002.

As an entity created by the U.N. treaty process, the ICC's jurisdiction would be any international crime like war crime, genocide, unprovoked aggression, crimes against humanity, and (theoretically) terrorism. States consent to participate on a case-by-case basis. The forum is supposed to be neutral and 18 judges are elected for nine-year terms. The court may sentence convicted offenders to incarceration for terms of up to 30 years or, in cases of extreme gravity, life imprisonment

Another basic problem of course is the questionable status of detainees in a war on terrorism. Captured terrorists may be held by one nation as "unlawful combatants" and deprived of POW (prisoner of war) status and Geneva convention protections. Such protections require viewing the terrorists as legitimate armies. Rule 117 of the ICC's *Rules of Procedure and Evidence* provides for detention in a "custodial state" and allows for a hearing on pretrial conditional release.

By definition, terrorists do not meet the four requirements necessary for combatant status (wear uniforms or other distinctive insignia, carry arms openly, be under command of a person responsible for group actions, and conduct their operations in accordance with laws of war). For this reason, *captured terrorists are not usually afforded prisoner of war status*" (Joint Chiefs of Staff Publication 3-07.2, Joint Tactics, Techniques and Procedures for Antiterrorism, Washington, DC: 17 March 1998).

THE GLOBALIZATION THEORY OF TERRORISM

Nassar (2004) has probably written the most interesting piece on globalization theory as it relates to terrorism, and the ideas are fairly robust precisely because globalization can be a complex subject at times. Globalization contributes to dreams, fantasies, and rising expectations, but at the same time, it leads to dashed hopes, broken dreams, and unfulfilled achievements. Terrorism breeds in the gap between expectations and achievements.

The thinking is very similar to strain theory in criminology or the rising expectations theory of prison riots, and about the only thing unique about globalization theory is that it adds a rich-poor dichotomy. Rich people (or nations) are seen as wanting power and wealth, and poor people (or nations) are seen as wanting justice.

From this perspective, then, rich people are part of the causal factor or root cause of terrorism, since they contribute to the conditions which give rise to it. Perpetrators of "terrorism" (always treated as an ill-defined concept in globalization theory) are never seen as born or raised with any specific predispositions toward it. In brief, globalization theory holds that if the oppressed and disgruntled poor people of the world were simply given the chance to find peaceful means for achieving justice, terrorism would not thrive.

Globalization theory is further tied into ideas about colonialism, imperialism, and neocolonialism. The first two words are often used interchangeably to describe a set of conditions (technically, extensions of sovereignty) where the mores, values, and beliefs of the colonizers are considered superior to those of the colonized. However, when the assumption is made that (imperial) power is a necessary thing to maintain cultural superiority, this is the usual meaning of imperialism.

Neocolonialism is a concept developed by Marxists and holders of certain conspiracy theories to refer to allegations about First World nations, international organizations, and/or multinational corporations employing economic, financial and trade policies to dominate less powerful countries. Onwudiwe (2001) is typical of the criminological approach taken when globalization ideas are incorporated into theories about terrorism, and it is probably safe to say that the approach remains relatively underdeveloped.

THE POLITICAL THEORY OF FASCISM AS A THEORY OF TERRORISM

Fascism is the one form of government with the most disagreement about a definition for it, which Passmore (2002) attempts to consolidate as an ultranationalist ideology that is unabashedly racist. The word comes from the Latin "fasces" which means to use power to scare or impress people. It generally refers to the consolidation of all economic and political power into some form of super-patriotism that is devoted to genocide or endless war with one's enemies.

Benito Mussolini, who practically invented the term in 1922, said it is the merger of state and corporate power. Adolf Hitler said that it is the clever and constant application of propaganda so that people can be made to see paradise as hell, and the other way around. So-called Islamo-Fascism can also be traced to the same time period as the birth of the Nazi ("national socialist") fascism in 1928 when the Muslim Brotherhood (Al Ikhwan Al Muslimun), parent organization of numerous terrorist groups, was formed in reaction to the 1924 abolition of the caliphate by the Turks.

Fascism supports terrorism at home and abroad. Charismatic leaders are usually given supreme powers to crack down on dissidents, peacemakers, and anyone who doesn't abide by the "cult of the individual" which worships a He-man mentality and the party line. With the frequent wars and militaristic ventures that come with fascism, an effort is made to demonize the enemy as sub-humans who deserve extinction. These enemies are also made into scapegoats for all the past problems a country has had. Fascism appeals to the frustrations and resentments of a race of people who think they ought to have a bigger place at the global table. When combined with an anti-western slant (the United States as Great Satan), fascism becomes a means of social identity (Pan-Africanism, Pan-Arabism, Islamo-Fascism) as well as a facilitator of terrorism against all western interests. Frustrated fascists who fail to gain control in their own countries have historically turned to terrorism.

They are most likely to turn to domestic terrorism since fascists do not believe that citizen rights are bestowed merely because someone inhabits a country. Nor do they believe that all human beings are possessed of equal rights. "Foreign" families and businesses (as they define them) are usually targeted for extermination by fascists. The enemies who are seen as the greatest threat are those who fascists see as corrupting or poisoning family and property relations.

Fascism is full of ironies and contradictions. On the one hand, it is anti-modern in its glorification of the land, a return to country life, and its fascination with peasant dress or costume. On the other hand, it is pro-modern in its worship of military technology, favoritism of big business, mass mobilization of people, promotion of commercialized sport, and its surprisingly liberal attitude toward the involvement of women in the movement. Science and scholarship also take on interesting twists under fascism. "Hard" sciences like biology and chemistry usually advance significantly, especially in areas such as genetic research. "Soft" sciences like sociology and psychology usually become usurped into mumbo-jumbo pseudoscientific ideas about a glorified folk culture and reasons for hating the enemy.

Just as anarchists have their May Day (May 1st) celebrations, fascists also tend to celebrate anniversaries. Many terrorists, of course, have been known to time their attacks to coincide with the date for an historical event or the birthday of someone special to them. For example, with ecoterrorism, that day is October 16, which coincides the the United Nation's World Food Day, and is usually when McDonald's restaurants are targeted for vandalism.

However, *the most important date in the study of terrorism is April 19.* A number of significant events have happened on that date. Right-wing domestic terrorist groups call it "Militia Day" because it was when the siege at Waco ended, it was when surveillance began at the Ruby Ridge compound in Idaho, and it marks the anniversary of the Oklahoma City bombing of the federal building. Neo-Nazi fascist groups celebrate April 19 because it was the day German Nazis started wiping out Jewish ghettos across Europe, as well as the following day being Adolf Hitler's birthday. Internationally, terrorist groups who regard themselves as "freedom fighters" and trace at least part of this justification to the American Revolution, take heart in the fact that the American Revolution started on April 19, 1775 at the Battle of Lexington. It remains to be seen if September 11 will replace April 19 as the most popular date for terrorism.

THE POLITICAL THEORY OF ANARCHISM AS A THEORY OF TERRORISM

Terrorism is most definitely not a form of governance, but anarchism is. Most anarchists reject terrorism in its vanguard varieties (for nationalist or religious purposes), but in a theoretical sense, anarchism justifies terrorism as a form of criminal action that attacks the values of an organized, complacent society. Anarchism is a theory of governance that rejects any form of central or external authority, preferring instead to replace it with alternative forms of organization such as shaming rituals for deviants, mutual assistance pacts between citizens, syndicalism (any non-authoritarian organizational structure that gives the greatest freedom to workers), iconoclasm (the destruction of cherished beliefs), libertarianism (a belief in absolute liberty), and plain old rugged individualism. Anarchism is often referred to as the nineteenth century roots of terrorism, the term first being introduced in 1840 by Pierre-Joseph Proudhon. *Anarchism defined* is the rejection of the state, of any form of coercive government, of any form of domination and exploitation. It is the notion of free and equal access to all the world's resources to enable positive freedom (*freedom to*) in place of negative freedom (*freedom from*, or the basis of most constitutional rights).

As a theory, anarchism holds a unique place in history because it was the first revolutionary movement to come up with systematic ideas about the purpose of agitation. You'll recognize some of these ideas as terrorist tactics, but it's important first to understand them in the context of anarchism. Proudhon contributed the idea of finding the "moment" as in when the moment is ripe for revolutionary action. Another anarchist, Mikhail Bakunin, popularized the idea of "propaganda by deed" or letting your actions speak for themselves, which was a theory originally developed by Carlo Pisacane, an Italian revolutionary who argued that ideas spring from deeds and not the other way around. Over the years, this notion has evolved into a fairly competent philosophy of the bomb as part of a propaganda campaign to stimulate awareness and sympathy with the cause, and in this respect has been noted as a defining feature of terrorism (Georges-Abeyie & Hass 1982). Bakunin's ideas strongly influenced anarchism because his concept of propaganda by deed also included a prohibition against large scale group action (it being better, he thought, for anarchist action to be individualized or done in small groups). Most anarchists operate on the principle of leaderless resistance, or acting on your own, with little knowledge or support of the groups they may belong to. Major anarchist figures, like Karl Heinzen and Johann Most, contributed the idea that murder, especially murder-suicide, constituted the highest form of revolutionary struggle. Both advocated the use of weapons of mass destruction. Other anarchists contributed different ideas, such as Peter Kropotkin's notion of "propaganda by word" or radicalizing the public by use of subversive publications. Anarchism (like fascism) has also had some influential female figures, and Emma Goldman (1869-1940) comes to mind as a early founder of free speech (the ACLU) and sexual freedom movements.

Minor figures in the history of anarchism, like Charles Gallo, Auguste Vaillante, Emile Henry, and Claudius Konigstein advocated the idea that to have the most effect, the targets must be innocents (in places such as crowded dance halls or shopping centers) or symbols of economic success (like banks and stock exchanges). It may be worth noting, in passing, that the famous Italian criminologist, Cesare Lombroso, developed his notion of the "born criminal" in part by being called in to examine the physical features of some minor anarchists who were really nothing more than criminals justifying their behaviour with anarchist talk.

Between 1875 and 1912, anarchists alone or in small groups managed to assassinate or attempt to assassinate the leaders of nine (9) different countries, including the U.S. (with President William McKinley in 1901). These crimes were just the most well-known acts of anarchism, as anarchists were involved in numerous ordinary crimes such as theft, robbery, murder, kidnapping, assault, and bombing. The most famous incident was the Haymarket riot in Chicago during 1886. During these peak years for classic anarchism, May Day celebrations became famous as all-out crime-rampant days. Police departments around the world became convinced there was an international conspiracy, and suspicious foreigners were locked up by the hundreds in many countries. Perfunctory trials were held, and many defendants were hanged or deported. The most famous of these trials was the 1920 case of Sacco and Vanzetti who were more antiwar and labor activists than anarchists. Anarchism in the classical sense was largely erased from the face of the earth by 1917 via a number of factors: the rise of communism and fascism (both of which are opposed to anarchism), strong xenophobic deportation (Red Scare) laws in democratic countries, and the fact that classic anarchism never became an organized movement. Twentieth-century terrorist groups which came later and claimed an ancestry with anarchism include: the Japanese Red Army, the British Angry Brigade, the German Baader-Meinhof Gang, the Weatherman in the United States, and the Mexican Zapatista movement (Kushner 2003). During the Spanish revolution of 1936, something called anarcho-syndicalism developed, which is a loose confederation of various protest groups. Those who call themselves anarchists today are more likely to be environmentalists or part of the anti-globalization movement who target for attack such institutions as the World Bank, International Monetary Fund, or World Trade Organization.

For purpose of balance, it is important to point out that anarchism today does not support terrorism. It has historically supported terrorism and even today might support assassination, but there are only weak theoretical links between the two, most strongly with the propaganda by deed concept. Anarchists hold to a doctrine that anarchy must be created in the act of self-liberation from oppressive and coercive relationships. You don't blow up the relationship as terrorists do; instead, you convince others that grounds for the existing relationship must be blown up. Anarchism is not about mad bombing or chaos. *Terrorists target people; anarchists target things* such as institutions and structures. Bakunin did not want the death of people but the destruction of things and positions of authority. Only a small minority of terrorists have ever been anarchists, and only a small minority of anarchists have ever been terrorists.

In fact, there is an area of study called anarchist criminology, a controversial subfield of critical criminology which celebrates the fact anarchism really has no workable definition. Anarchist criminology advocates the abolishment of criminal justice systems. It argues that much harm has been committed in the name of reasonableness, and anarchist criminology is committed to promoting the unthinkable and unreasonable. Like other subfields of critical criminology, anarchist criminology views the state as an inherently oppressive entity, and anarchist justice not only promotes social justice (equal access to all resources), but protects diversity and difference among people (Ferrell 1999).

10

Al-Qaeda Unique among Terrorist Organizations

Four characteristics distinguish al-Qaeda from its predecessors in either nature or degree: its fluid organization, recruitment methods, funding, and means of communication.

FLUID ORGANIZATION

The al-Qaeda of September 2001 no longer exists. As a result of the war on terrorism, it has evolved into an increasingly diffuse network of affiliated groups, driven by the worldview that al-Qaeda represents. In deciding in 1996 to be, essentially, a "visible" organization, running training camps and occupying territory in Afghanistan, al-Qaeda may have made an important tactical error; this, in part, explains the immediate success of the U.S.-led coalition's war in Afghanistan.

Since then, it has begun to resemble more closely a "global jihad movement," increasingly consisting of web-directed and cyber-linked groups and ad hoc cells. In its evolution, al-Qaeda has demonstrated an unusual resilience and international reach. It has become, in the words of Porter Goss, "only one facet of the threat from a broader Sunni jihadist movement." No previous terrorist organization has exhibited the complexity, agility, and global reach of al-Qaeda, with its fluid operational style based increasingly on a common mission statement and objectives, rather than on standard operating procedures and an organizational structure.

Al-Qaeda has been the focal point of a hybrid terrorist coalition for some time, with ties to inspired freelancers and other terrorist organizations both old and new. Some observers argue that considering al-Qaeda an organization is misleading; rather it is more like a nebula of independent entities (including loosely associated individuals) that share an ideology and cooperate with each other. The original umbrella group, the International Islamic Front for Jihad against Jews and Crusaders, formed in 1998, included not only al-Qaeda but also groups from Algeria, Bangladesh, Egypt, and Pakistan.

A sampling of groups that are connected in some way includes the Moro Islamic Liberation Front (Philippines), Jemaah Islamiyah (Southeast Asia), Egyptian Islamic Jihad (which merged with al-Qaeda in 2001), al-Ansar Mujahidin (Chechnya), al-Gama'a al-Islamiyya (primarily Egypt, but has a worldwide presence), Abu Sayyaf (Philippines), the Islamic Movement of Uzbekistan, the Salafist Group for Call and Combat (Algeria), and Harakat ul-Mujahidin (Pakistan/Kashmir). Some experts see al-Qaeda's increased reliance on connections to other groups as a sign of weakness; others see it as a worrisome indicator of growing strength, especially with groups that formerly focused on local issues and now display evidence of convergence on al-Qaeda's Salafist, anti-U.S., anti-West agenda.

The nature, size, structure, and reach of the coalition have long been subject to debate. Despite claims of some Western experts, no one knows how many members al-Qaeda has currently or had in the past. U.S. intelligence sources place the number of individuals who underwent training in camps in Afghanistan from 1996 through the fall of 2001 at between 10,000 and 20,000; the figure is inexact, in part, because of disagreement over the total number of such camps and because not all attendees became members. The International Institute for Strategic Studies in 2004 estimated that 2,000 al-Qaeda operatives had been captured or killed and that a pool of 18,000 potential al-Qaeda operatives remained. These numbers can be misleading, however: it would be a mistake to think of al-Qaeda as a conventional force, because even a few trained fighters can mobilize many willing foot soldiers as martyrs.

Methods of Recruitment

The staying power of al-Qaeda is at least in part related to the way the group has perpetuated itself; in many senses, al-Qaeda is closer to a social movement than a terrorist group. Involvement in the movement has come not from pressure by senior al-Qaeda members but mainly from local volunteers competing to win a chance to train or participate in some fashion. The process seems to be more a matter of "joining" than being recruited, and thus the traditional organizational approach to analyzing this group is misguided.

But the draw of al-Qaeda should also not be overstated: in the evolving pattern of associations, attraction to the mission or ideology seems to have been a necessary but not sufficient condition. Exposure to an ideology is not enough, as reflected in the general failure of al-Qaeda to recruit members in Afghanistan and Sudan, where its headquarters were once located. As psychiatrist Marc Sageman illustrates, social bonds, not ideology, apparently play a more important role in al-Qaeda's patterns of global organization.

Sageman's study of established links among identified al-Qaeda operatives indicates that they joined the organization mainly because of ties of kinship and friendship, facilitated by what he calls a "bridging person" or entry point, perpetuated in a series of local clusters in the Maghreb and Southeast Asia, for example. In recent years, operatives have been connected to al-Qaeda and its agenda in an even more informal way, having apparently not gone to camps or had much formal training: examples include those engaged in the London bombings of July 7 and 21, 2005, the Istanbul attacks of November 15 and 20, 2003, and the Casablanca attacks of May 16, 2003. This loose connectedness is not an accident: bin Laden describes al-Qaeda as "the vanguard of the Muslim nation" and does not claim to exercise command and control over his followers. Although many groups boast of a connection to al-Qaeda's ideology, there are often no logistical trails and thus no links for traditional intelligence methods to examine. This explains, for example, the tremendous difficulty in establishing connections between a radical mosque, bombers, bomb makers, supporters, and al-Qaeda in advance of an attack (not to mention after an attack).

Another concern has been the parallel development of Salatist networks apparently drawing European Muslims into combat against Western forces in Iraq. The European Union's counterterrorism coordinator, Gijs de Vries, for example, has cautioned that these battle-hardened veterans of the Iraq conflict will return to attack Western targets in Europe.

The Ansar al-Islam plot to attack the 2004 NATO summit in Turkey was, according to Turkish sources, developed in part by operatives who had fought in Iraq. A proportion of those recently drawn to the al-Qaeda movement joined after receiving a Salafist message disseminated over the internet. Such direct messages normally do not pass through the traditional process of vetting by an imam. European counterterrorism officials thus worry about members of an alienated diaspora— sometimes second-and third-generation immigrants—who may be vulnerable to the message because they are not thoroughly trained in fundamental concepts of Islam, are alienated from their parents, and feel isolated in the communities in which they find themselves. The impulse to join the movement arises from a desire to belong to a group in a context where the operative is excluded from, repulsed by, or incapable of successful integration into a Western community.

Thus, with al-Qaeda, the twentieth-century focus on structure and function is neither timely nor sufficient. Tracing the command and control relationships in such a dramatically changing movement is enormously difficult, which makes comparisons with earlier, more traditional terrorist groups harder but by no means impossible; one detects parallels, for example, between al-Qaeda and the global terrorist movements that developed in the late nineteenth century, including anarchist and social revolutionary groups.

Means of Support

Financial support of al-Qaeda has ranged from money channelled through charitable organizations to grants given to local terrorist groups that present promising plans for attacks that serve al-Qaeda's general goals. The majority of its operations have relied at most on a small amount of seed money provided by the organization, supplemented by operatives engaged in petty crime and fraud. Indeed, beginning in 2003, many terrorism experts agreed that al-Qaeda could best be described as a franchise organization with a marketable "brand." Relatively little money is required for most al-Qaedaassociated attacks. As the International Institute for Strategic Studies points out, the 2002 Bali bombing cost less than $35,000, the 2000 USS *Cole* operation about $50,000, and the September 11 attacks less than $500,000. Another element of support has been the many autonomous businesses owned or controlled by al-Qaeda; at one point, bin Laden was reputed to own or control approximately eighty companies around the world. Many of these legitimately continue to earn a profit, providing a self-sustaining source for the movement. International counterterrorism efforts to control al-Qaeda financing have reaped at least $147 million in frozen assets. Still, cutting the financial lifeline of an agile and low-cost movement that has reportedly amassed billions of dollars and needs few resources to carry out attacks remains a formidable undertaking.

Choking off funds destined for al-Qaeda through regulatory oversight confronts numerous challenges. Formal banking channels are not necessary for many transfers, which instead can occur through informal channels known as "alternative remittance systems," "informal value transfer systems," "parallel banking," or "underground banking." Examples include the much-discussed *hawala* or *hundi* transfer networks and the Black Market Peso Exchange that operate through family ties or unofficial reciprocal arrangements. Value can be stored in commodities such as diamonds and gold that are moved through areas with partial or problematical state sovereignty. Al-Qaeda has also used charities to raise and move funds, with a relatively small proportion of gifts being siphoned off for illegitimate purposes, often without the knowledge of donors. Yet efforts to cut off charitable ºows to impoverished areas may harm many genuinely needy recipients and could result in heightened resentment, which in turn may generate additional political support for the movement. Al-Qaeda's fiscal autonomy makes the network more autonomous than its late-twentieth-century state-sponsored predecessors.

Means of Communication

The al-Qaeda movement has successfully used the tools of globalization to enable it to communicate with multiple audiences, including potential new members, new recruits, active supporters, passive sympathizers, neutral observers, enemy governments, and potential victims. These tools include mobile phones, text messaging, instant messaging, and especially websites, email, blogs, and chat rooms, which can be used for administrative tasks, fund-raising, research, and logistical coordination of attacks. Although al-Qaeda is not the only terrorist group to exploit these means, it is especially adept at doing so.

A crucial facilitator for the perpetuation of the movement is the use of websites both to convey messages, *fatwas,* claims of attacks, and warnings to the American public, as well as to educate future participants, embed instructions to operatives, and rally sympathizers to the cause. The internet is an important factor in building and perpetuating the image of al-Qaeda and in maintaining the organization's reputation. It provides easy access to the media, which facilitates al-Qaeda's psychological warfare against the West. Indoctrinating and teaching new recruits is facilitated by the internet, notably through the dissemination of al-Qaeda's widely publicized training manual (nicknamed "The Encyclopedia of Jihad") that explains how to organize and run a cell, as well as carry out attacks. Websites and chat rooms are used to offer practical advice and facilitate the fraternal bonds that are crucial to al-Qaeda. In a sense, members of the movement no longer need to join an organization at all, for the individual can participate with the stroke of a few keys. The debate over the size, structure, and membership of al-Qaeda may be a quaint relic of the twentieth century, displaced by the leveling effects of twenty-first-century technology. The new means of communication also offer practical advantages. Members of al-Qaeda use the web as a vast source of research and data mining to scope out future attack sites or develop new weapons technology at a low cost and a high level of sophistication. On January 15, 2003, for example, U.S. Secretary of Defence Donald Rumsfeld quoted an al-Qaeda training manual retrieved by American troops in Afghanistan that advised trainees that at least 80 percent of the information needed about the enemy could be collected from open, legal sources.

ORGANIZATION STRUCTURE OF AL-QAEDA

Though the current structure of al-Qaeda is unknown, information mostly acquired from Jamal al-Fadl provided American authorities with a rough picture of how the group was organized. While the veracity of the information provided by al-Fadl and the motivation for his cooperation are both disputed, American authorities base much of their current knowledge of al-Qaeda on his testimony. Osama bin Laden is the emir and Senior Operations Chief of al-Qaeda (although originally this role may have been filled by Abu Ayoub al-Iraqi), advised by a Shura Council, which consists of senior al-Qaeda members, estimated by Western officials at about twenty to thirty people. Ayman al-Zawahiri is al-Qaeda's Deputy Operations Chief and Abu Ayyub al-Masri is possibly the senior leader of al-Qaeda in Iraq.

- The Military Committee is responsible for training operatives, acquiring weapons, and planning attacks.
- The Money/Business Committee runs business operations, provides air tickets and false passports, pays al-Qaeda members, and oversees profit-driven businesses. In the 9/11 Commission Report, it is estimated that al-Qaeda requires $30,000,000 USD per year to conduct its operations.
- The Law Committee reviews Islamic law and decides if particular courses of action conform to the law.
- The Islamic Study/Fatwah Committee issues religious edicts, such as an edict in 1998 telling Muslims to kill Americans.
- In the late 1990s there was a publicly known Media Committee, which ran the now-defunct newspaper *Nashrat al Akhbar (Newscast)* and handled public relations.
- In 2005, al Qaeda formed As-Sahab, a media production house, to supply its video and audio materials.

The number of individuals belonging to the organization is also unknown. According to the controversial BBC documentary *The Power of Nightmares,* al-Qaeda is so weakly linked together that it is hard to say it exists apart from Osama bin Laden and a small clique of close associates. The lack of any significant numbers of convicted al-Qaeda members despite a large number of arrests on terrorism charges is cited by the documentary as a reason to doubt whether a widespread entity that meets the description of al-Qaeda exists at all. Therefore the extent and nature of al-Qaeda remains a topic of dispute.

Its rank and file has been described as changing from being "predominantly Arab," in its first years of operation, to "largely Pakistani," as of 2007. It has been estimated that 62% of al-Qaeda members have university education.

Organization v. Concept

When asked about the possibility of Al Qaeda's connection to the 7 July 2005 London bombings in 2005, Metropolitan Police Commissioner Sir Ian Blair said: "Al Qaeda is not an organization. Al Qaeda is a way of working... but this has the hallmark of that approach.... Al Qaeda clearly has the ability to provide training... to provide expertise... and I think that is what has occurred here."

What exactly al-Qaeda is, or was, remains in dispute. In the BBC documentary *The Power of Nightmares,* writer and journalist Adam Curtis contends that the idea of al-Qaeda as a formal organization is primarily an American invention. Curtis contends the name "al-Qaeda" was first brought to the attention of the public in the 2001 trial of Osama bin Laden and the four men accused of the 1998 United States embassy bombings in East Africa. As a matter of law, the U.S. Department of Justice needed to show that Osama bin Laden was the leader of a criminal organization in order to charge him *in absentia* under the Racketeer Influenced and Corrupt Organizations Act, also known as the RICO statutes. The name of the organization and details of its structure were provided in the testimony of Jamal al-Fadl, who claimed to be a founding member of the organization and a former employee of Osama bin Laden. To quote the documentary directly:

The reality was that bin Laden and Ayman Zawahiri had become the focus of a loose association of disillusioned Islamist militants who were attracted by the new strategy. But there was no organization. These were militants who mostly planned their own operations and looked to bin Laden for funding and assistance. He was not their commander. There is also no evidence that bin Laden used the term "al-Qaeda" to refer to the name of a group until after September the 11th, when he realized that this was the term the Americans had given it.

Questions about the reliability of al-Fadl's testimony have been raised by a number of sources because of his history of dishonesty and because he was delivering it as part of a plea bargain agreement after being convicted of conspiring to attack U.S. military establishments. Sam Schmidt, a defence lawyer from the trial, had the following to say about al-Fadl's testimony.

AL QAEDA'S LEADERSHIP AND EXTREMIST MUSLIM IDEOLOGY

In looking at the dominant characteristics of a belligerent, Clausewitz indicated that a centre of gravity in a popular uprising is the "personalities of the leaders and public opinion." Al Qaeda's leader, Osama Bin Laden, fits the Clausewitzian definition of a personality leading a popular uprising. Only today, this uprising is on a global scale with the objective of overthrowing the world order. Bin Laden rallies Muslim extremists. His charisma, vision, wealth, and leadership abilities are the reasons Al Qaeda is an effective terrorist organization striking fear across the globe while winning admiration among many in the Muslim world. Author Rohan Gunaratna in describing Bin Laden's capabilities:

In the spectrum of contemporary terrorist leaders Osama bin Laden *has no equal*. As a leader who has employed violence in pursuit of his political aims and objectives, he stands out in many ways. First, he is the only leader to have built a truly multinational terrorist group that can strike anywhere in the world. For over a decade *Osama has inspired, instigated and supported Islamist guerrillas and terrorists,* bringing about many deaths and much human suffering. In the World Trade Centre attack alone, the victims were from nearly 100 different nationalities. Second, *he has built a popular following throughout the Islamic world, being almost revered* in Muslim circles in Asia, Africa and the Middle East and among the first- and second-generation migrants in North America, Europe and Australia. *Nor has his popularity waned* despite evidence that he masterminded the worst terrorist attack in history. *He continues to be regarded as the supreme symbol of resistance to US imperialism.* Third, Osama's disposition towards his enemies has not mellowed in the face of the imminent threat to his own life and to his organisation. Even after the US cruise missile attacks in 1998 and intervention in Afghanistan in late 2001, the tone of his statements has remained constant, if not more strident. To his admirers *he sets an example of fearlessness; he is unrelenting; neither he nor Al Qaeda will compromise.*

It is interesting to note that Clausewitz connected leaders of popular uprisings with public opinion. He did not expand on this idea in his book *On War,* but, his phrasing of "personalities of leaders and public opinion," clearly links these two elements as a single centre of gravity candidate. Although Clausewitz never could have imagined the world as it exists today, his observations and words still resonate by relating to the Gunaratna's description above of Bin Laden and that segment of the Muslim population that supports his extremist Muslim ideology. Thus, with Bin Laden, coupled with extremist ideology, as the strategic centre of gravity for Al Qaeda, the United States must "direct its energies" at both. Echevarria offers the counter to this by saying:

... the avowed "hatred of apostasy," rooted in a radical brand of Islam – rather than Osama bin Laden or another individual leader—probably serves as the group's COG. Admittedly, bin Laden laid much of the groundwork to establish Al Qaeda, but it does not appear that his removal will cause his organization to collapse. Most analysts and intelligences sources claim that *if bin Laden were captured or killed, another leader would simply take his place.* That leader can only turn out to be either more or less effective than bin Laden. Thus, Al Qaeda's leadership really amounts to a centre of critical capability—something we want to neutralize but not something, in itself, that will end the war. In my opinion, Bin

Laden is not replaceable—another leader cannot "simply take his place." Bin Laden possesses characteristics of a successful commander who not only knows the rules of the game, but he is "the one who through his genius created them." Neutralizing this "genius," who is clearly a talented yet ruthless and evil leader, will achieve "significant" results that will commence the unraveling of Al Qaeda. The author Peter Bergen, CNN's terrorism analyst, notes that if Bin Laden is captured or killed, Al Qaeda will be dealt a blow. Bergen goes on to say:

Others down the chain of command might hate the United States as much or more, but it was bin Laden's charisma and organizational skills that created his transnational terrorist concern. In death bin Laden will certainly become a martyr for his immediate followers.

But the most obvious statement you can make about martyrs is that they are dead, and that would immediately make bin Laden less potent. Bin Laden's al-Qaeda occupies the space that exists somewhere in between a cult and a genuine mass movement. Cults usually disappear with the deaths of their leaders: think of Jim Jones or David Koresh. So too will "bin Ladenism" eventually join what President Bush has called "history's unmarked grave of discarded lies."

In identifying the "hatred of apostasy" as the possible centre of gravity, Echevarria suggests that the strategy to defeat Al Qaeda "will mean employing the diplomatic and informational elements of national power as deliberately, if not more so, as the military one." I agree that the United States will need to employ these two elements of power as well as the economic element of power to effect the Islamist attitude and defiance. But, identifying the "hatred of apostasy" as the sole centre of gravity seems to be an intangible thing to attack. In my strategic judgment I suggest it be the other way around. Neutralizing the Al Qaeda leadership should be the first priority and the "hub of all power and movement at which our energies should be directed." To effect defeat of Al Qaeda by concentrating on influencing the will of disaffected Islamists may take a generation or longer to accomplish. We have a more immediate need to conduct moral and physical harm on the Al

Qaeda leadership now before they can orchestrate more hate and another major attack on us. As Bin Laden provides the motivation of "hatred of apostasy," fueling a world-wide uprising, his critical requirements include his personal safety and that of key Al Qaeda deputies within the command and control element, his ability to periodically communicate direction and targets for terrorists cells, and his ability to communicate his Islamist message to the world and gain support for his movement.

Bin Laden also requires resources (financing, weapons, etc.) and a place to hide. Al Qaeda's operations are also enhanced by the cooperation of other terrorist groups and entities sympathetic to Bin Laden's cause through material assistance and shared information and intelligence. Bin Laden is vulnerable to U.S. or allied surveillance and attack if he can be located. He also could be rendered irrelevant if the Islamist movement that supports him could be thwarted. If Bin Laden is killed, his martyrdom would probably not last because martyrs do not feed or take care of people. On the other hand, martyrs can become powerful images; an information campaign would be necessary to counter this. If he is captured alive, he should be taken out of the limelight and tried in front of a tribunal without public access and media coverage.

The critical requirement for a "popular uprising" as in Al Qaeda's Islamist movement, is a charismatic and visionary leader like Bin Laden. In addition, the movement requires something to hate (like Western culture) and is further fueled by repression and poverty and the lack of opportunity.

The movement is further organized by the effort to educate and institutionalize the radical form of Islam through a "network of fundamentalist schools (*madrassas*), some of which radicalize and recruit youngsters for entrance into terrorists networks. Funded through Islamic charities and often espousing extreme views, *madrassas* will remain a key source of trouble in the years ahead."

The movement and its ideology are vulnerable to "fighting an idea with a better idea." And, these ideas would include improved human rights, democratization of all nations in the Middle East, resolution of the Israeli/Palestian issue, and stabilization of the Middle East region and economic development. It will take a generation or longer, but the United States must lead this effort.

1993 WORLD TRADE CENTRE BOMBING

In 1993, Ramzi Yousef used a truck bomb to attack the World Trade Centre in New York City. The attack was intended to break the foundation of Tower One knocking it into Tower Two, bringing the entire complex down. Yousef hoped this would kill 250,000 people. The towers shook and swayed but the foundation held and he succeeded in killing only six people (although he injured 1,042 others and caused nearly $300 million in property damage). After the attack, Yousef fled to Pakistan and later moved to Manila. There he began developing the Bojinka Plot plans to blow up a dozen American airliners simultaneously, to assassinate Pope John Paul II and President Bill Clinton, and to crash a private plane into CIA headquarters. He was later captured in Pakistan. None of the U.S. government's indictments against Osama bin Laden have suggested that he had any connection with this bombing, but Ramzi Yousef is known to have attended a terrorist training camp in Afghanistan. After his capture, Yousef declared that his primary justification for the attack was to punish the United States for its support for the Israeli occupation of Palestinian territories and made no mention of any religious motivations.

Late 1990s

On November 13, 1995, a van containing a hundred pounds of Semtex explosive blew up near the communications centre for the Saudi National Guard in downtown Riyadh, Saudi Arabia, where some American military contractors and Army officers had been training the Saudi National Guard. Seven people were killed, and sixty people were injured. The Saudi government arrested four men, "torturing confessions" out of them that they had been inspired by bin Laden's speeches and trained at al-Qaeda's camp in Afghanistan, and quickly executed them. It is unclear if they had anything to do with the crime. As with many bombings suspected to be the work of al-Qaeda, bin Laden praised the attacks but denied authorizing the attack or training the bombers.

The U.S. embassy bombings in East Africa, resulting in upward of 300 deaths, mostly locals. A barrage of cruise missiles launched by the U.S. military in response devastated an al-Qaeda base in Khost, Afghanistan, but the network's capacity was unharmed. Bin Laden then turned his sights towards the United States Navy. In October 2000, al-Qaeda militants in Yemen bombed the missile destroyer U.S.S. Cole in a suicide attack, killing 17 U.S. servicemen and damaging the vessel while it lay offshore. Inspired by the success of such a brazen attack, al-Qaeda's command core began to prepare for an attack on the United States itself.

September 11 Attacks

The September 11 attacks were the most devastating terrorist acts in American and world history, killing approximately 3,000 people. Two commercial airliners were deliberately flown into the World Trade Centre towers, a third into The Pentagon, a fourth, originally intended to target the United States Capitol crashed in Pennsylvania. The attacks were conducted by al-Qaeda, acting in accord with the 1998 *fatwa* issued against the United States and its allies by military forces under the command of bin Laden, al-Zawahiri, and others. Evidence points to suicide squads led by al-Qaeda military commander Mohamed Atta as the culprits of the attacks, with bin Laden, Ayman al-Zawahiri, Khalid Shaikh Mohammed, and Hambali as the key planners and part of the political and military command. Messages issued by bin Laden after September 11, 2001 praised the attacks, and explained their motivation while denying any involvement. Bin Laden legitimized the attacks by identifying grievances felt by both mainstream and Islamist Muslims, such as the general perception that the United States was actively oppressing Muslims. Bin Laden asserted that America was massacring Muslims in 'Palestine, Chechnya, Kashmir and Iraq' and that Muslims should retain the 'right to attack in reprisal'. He also claimed the 9/11 attacks were not targeted at women and children, but 'America's icons of military and economic power'. Evidence has since come to light that the original targets for the attack may have been nuclear power stations on the east coast of the U.S. The targets were later altered by al-Qaeda, as it was feared that such an attack "might get out of hand".

AL-QAEDA'S OPERATIONS MANUAL

In the early 1990s, al-Qaeda produced the Encyclopedia of the Afghan Jihad, a detailed how-to guide for using handguns, explosives, and biological and chemical weapons, in print and on CD-ROM. Materials belonging to a captured al-Qaeda operative in England detailed techniques for forgery, surveillance, and espionage.

Location/Area of Operation

Al-Qaeda has cells worldwide and is reinforced by its ties to Sunni extremist networks.

Coalition attacks on Afghanistan since October 2001 have dismantled the Taliban–al-Qaeda's protectors–and led to the capture, death, or dispersal of al-Qaeda operatives. Some al-Qaeda members at large probably will attempt to carry out future attacks against US interests. Other known areas of operation: United States, Yemen, Germany, Pakistan.

Al-Qaeda is a multi-national network possessing a global reach and has supported through financing, training and logistics, Islamic militants in Afghanistan, Algeria, Bosnia, Chechnya, Eritrea, Kosovo, the Philippines, Somalia, Tajikistan, and Yemen, and now Kosovo. Additionally, al-Qaeda has been linked to conflicts and attacks in Africa, Asia, Europe, the former Soviet Republics, the Middle East, as well as North and South America.

The headquarters of al-Qaeda are not known anymore.

- From 1991 to 1996, al-Qaeda worked out of Sudan.
- From 1996 until the collapse of the Taliban in 2001, al-Qaeda operated out of Afghanistan and maintained its training camps there.
- U.S. intelligence officials now think al-Qaeda's senior leadership is trying to regroup in lawless tribal regions just inside Pakistan, near the Afghan border, inside Pakistani cities or in Iran.
- In May 2003, administration officials claimed that senior al-Qaeda figures were in Iran and urged Tehran to

apprehend them. Sa'ad bin Laden, Usama bin Laden's son, in an October 2003 report, is said be among those in Iran.

- Al-Qaeda has autonomous underground cells in some 100 countries, including the United States, officials say. Law enforcement has broken up al-Qaeda cells in the United Kingdom, the United States, Italy, France, Spain, Germany, Albania, Uganda, and elsewhere.

Strength

It is impossible to known precisely, due to the decentralized stucture of the organization. Al-Qaeda may have several thousand members and associates. It trained over 5,000 militants in camps in Afghanistan since the late 1980s. It also serves as a focal point for a worldwide network that includes many Sunni Islamic extremist groups, some members of al-Gama'a al-Islamiyya, the Islamic Movement of Uzbekistan, and the Harakat ul-Mujahidin.

External Aid

Bin Laden, member of a billionaire family that owns the Bin Ladin Group construction empire, is said to have inherited tens of millions of dollars that he uses to help finance the group. Al-Qaeda also maintains moneymaking front businesses, solicits donations from like-minded supporters, and illicitly siphons funds from donations to Muslim charitable organizations. US efforts to block al-Qaeda funding has hampered al-Qaeda's ability to obtain money.

Al-Qaeda has cooperated with a number of known terrorist groups worldwide including:

- Armed Islamic Group
- Salafist Group for Call and Combat and the Armed Islamic Group
- Egyptian Islamic Jihad (Egypt)
- Al-Gama'a al-Islamiyya
- Jamaat Islamiyya
- The Libyan Islamic Fighting Group
- Bayt al-Imam (Jordan)

- Lashkar-e-Taiba and Jaish-e-Muhammad (Kashmir)
- Asbat al Ansar
- Hezbollah (Lebanon)
- Al-Badar
- Harakat ul Ansar/Mujahadeen
- Al-Hadith
- Harakat ul Jihad
- Jaish Mohammed-JEM
- Jamiat Ulema-e-Islam
- Jamiat-ul-Ulema-e-Pakistan
- Laskar e-Toiba-LET
- Moro Islamic Liberation Front (the Philippines)
- Abu Sayyaf Group (Malaysia, Philippines)
- Al-Ittihad Al Islamiya-AIAI (Somalia)
- Islamic Movement of Uzbekistan
- Islamic Army of Aden (Yemen)

These groups share al-Qaeda's Sunni Muslim fundamentalist views. Some terror experts theorize that Al-Qaeda, after the loss of it Afghanistan base, may be increasingly reliant on sympathetic affiliates to carry out it agenda. Intelligence officials and terrorism experts also say that al-Qaeda has stepped up its cooperation on logistics and training with Hezbollah, a radical, Iran-backed Lebanese militia drawn from the minority Shiite strain of Islam.

Al-Arabiyah television reported on 20 October 2004 that Jama'at Al-Tawhid wa Al-Jihad hadr released a statement claiming it has officially joined the Al-Qaeda terrorist network. Al-Jazeera broadcast a statement by the group identifying itself as Tanzim Qa'idat Al-Jihad in Bilad al-Rafidayn (Organization of Jihad's Base in the Country of the Two Rivers). Iraq is commonly known as the land of the two rivers, the Tigris and Euphrates. The statement has not been verified. Usama bin Laden'd 29 October 2004 video broadcast on the Arab TV network Al Jazeera made no mention of Zarqawi, suggesting that the report a few days earlier that Zarqawi and Bin Laden had joined forces were in error.

AL-QAEDA'S STRATEGIC, IDEOLOGICAL AND STRUCTURAL ADAPTATIONS SINCE 9/11

Approaching the tenth anniversary of the 9/11 attacks, there is a growing sense among counterterrorism analysts from the policy community and academia that Al-Qaeda has substantially weakened in the last decade and is destined to lose the battle against its enemies, and in particular the United States. Indeed, signs that Al-Qaeda is flagging are ample, and include its loss of Osama bin Laden and important operational leaders; defeat or near defeat of various Al-Qaeda franchises outside of Pakistan; a large number of ideological challenges levelled against the group by some of its former allies; and the series of protests that shook several Middle Eastern and North African states beginning in early 2011. Because the revolts in Tunisia, Egypt, Yemen, Bahrain, Syria, and other countries were mostly nonviolent, they provided a striking counterexample to Al-Qaeda's emphasis on violent regime change in the Middle East.

These organizational setbacks are significant, but must be viewed in the context of Al-Qaeda's success in spawning an expansionist global jihadist movement. Ten years into the fight against Al-Qaeda, that movement's overarching narrative continues to attract followers from a multitude of countries. All the while, the interplay of Al-Qaeda Core (AQC) with its affiliated groups, associated groups, and inspired adherents provides an increasing number of pathways to violence. A number of successful and unsuccessful plots in the past decade, and especially the last two years, serve as a stark reminder that the global jihad remains devoted to striking its enemies, often with ingenuity. The examples listed below span the breadth of the movement; taken together, these representative plots allude to the tactical, geographic, and organizational variability of the violence emanating from the global jihad.

AL-QAEDA

The August 2006 plot to blow up transatlantic airliners using liquid explosives—an attack most likely timed to coincide with the fifth anniversary of 9/11—served as a striking example of Al-

Qaeda's ongoing attempts to inflict significant pain on the United States five years after 9/11. Its interdiction may have forced Al-Qaeda's external operations branch to be more risk averse, but not to desist. In November of 2009, this branch trained three separate cell leaders, all from separate Western nations, on bomb-making techniques. After training them, AQC redeployed them to the United States, the United Kingdom, and Norway, where the operatives led respective terrorist cells in a geographically distributed complex suicide attack—an adaptation of Al-Qaeda's trademark complex attack. The successive deaths of Al-Qaeda's primary external operations planners at the time, Saleh al-Somali and Rashid Rauf, did not prevent the plots from progressing, albeit unsuccessfully.

Affiliated Organizations

On 27 August 2009, Abdullah Hassan Talea Asiri, a Saudi national and member of Al-Qaeda in the Arabian Peninsula (AQAP), attempted to assassinate Assistant Interior Minister of Saudi Arabia, Prince Muhammad bin Nayef, using a Pentaerythritol tetranitrate (PETN)-based explosive device hidden in his underwear. On Christmas Day 2009, AQAP-trained Nigerian citizen Umar Farouk Abdulmutallab used the same compound when he attempted to detonate explosives hidden in his underwear on Northwest Airlines flight 253. A third variation of the AQAP attack placed PETN within printer cartridges shipped in cargo planes intended to detonate over the continental United States in a plot discovered in late 2010.

Associated Organizations

On 30 December 2009, a Saudi national named Humam Khalil al-Balawi wore a bomb vest into a CIA outpost in Khost, Afghanistan, killing himself, 7 CIA employees and one Jordanian intelligence officer.

Balawi, a formerly imprisoned Al-Qaeda devotee and an infamous jihadist blogger known by the pen name Abu Dujana al-Khorasani, had been recruited as an informer for the Jordanian General Intelligence Directorate (GID), but played a sophisticated double game on behalf of the *Tehriki Taliban Pakistan* (TTP). In a second TTP plot in May 2010, a Pakistani-American citizen, Faisal Shahzad, demonstrated effective operational security and planning but poor bomb-making skills when he targeted New York's Times Square with a crude vehicle-borne improvised explosive device (VBIED).

Adherents

In November of 2009, Nidal Malik Hasan, a U.S. Army Officer with only tangential personal ties to a radical cleric and no known organizational affiliation to Al-Qaeda, conducted a firearms attack at a deployment centre on Fort Hood, killing thirteen individuals and wounding over thirty others. Al-Qaeda and its Yemen-based affiliate both endorsed the action, but neither entity claimed the alleged assailant as a group member. In 2010 in Portland, Oregon, Mohamed Osman Mohamud, a naturalized Somali-American citizen attempted to detonate a VBIED at a Christmas tree lighting ceremony.

In March of 2011, authorities in the United States arrested Khalid al-Dawsari, a Saudi Arabian student who, acting alone, procured explosive materials for use against targets in the United States. This anecdotal survey of plots illuminates the contours of a multi-faceted threat fostered by, but not unique to, the Al-Qaeda organization. To describe how this multifaceted threat has evolved over the last decade, this chapter will first recount some of the more salient examples of Al-Qaeda's post-9/11 strategic, ideological, and structural adaptations. It will then offer a balance sheet of Al-Qaeda's contemporary strengths and weaknesses. Ultimately, the aggregation of Al-Qaeda's adaptations since 9/11 has brought about an evolutionary change in the landscape of anti-Western Islamist militancy, ushering in an era of global jihadism beyond Al-Qaeda.

AL QAEDA UNDER ATTACK

In recent years, al Qaeda has come under attack by leading Muslim voices in the form of criticism of its theological, jurisprudential, and strategic reasoning. The criticism has been particularly strident regarding al Qaeda's violence against fellow

Muslims. Among the harshest attacks coming from outside the salafi-jihadi movement are those from Saudi cleric Salman al-Awda and Egyptian cleric Yusuf al-Qaradawi. In a September 14, 2007, open letter titled "A Ramadan Letter to Osama bin Laden," al-Awda asked bin Laden: "How much blood has been spilled? How many innocent children, women, and old people have been killed, maimed, and expelled from their homes in the name of 'al Qaeda'?"6 Al-Awda reportedly had been an important early influence on bin Laden's religious views. In June 2009, al-Qaradawi, a highly influential Qatar-based cleric who is chairman of the International Federation of Muslim Scholars, published a book in which he repudiated al Qaeda's concept of jihad as a "mad declaration of war upon the world." This work, by a popular, mainstream Islamic cleric who has a weekly program on al-Jazeera television and who retains a storied ability to serve as a barometer of broader mainstream Muslim opinion, suggested that the mainstream tide might have turned against al Qaeda.

In many ways, the attacks on al Qaeda and "revisions" of jihadi doctrine from within the salafi-jihadi movement have been even more scathing, and there should be little doubt that these high-profile defections from the movement have raised doubts about al Qaeda among its cadres and sympathizers. In April 2007, the Kuwaiti salafi-jihadi scholar Hamid al-Ali issued a *fatwa* (religious ruling) against the establishment of the Islamic State of Iraq, implicitly criticizing al Qaeda's affiliate in Iraq for its violence. "The spreading of bigotry and rancor, even if wrapped in the cloak of religion, is the work of the devil and of people who follow their own caprice. It must be avoided. Everyone must keep distance from such a dangerous path," wrote al-Ali. Late 2007 saw the release of a book by Sayyid Imam Abd al-Aziz al-Sharif, the former Egyptian Islamic Jihad Organization ideologue and author of a classic jihadi manual. In his book, Sayyid Imam extensively revised his earlier positions on the jurisprudence of jihad, making violent jihad impermissible under most circumstances. This was an especially important attack from within the salafi-jihadi camp, as Sayyid Imam had formerly been the ideological mentor to Ayman al-Zawahiri. Sayyid Imam's *volte-face* on the permissibility of jihad sent shock waves through the salafi-jihadi community and led to a public dispute with al-Zawahiri. Also in late 2007, former Libyan Islamic Fighting Group leader Nu'man Bin 'Uthman issued his opening salvo against al Qaeda, framing his criticisms in both strategic and jurisprudential terms.

In January 2009, the Egyptian Islamic Group—a prominent former jihadi group, most of whose leadership declared a unilateral cease-fire in the late 1990s and formally renounced violence in March 2002—issued a statement urging al Qaeda to observe a cease-fire until it could assess the intentions of the recently elected Obama administration. 15 In September 2009, the Libyan Islamic Fighting Group released a new "code" for jihad in the form of a 417-page religious document that served as an extended critique and recantation of al Qaeda's reading of the jurisprudence of jihad.

In November 2010, former al Qaeda spokesman Suleman Abu Ghaith released a book that constituted another damning indictment of al Qaeda from a former insider. Echoing other critics, Abu Ghaith emphasized that after having pledged allegiance to Taliban leader Mullah Mohammed Omar while in Afghanistan, bin Laden violated Islamic law by failing to abide by Omar's instructions not to attack the United States. This violation, according to Abu Ghaith and others, made bin Laden an unfit leader who deserved punishment.

Finally, in late 2010, al Qaeda's former military planner Sayf al-Adl wrote a number of letters calling upon al Qaeda's leaders to conduct a comprehensive review of their operations, including the 9/11 attacks, for the purpose of "assessing the past stage, learning the lessons, and drawing up a strategy for the future." The letters were highly critical of al Qaeda's past mistakes, but it is also alarming that al-Adl appeared to be advocating that the group emphasize a strategy focused on attacking the United States rather than local Muslim regimes. In the wake of bin Laden's death, al-Adl was appointed al Qaeda Central's acting chief until al Qaeda's Shura Council could choose a more permanent successor.
Implications for U.S. Strategy and Policy

Suspicions of U.S. intentions run deep in many parts of the Muslim world, and it can be difficult to overcome the undercurrent of sheer resentment of U.S. superpower status, whatever

Washington does, but al Qaeda's current situation nonetheless presents opportunities, especially now, given the death of the charismatic and organizationally adept bin Laden and the opening of political space in some Muslim countries as a result of the Arab Spring. With al Qaeda already under considerable pressure from within the Muslim community, what, if any, fruitful role can the United States play in what is essentially an intra-Muslim debate about the nature of Islam and the permissibility of violent jihad? In short, U.S. strategy and policy should take the long view, which means focusing on three objectives: (1) reducing or eliminating the irritants that fuel support for al Qaeda, (2) promoting universal democratic and humanitarian values, and (3) avoiding actions and rhetorical missteps that reinforce al Qaeda's narrative.

Reducing or eliminating the irritants that fuel support for al Qaeda. Al Qaeda's grand strategy is based on the dual assumptions that attacks on the United States can lure it into intervening militarily in Muslim lands and that Muslims can then more easily be mobilized into jihad beneath al Qaeda's banner. With a withdrawal of U.S. military forces from Iraq by the end of 2011 and substantial reductions of forces in Afghanistan envisioned to begin by the end of 2014, this irritant will diminish, and al Qaeda will find it increasingly difficult to exploit this issue in mobilizing jihadists. It bears mentioning that bin Laden's own radicalization appears to have been fuelled by the 1991 Gulf War, the deprivations experienced by Iraqis in the war's aftermath, and the prolonged presence of U.S. troops in Saudi Arabia following that war. Future decisions to deploy or permanently station U.S. military forces in Muslim lands must be carefully weighed against their potential consequences for fuelling recruitment and mobilization into al Qaeda extremism. In a similar vein, the United States can weaken al Qaeda's ability to exploit the Palestinian issue by continuing efforts to expand the writ and influence of the Palestinian Authority and to promote a broader settlement between Israel and the Palestinians. Al Qaeda has judged that the Israeli occupation of Palestine is the issue that is most salient to Muslims worldwide—and the most easily exploited in its propaganda and recruitment efforts. Thus, despite the current impasse in Israeli-Palestinian negotiations, it is crucial that the United States continue its decades-long effort to promote a broader settlement.

Promoting universal democratic and humanitarian values. By promoting and supporting democratic reform in the Muslim world, the United States aligns itself with the aspirations of most ordinary Muslims and is better positioned to marginalize al Qaeda because of the organization's outright rejection of democracy and peaceful political competition. The overthrow of corrupt and despotic leaders and the opening of political space, as occurred in the recent revolutions in Tunisia, Egypt, and Libya, can help sap support for al Qaeda's extremism and channel energies toward peaceful political competition. Efforts by the United States to secure the release of political prisoners also can provide tangible signs of the U.S. commitment to democratic values. Finally, by providing humanitarian assistance and disaster relief, as it did following the December 2004 Indian Ocean tsunami that struck Indonesia and other nations in the region and the October 2005 earthquake that struck Pakistan, the United States can soften its image abroad, build goodwill in Muslim nations, and help to inoculate their populations against al Qaeda propaganda and rhetoric promoting violence against America.

Avoiding actions and rhetorical missteps that reinforce al Qaeda's narrative. U.S. efforts to directly influence intra-Muslim debates over the nature of Islam and the permissibility of violent jihad seem highly unlikely to be effective. The theological and jurisprudential conditions and constraints that bear on the conduct of violent jihad are complex and subtle, and official U.S. efforts to opine on or influence such matters carry grave risks of both alienating potential friends and allies within the Muslim world and reinforcing al Qaeda's narrative that the United States aims to refashion Islam into a moderate or even secular form. U.S. deeds of the types outlined above matter far more than words, but U.S. words can also cause great harm. Characterizing U.S. efforts against al Qaeda as part of a "crusade" or clash of civilizations may play well with some domestic audiences, but ultimately, it is likely to reinforce al Qaeda's narrative of an Islam that is under attack by the non-Muslim world.

This is clearly not a strategy for quick, short-term results. Rather, as was the case with the earlier U.S. sustained effort to promote democracy, markets, and individual freedom over totalitarian communism, it is a strategy that is likely to require decades or generations of effort. However, only by taking the long view will the United States be able to establish conditions that favour the triumph of a merciful, compassionate, and tolerant Islam over the violent nihilism of al Qaeda and its fellow travellers. A Psychological Triumph. There is very little concrete evidence upon which to base such dire forecasts. The threat of nuclear terror floats far above the world of known facts. How has al Qaeda managed to pull off this stunning feat of psychological legerdemain?

The dramatic impact of terrorism provides part of the answer. What distinguishes terrorism from other modes of armed conflict is the separation between the actual targets of terrorist violence and the targets of the psychological terror. Because terrorists cannot hope to defeat their foes in open battle, they deliberately aim spectacular attacks at vulnerable civilian targets, hoping to create an atmosphere of terror, which will induce the public audience to exaggerate the terrorists' strength and dissuade governments from pursuing policies opposed by the terrorists because of the perceived price. Terrorist attacks also create political crises, provoking overreaction and compelling governments to divert vast resources to security in order to maintain public confidence that they will be protected, even while knowing that absolute security is not possible. This is the very essence of terrorism. And it often works. The trajectory of contemporary terrorist violence also has contributed to fears of mass destruction.

As war has become less lethal, terrorism has become more lethal. In the decades since World War II, military power has moved away from the industrial-scale slaughter of total war, placing greater emphasis on reducing collateral casualties to a minimum. The development of increasingly precise weapons has facilitated this effort. Domestic genocide, particularly the targeting of specific ethnic groups, has been the exception to this rule. Meanwhile, contemporary terrorists have moved in the opposite direction, toward large-scale indiscriminate violence, escalating from small, mostly symbolic bombings involving few casualties in the 1970s to truck bombs aimed at killing hundreds in the 1980s and 1990s to the attacks on September 11, 2001, that killed thousands. From this cataclysmic event, it was easy to extrapolate the idea of Osama bin Laden using a nuclear weapon if he had one. The 9/11 terrorist attacks fundamentally altered perceptions of plausibility. With box cutters and mace, terrorists turned commercial airliners into guided missiles that brought down skyscrapers. People feared that al Qaeda would try to launch more 9/11-scale attacks if it could, or perhaps even more-ambitious attacks. Terrorist scenarios that had been deemed far-fetched before 9/11 became operative presumptions after 9/11. In this environment, no terrorist scheme could be dismissed. Nuclear terrorism ascended to a clear and present danger.

There are vast differences between chemical, biological, radiological, and nuclear weapons. In its final report, written before 9/11, the National Commission on Terrorism chose wisely to avoid the collective term "weapons of mass destruction." Aggregating such weapons confuses a low threshold for occurrence—terrorists already have employed chemical and biological weapons, with modest results—with a high potential for theoretical casualties, thereby exaggerating both probability and likely consequences. Realistically, only biological and nuclear weapons have a capacity for true mass destruction. And nuclear weapons differ from biological weapons in that biological weapons also may be used to kill just a few, as the anthrax letters did. It is hard to imagine a minor nuclear attack. Absence of Warning

Paradoxically, the absence of evidence heightens the threat. Many believe that the public will have no warning of an impending terrorist nuclear attack. Although there are two diametrically opposite views of U.S. intelligence capabilities, both fuel nuclear terror. The first view of U.S. intelligence credits it with omniscience but remains suspicious that Washington is deliberately withholding information to avoid causing public panic. This is a popular theme among conspiracy-driven books and articles on nuclear terrorism that promise to tell the reader what the government will not. In fact, since 9/11, the government has routinely passed threat information—some of it vague, even dubious—on to the public. Yet it is also true that since the 1970s, there have been scores of undisclosed nuclear threats to American cities. The Federal Bureau of Investigation (FBI) and U.S. Department of Energy nuclear emergency teams have mobilized to conduct secret searches. All of the threats were found to be apparent hoaxes, but none of this was published at the time. As an example, just after 9/11, the CIA received intelligence from a source appropriately code-named Dragonfire that terrorists had planted a nuclear device in New York City. The federal government initiated a search without informing the public or local authorities. Nothing was found—the source was mistaken. But given this record, it is conceivable that if the government received credible intelligence that al Qaeda or another terrorist organization had acquired a nuclear weapon, it might not reveal it.

The second view of U.S. intelligence is that it cannot be depended upon to provide advance warning of a terrorist nuclear attack. We will know it only when we see the bright yellow flash. After all, American intelligence officials were surprised to discover in 1991 that Iraq had come closer to developing nuclear weapons than they had imagined. U.S. intelligence did not foresee 9/11. It failed to predict the testing of nuclear weapons by India, Pakistan, and North Korea, but prior to the Iraq War, it reported with confidence that Iraq had weapons of mass destruction when it had none. While this recitation is not entirely fair to the intelligence community, perceived past failures of intelligence do not inspire confidence.

Lacking hard evidence that terrorists have nuclear weapons or material, intelligence analysts instead pore over al Qaeda's public statements for warnings or other clues about its interest in nuclear weapons. They argue over whether *fatwas*—religious rulings—authorizing al Qaeda to kill millions should be interpreted as the obligatory warning required by Islamic concepts of warfare. They debate whether terrorists might be deterred from acquiring or using nuclear weapons. These are legitimate lines of inquiry, but they also reify the threat, treating a hypothetical—al Qaeda's or any terrorists' possession of nuclear weapons—as if it were a concrete fact, or at least an inevitable development. Spinning Nuclear Fantasies

Al Qaeda's efforts to obtain nuclear weapons were accompanied by an active communications effort, which implied that the terrorist group was further along in its quest than it actually was. This public communications campaign intensified as al Qaeda's central leadership came under increasing pressure after 9/11. In earlier interviews, Osama bin Laden, when asked by reporters about weapons of mass destruction, coyly responded that their acquisition was a religious duty. But in an interview with a Pakistani reporter in November 2001, as the Taliban and al Qaeda were being bombed by American warplanes, bin Laden and Ayman al-Zawahiri were said to have claimed that al Qaeda had chemical and nuclear weapons, although the reporting of this interview raised doubts. The first published version had bin Laden saying only that al Qaeda would survive even if the United States used chemical or nuclear weapons against it; subsequent versions of the same interview introduced the claim that al Qaeda itself already had such weapons.

Neither of al Qaeda's two top leaders made many public mentions of nuclear weapons after the 2001 interview, but in 2002, an al Qaeda spokesman posted a message on the Internet claiming that because the United States was responsible for the deaths of millions of Muslims, al Qaeda, in accordance with Islamic law, had the right to kill 4 million Americans. This was amended by a fugitive Saudi cleric who issued a religious ruling in 2003 authorizing al Qaeda to kill 10 million Americans.

Exactly why al Qaeda elicited the two statements about killing millions of Americans is not known, but the statements excited the organization's followers and alarmed analysts in the United States. The two communications prompted a lively discourse among jihadists about al Qaeda's nuclear posture and strategy, as if its possession of nuclear weapons were real. Analysts in the United States, meanwhile, interpreted the two statements as providing the necessary warning before attack required by the Islamic code of warfare. They noted that the only way al Qaeda could achieve this magnitude of casualties was with nuclear, or possibly biological, weapons. It was seen as a signal. Al Qaeda's communications campaign was not a centrally directed effort but, rather, a distributed project, a new phenomenon made possible by the Internet. A chorus of online jihadists carried on the campaign, issuing threats and adding lurid landscapes of fireballs and mushroom clouds over Manhattan and Washington. These were the fantasies of the powerless, vicarious participation in al Qaeda's terrorist campaign. Psychologically satisfying to their jihadist authors, they kept Western government officials on edge.

Al Qaeda's nuclear threats also commanded the attention of the U.S. news media, which, for reasons of commercial competition, has veered off into the realm of shock and entertainment in the years since 9/11. Editorial constraint yielded to drama. The line between news and fiction blurred. Here was the stuff of suspense novels, with Western civilization hanging in the balance. What could make for a better story? Nuclear terror acquired a life of its own.

DRIVEN BY OUR IMAGINATION

A receptive audience, Americans have been avid consumers of nuclear terror. It has revived Cold War anxieties. It has resonated with many who anticipate the Apocalypse, confirming their belief that we are in the end times. It has acted as a condenser for the nation's broader apprehensions about economic and political decline, its fear of being taken over by alien cultures. "Nuclear terrorism" and "nuclear terror" have different domains of meaning. Terrorism is action, and it can include the mere threat of action, which can produce its own powerful effect. Terror is the effect. Nuclear terrorism today is about the possibility that terrorists will acquire and use nuclear weapons, while nuclear terror is about the *anticipation* of that event. Nuclear terrorism is driven by terrorist capabilities. Nuclear terror is driven by our imagination.

The history of nuclear terrorism can be quickly summarized: It hasn't happened. Terrorists are not known to have acquired and certainly have not used nuclear weapons—although many would hasten to add "yet." But nuclear terror is real, and it has become deeply embedded in our popular culture and policymaking circles. This fear does not come free. It adds another layer to our already considerable national anxieties. It fans xenophobia. It corrodes our commitment to liberty. It demands obedience to an orthodoxy that cannot be challenged without provoking accusations of being dangerously naïve or soft on terrorism. And yet, paradoxically, despite the widespread apprehension that within a very few years, terrorists armed with nuclear weapons will destroy an American city, we still live in those cities. Even those who warn us that nuclear terrorists are coming have not removed themselves from danger. The government did not invent the bogeyman of nuclear terrorism to compensate for the end of the Cold War or to perpetuate the military-industrial complex, as some cynics suggest. Concern about the nuclear threat is genuine, and we should be grateful for the many officials who work tirelessly to prevent nuclear attacks from any quarter. But we should also be careful about how we allow the threat of nuclear terrorism to be harnessed to serve a variety of purposes, some of which are more useful than others.

Showing, Not Just Telling

In propounding this war against Islam, America's enemies often use outright lies and fabrications. But they also know that their message is most convincing and most motivating when it draws on real events. It is one thing to tell recruits that America is at war against Islam and another to show actions that seem to prove it. Consequently, al Qaeda has been eager to take advantage of America's own policies, pronouncements, and behaviours to crudely and unfairly illustrate its message. Even before Abu Ghraib, the U.S. war in Iraq was seen by some as reason enough to join the militant cause. In the eyes of jihadists, the Iraq War was unjustified and constituted a foreign and infidel occupation of Muslim lands. In this sense, the motivations of foreign fighters entering Afghanistan in the 1980s were little different from those of fighters coming into Iraq. Simplistic and false accusations that the United States entered Iraq to "take its oil," the real fact that the United States ignored many pleas of the international community before invading, and the U.S. failure to establish security following a successful invasion were further used to tarnish the image of the United States.

Al Qaeda uses U.S. operations in Afghanistan to similar effect. In the wake of 9/11, it was necessary to attack al Qaeda at its Afghan base, and establishing stability and security remains an imperative. But the war drags on. The rallying cry of an infidel occupation of a Muslim land is a common jihadist refrain that not only motivates foreign fighters and some Taliban but also galvanizes recruits in the West. This refrain was the argument used by Nidal Hassan, the sole suspect in the shootings at Fort Hood, Texas, whose PowerPoint presentation to classmates at the Uniformed Services University of the Health Sciences spoke of the war against Islam, the U.S. campaign in Afghanistan, and a Muslim's duty. The very nature of the Iraqi and Afghan conflicts, wars fought among civilian populations in an urban landscape, has inevitably led to accusations of abuse. Insurgents and terrorists in both countries have foresworn distinguishing uniforms and shamefully hide behind civilian populations. U.S. forces by no means intend civilian casualties and go to great lengths to avoid them. But when mistakes happen, al Qaeda pounces. The isolated and worst-case scenarios are used to allege a systematic campaign of abuse. Aiding these arguments, at times, has been a slow and feeble response that in the cases of Abu Ghraib, the deaths of civilians in Haditha, and other civilian casualty events has failed to quickly investigate accusations and admit wrongdoing. Perceptions of abuse of Muslims were what motivated Carlos Bledsoe, the convicted attacker at the military recruiting centre in Little Rock, Arkansas, who asserted that he was defending Muslims against U.S. military actions in the Middle East.

Shooting Oneself

After 9/11, the United States took an aggressive stance toward detainees, who were given the status of unlawful combatants and denied prisoner-of-war status, held without trial or habeas corpus, and, in some instances, subjected to torture and harsh interrogations. The status of detainees in a war without uniforms or nation-states has fostered a complex debate with merit on both sides. But complex and nuanced arguments are quickly stripped away once they are put through al Qaeda's propaganda machine, and our detainee policy, as evidenced by opinion polling conducted by World Public Opinion and others, has been perceived as still more evidence of U.S. ill intent. Al Qaeda has also taken advantage of U.S. political statements and bravado. President George W. Bush announced the "Global War on Terror" nine days after 9/11 to define the conflict of a new age. However, the term *terror* is much broader than *terrorism*, so instead of al Qaeda being the focus of the fight, America's adversary became a conflated mix of groups that often had little association with the militant network that had attacked it. Many Muslims throughout the Middle East and beyond came to perceive the sweeping term as evidence that Islam itself was the target of American retribution. While certainly not intended, U.S. pronouncements sowed confusion where none was required.

Extremists have also been delighted with the ill-conceived anti-Muslim attitudes and behaviour of a small minority of Americans. The most extreme example was the "Burn a Koran Day" that was to be hosted by a small fringe church in Gainesville, Florida. The event was canceled at the last minute at the urging of U.S. officials, but its mere planning and publicity stirred resentment against the United States and spurred violent threats on extremist websites. In a similar fashion, many Americans found controversy in plans to build a Muslim community centre and mosque near Ground Zero. Pernicious anti-Muslim statements have become increasingly common in American blogs, talk radio shows, and even political rallies. These bigoted sentiments play right into al Qaeda's hands, not only seeming to prove its point to future extremists but also alienating an American Muslim population that has played a critical role in clamping down on homegrown extremism.

Today's media environment works to al Qaeda's advantage. At one time, extremists had to compile elaborate videotapes depicting horrendous abuse of Muslims and then pass them from one person to the next. For many, the message was compelling, but the dissemination process was slow. Today, however, an image from a distant battlefield or small-town America can be instantly uploaded on YouTube and onto jihadist websites. The videos go viral and pass from one to many. Jihadist websites wrap these images in a narrative that argues that such pictures are not the exception but the rule. The images are accompanied by stirring music and grand exhortations. The number of jihadist websites and chat rooms has proliferated into the thousands, reaching Arabic and English speakers alike. A visit to the Internet has become a first and potent step in the slow process of radicalization. The discontent and angry can while away hours in front of the computer screen. They easily ignore other web content that fails to justify their extremist views. They gain reassurance that their perceptions, albeit misplaced, were right all along. They interact in chat rooms and web forums where their anger is reinforced in a virtual social environment. Many view attack videos that illustrate an exciting and seemingly efficacious outlet for discontent. Surely, most would-be jihadists just sit and stew in a virtual world. Others, though, gain real-world connections and find solace among peer groups that cycle the anger further and galvanize the will. The radicalization of a few is fed by the resentment of many.

Opinion polls throughout the Middle East testify to the unfavourable perceptions of U.S. policy. Large majorities hold negative opinions of the United States and believe that it intends to weaken and divide Islam. Majorities claim that the West does not respect Islam. Most in the Arab and Muslim world do not support terrorist attacks, but their overall opinions matter because they expand the pool of individuals who may be open and receptive to one of al Qaeda's core messages. The overall perceptions create a social environment in which hatred seems acceptable and may in fact be reinforced in everyday conversation. For some who become so imbued with this ideology, the only step left is to act.
The Ongoing Challenge

The strategic dilemma about how best to tackle al Qaeda's havens now being confronted by the Obama administration has confounded its predecessors of both political parties for more than two decades. The Clinton administration faced similar challenges after the 1998 U.S. embassy bombings in Kenya and Tanzania that were planned and executed by al Qaeda operatives, killing 231 people, including 12 Americans. As they are today, the policy instruments available in 1998 were limited because the U.S. security apparatus had been built around threats from states, not non-state actors. Two weeks after the embassy bombings, President Clinton approved retaliatory attacks with cruise missiles against al Qaeda training camps and facilities in Afghanistan and Sudan.

In announcing these attacks, Clinton gave the following justification: "The United States does not take this action lightly. Afghanistan and Sudan have been warned for years to stop harboring and supporting these terrorist groups. But countries that persistently host terrorists have no right to be safe havens." The immediate response to an attack against U.S. interests overseas during the Clinton administration was to attack al Qaeda's training camps and facilities and to punish those countries harboring its operatives.

Why? In its in-depth exploration of the 1998 embassy bombings and the U.S. response, the 9/11 Commission concluded that senior U.S. officials had considered multiple avenues of response, both in the immediate aftermath and for a continuing campaign against al Qaeda, but most were discarded because of a perceived lack of feasibility or for the sake of general caution.

Thus, arguably, cruise missiles were chosen as the immediate response because a cruise-missile attack was something the United States could do. Subsequently, the United States adopted a plan to capture Osama bin Laden, a plan that was given only a 15-percent chance of success by the CIA at the time. The George W.

Bush administration faced similar problems. In her April 2004 testimony before the 9/11 Commission, National Security Adviser Condoleezza Rice described the dilemma as she saw it prior to the 9/11 attacks: "Integrating our counterterrorism and regional strategies was the most difficult and the most important aspect of the new strategy to get right. Al Qaeda was both a client of and a patron to the Taliban, which in turn was supported by Pakistan. Those relationships provided Al Qaeda with a powerful umbrella of protection and we had to sever that."

Safe havens again. Administration after administration—Republican and Democrat—have returned to terrorist havens as the key hurdle to overcome. And yet experts have disagreed about whether havens are important for al Qaeda to pursue its global strategy. In his October 2009 testimony before the Armed Services Committee of the U.S. House of Representatives, noted terrorism expert Paul Pillar argued that an expansion of military efforts in Afghanistan was unwarranted: "It is not apparent to me how a move of al Qaeda or parts of it from one side of the Durand line to the other would substantially affect the threat the group poses to U.S. interests.

Any such threat would be no less from Waziristan [Pakistan] than it would be from Nuristan [Afghanistan]." Just one month earlier, in his own testimony before the Senate Foreign Relations Committee, John Nagl, president of the Centre for a New American Security, argued the exact opposite: "American efforts now focus on Pakistan as a launching pad for transnational terrorists and insurgents fighting in Afghanistan. But the problem runs both ways: a failed Afghanistan would become a base from which the Taliban and al Qaeda militants could work to further destabilize the surrounding region."

Last year, several RAND researchers examined al Qaeda strategic documents to discern the views of al Qaeda's senior leaders on the need for physical sanctuary or lack thereof. (We felt that, strangely, in this debate among experts, the perspectives of al Qaeda's senior leaders had been absent.) Included among the al Qaeda documents studied was a work by one of its forefathers, Abdullah Azzam; statements released in the mid-1990s by al Qaeda's Advisory and Reform Committee in London; and more recent treaties by strategist Abu Musab al-Suri, as well as guidance provided by second-in-command Ayman al-Zawahiri to Al Qaeda in the Arabian Peninsula released in its magazine, *Sada al-Malahim*. Our analysis led us to conclude that while al Qaeda could learn to function without a physical sanctuary, its leaders believe that they need a safe location from which to pursue a global strategy, and thus they behave accordingly.

On the basis of this review, it is reasonable to conclude that consecutive White House administrations have focused on havens. Unfortunately, the only solution before us still is to invade and occupy a sanctuary, which brings us back to the familiar strategic dilemma: Just because havens might represent viable targets does not mean that we can eliminate them. Counter Resentment, Counter Terrorism

In this war of ideas, perceptions can matter more than reality. It is surely fair to argue that American service personnel entering Iraq did so to remove a brutal dictator who killed hundreds of thousands of Muslims, and it is certainly true that U.S. involvement in Afghanistan is intended to bring stability to a war-torn country and that the attitudes of a few Americans do not represent those of a tolerant American society. Unfortunately, the enemy will spin what it can spin, and it will take the worst example and hold it up as emblematic of all that America is. These perceptions—and the ease with which they can be disseminated—demand that we as Americans continuously hold ourselves to an ever-higher standard.

Nothing written here is new to the United States. The inflaming consequences of the war in Iraq are well understood. The U.S. military, previously unaccustomed to dealing with insurgents and civilians alike, has significantly reduced civilian casualties, markedly improved oversight of detention facilities, and gained a hard-earned focus on interacting with and protecting civilian populations. The torture of detainees is no longer permitted, and those at the Guantanamo Bay detention camp are increasingly having their days in court. The United States increasingly speaks of engagement with the Muslim world and favors international cooperation over unilateral action. These changes have not gone unnoticed.

In moving forward, the United States must continue to be driven by the better angels of its nature. U.S. leaders must think through their policies in advance to understand how they will affect and be interpreted by the Muslim world. The United States must not seek shortterm gains at the expense of long-term counterterrorism and humanitarian objectives. The U.S. military must continually orient the force to execute missions successfully and carefully in civilian-populated areas.

Mistakes and misconduct, when uncovered, should be followed by public acknowledgment and assurances that they will not be repeated. Politicians and civic and religious leaders must work together to quash the seeds of hatred that threaten American unity.

Abu Ghraib was a stain on the character of America, but it is a stain that must not be repeated or be allowed to define who America is to the world. A picture is indeed worth a thousand words, but we as a nation can determine how the future pictures will be drawn. Misperceptions about U.S. intent will still abound and will feed the hardened hearts of a few. The war against al Qaeda will be long. The fight in Afghanistan will continue. Terrorist networks will be hunted. Mistakes will surely be made, and well-meaning actions and statements will be deliberately misrepresented. We as Americans must be prepared for this. But more to the point, we must disprove the claims of our enemies by our deeds.

Bibliography

Allison, Graham: *Nuclear Terrorism: The Ultimate Preventable Catastrophe*, New York: Times Books, 2004.

Aurobindo, Sri : *The Foundations of Islamic Culture*, New York, 1973.

Basrur, Rajesh M., and Hasan-Askari Rizvi, *Nuclear Terrorism and South Asia*, Albuquerque, NM: Sandia National Laboratories, February 2003.

Brig Gurmeet Kanwal: *'Proxy War ' in "Pakistans's Proxy War"*, Lancer Publishers and Distributors,2002.

Bruce Hoffman: *Inside Terrorism*, Columbia University Press, 2006.

Daniel Byman: *Deadly Connections: States that Sponsor Terrorism*, Cambridge University Press, 2005.

Fatima, T. : *Islamic Law and Judiciary*, Deep & Deep Publications, New Delhi, 2001.

Friedman, G.: *The Future of War of Cyber Crimes*, N.Y., Random House, 1996.

Ghose, S.K.: *Politics of Violence: Dawn of a Dangerous Era*, Springfield, Nataraj, 1992.

Hoffman, Bruce: *Inside Terrorism and Internet Crime*, New York: Columbia University Press, 1998.

Janowitz, M.: *The Professional Soldier: A Social and Political Portrait*, N.Y., The Free Press, 1960.

John L. Esposito: *Islam: The Straight Path*, Oxford : Oxford University, England, 1991,

Kaplan, David, *The Cult At the End of the World*, New York: Crown Publishers, 1996.

Keane J.: *Democracy and Cyber Crimes*, London, Verso, 1988.

Laquer, Walter, *The New Terrorism: Fanaticism and the Arms of Mass Destruction*, Oxford: Oxford University Press, 1999.

Levitas, D.: *The terrorist next door: The militia movement and the radical right*, New York: Thomas Dunne Books, 2002.

Odum, Howard T. : *Environment, Power and Society*, New York, Wiley-Interscience, 1971.

Oudha, Abdul Qadir : *Criminal Law of Islam*, Kitab Bhavan, New Delhi, 1999.

Paul A. Leventhal, *Preventing Nuclear Terrorism: The Report and Papers of the International Task Force on Prevention of Nuclear Terrorism*, Lanham, MD: Rowman & Littlefield, 1987.

Poole, Lane, S. : *The Mohammedan Dynasties*, MacMillan & Co., London, 1895.

Qureshi, A. Iqbal : *Islam and the Theory of Interest*, Kitab Bhavan, New Delhi, 1994.

Rizvi, Hasan Askari : *Islami Reassertion : a Socio Political Study*, Progressive Publishers, Lahore, 1981.

Robert M. Young: *Darwinian Evolution and Human History*, Historical Studies on Science and Belief, 1980.

Saeed Shafaqat: *Civil-Military Relations in Pakistan: From Zulfikar Ali Bhutto to Benazir Bhutto*, West View Press 1997.

Schroeer, Dietrich, *Science, Technology, and the Nuclear Arms Race*, Ontario: John Wiley & Sons, 1984.

Spindlove, J. R.: *Terrorism today: The past, the players, the future*, Upper Saddle Creek, NJ: Prentice Hall, 2000.

Thomas Arnold: *The Spread of Islam in the World, A History of Peaceful Preaching*, Goodword Books, 2001.

Thomas Arnold: *The Spread of Islam in the World, A History of Peaceful Preaching*, Goodword Books, 2001.

Whitaker, D. J.: *The Terrorism Reader*, New York: Routledge, 2001.

White, J. R.: *Terrorism: An introduction: 2002 update*, Belmont, CA: Wadsworth, 2002.

Index

O

P

R

S

T

U

❑❑❑